Annuals & Bulbs

Annuals & Bulbs

CONSULTANT EDITOR

Geoffrey Burnie

BARNES & NOBLE BOOKS
NEW YORK

This edition published by Barnes & Noble, Inc.,
by arrangement with Fog City Press

2003 Barnes & Noble Books

M 10 9 8 7 6 5 4 3 2 1

ISBN 0-7607-4088-7

FOG CITY PRESS
CHIEF EXECUTIVE OFFICER John Owen
PRESIDENT Terry Newell
PUBLISHER Lynn Humphries
MANAGING EDITOR Janine Flew
ART DIRECTOR Kylie Mulquin
COVER DESIGN John Bull
PICTURE EDITOR Tracey Gibson
EDITORIAL COORDINATORS Paul McNally, Kiren Thandi
PRODUCTION MANAGER Caroline Webber
PRODUCTION COORDINATOR James Blackman
SALES MANAGER Emily Jahn
VICE PRESIDENT INTERNATIONAL SALES Stuart Laurence
EUROPEAN SALES DIRECTOR Vanessa Mori

LIMELIGHT PRESS PTY LTD
PROJECT MANAGEMENT Helen Bateman/Jayne Denshire
PROJECT EDITOR Liz Connolly
PROJECT DESIGNER Patricia Ansell
CONSULTANT EDITOR Geoffrey Burnie

A catalog record for this book is available from the
Library of Congress, Washington, DC.

Color reproduction by Bright Arts Graphics (S) Pte Ltd
Printed by LeeFung-Asco Printers

Printed in China

A Weldon Owen Production

Contents

How to Use This Book

This book will guide you through the whole process of planning and planting a fabulous flower garden, from learning about your site and picking the best plants to creating easy-care plantings for all purposes.

Illustrations highlight individual plants and techniques and methods for caring for your plants to get the optimum results.

Clear and simple step-by-step instructions will help guide you through various practical garden projects.

COVER UP

Row covers can be very handy for protecting young seedlings from frosts or unwanted animal pests.

HANDLE WITH CARE

Lady's purse *Calceolaria* Herbeohybrida Group is notoriously tender and so best kept for indoor gardens. It can be enjoyed outside in warmer climates, in sheltered sites with filtered light.

PROTECTING YOUR PLANTS

If temperatures are unseasonably warm, your transplants may like a few days of sun protection, especially during the afternoon. Use the lath fencing you used for hardening them off (see "Hardening Off" on page 42 for details), or shelter them with sheets of newspaper clipped to stakes or cages. Mist seedlings occasionally if they wilt, but don't add a lot of extra water to the soil; swampy soil is as bad as dry soil for tender roots.

If late frosts threaten, protect plants through the night with overturned cans, buckets or clay flower pots. Floating row covers (weigh down the edges with rocks or boards) can provide a few degrees of frost protection and also protect young plants from birds and other troublesome animal pests.

Sometimes, soil-dwelling caterpillars, called cutworms, will feed on seedlings at night, eating them off right at ground level. To protect young plants, you can surround them with a metal or cardboard collar. Slip sections of paper towel rolls over seedlings or open-ended soup or juice cans over transplants. Press the collar into the soil, so at least 1 inch (2.5 cm) is below the soil and several inches are left above. Remove after 2 or 3 weeks, or mulch over them and remove at the end of the season; paper collars will break down on their own.

Remember, too, that it isn't just unwanted attention from animal pests or damage from extremes of hot and cold that threaten young plants; spacing them according to their growth habit is also important. Most annuals grow better when they aren't overcrowded. Crowding leads to competition for water and nutrients and it also makes them more inviting to insect pests. It also interferes with air circulation, providing ideal conditions for diseases to develop (see "Managing Pests and Diseases" on pages 52–55 for more details).

Finally, remember to wet the soil, not the leaves, when you water as this can also lead to problems.

46 GARDENING WITH ANNUALS

STEP-BY-STEP GUIDE TO TRANSPLANTIN

1. Dig a hole, then carefully remove the plant from its temporary container.
2. Set the plant in the hole base of the stem is level the surface of the soil.
3. Gently but firmly, press down the soil around the base of the plant so it is stable.
4. Water the plant thoroughly with a fine spray to wet the soil around the plant's roots.

PLANTING TIME 47

Beautiful, full-color photographs give inspiration and guidance in planning and planting your garden.

Simple explanations and general information about different aspects of gardening, providing invaluable hints and easy solutions for common garden questions.

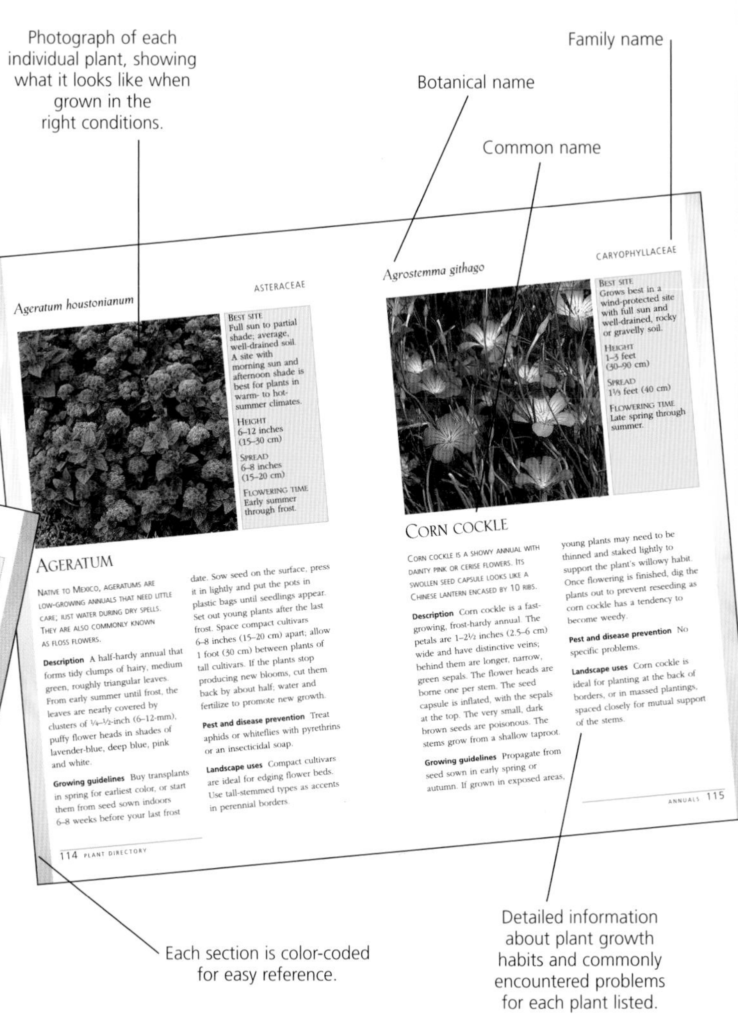

Ageratum houstonianum

ASTERACEAE

BEST SITE
Full sun to partial shade; average, well-drained soil. A site with morning sun and afternoon shade is best for plants in warm- to hot-summer climates.

HEIGHT
6–12 inches (15–30 cm)

SPREAD
6–8 inches (15–20 cm)

FLOWERING TIME
Early summer through frost.

AGERATUM

NATIVE TO MEXICO, AGERATUMS ARE LOW-GROWING ANNUALS THAT NEED LITTLE CARE; JUST WATER DURING DRY SPELLS. THEY ARE ALSO COMMONLY KNOWN AS FLOSS FLOWERS.

Description A half-hardy annual that forms tidy clumps of hairy, medium green, roughly triangular leaves. From early summer until frost, the leaves are nearly covered by clusters of $\frac{1}{4}$–$\frac{1}{2}$-inch (6–12-mm), puffy flower heads in shades of lavender-blue, deep blue, pink and white.

Growing guidelines Buy transplants in spring for earliest color, or start them from seed sown indoors 6–8 weeks before your last frost date. Sow seed on the surface, press it in lightly and put the pots in plastic bags until seedlings appear. Set out young plants after the last frost. Space compact cultivars 6–8 inches (15–20 cm) apart; allow 1 foot (30 cm) between plants of tall cultivars. If the plants stop producing new blooms, cut them back by about half; water and fertilize to promote new growth.

Pest and disease prevention Treat aphids or whiteflies with pyrethrins or an insecticidal soap.

Landscape uses Compact cultivars are ideal for edging flower beds. Use tall-stemmed types as accents in perennial borders.

114 PLANT DIRECTORY

Agrostemma githago

CARYOPHYLLACEAE

BEST SITE
Grows best in a wind-protected site with full sun and well-drained, rocky or gravelly soil.

HEIGHT
1–3 feet (30–90 cm)

SPREAD
1$\frac{1}{3}$ feet (40 cm)

FLOWERING TIME
Late spring through summer.

CORN COCKLE

CORN COCKLE IS A SHOWY ANNUAL WITH DAINTY PINK OR CERISE FLOWERS. ITS SWOLLEN SEED CAPSULE LOOKS LIKE A CHINESE LANTERN ENCASED BY 10 RIBS.

Description Corn cockle is a fast-growing, frost-hardy annual. The petals are 1–2$\frac{1}{2}$ inches (2.5–6 cm) wide and have distinctive veins; behind them are longer, narrow, green sepals. The flower heads are borne one per stem. The seed capsule is inflated, with the sepals at the top. The very small, dark brown seeds are poisonous. The stems grow from a shallow taproot.

Growing guidelines Propagate from seed sown in early spring or autumn. If grown in exposed areas, young plants may need to be thinned and staked lightly to support the plant's willowy habit. Once flowering is finished, dig the plants out to prevent reseeding as corn cockle has a tendency to become weedy.

Pest and disease prevention No specific problems.

Landscape uses Corn cockle is ideal for planting at the back of borders, or in massed plantings, spaced closely for mutual support of the stems.

ANNUALS 115

For zonal information, refer to Plant Hardiness Zone Maps, starting on page 308.

Part One

Background Basics

UNDERSTANDING ANNUALS

Some of the best-known annuals have achieved their popularity because of their free-flowing nature. If you remove spent flowers to prevent seed formation, they'll bloom until the cold weather arrives.

ALL ABOUT ANNUALS

True annuals germinate, grow, flower, set seed and die in one growing season. Their single goal is to reproduce themselves. This is good news for the gardener, since it means that most annual plants will flower like mad to achieve this.

The first frost usually kills the plants and signals the end of the bloom season for that year. Although you'll need to replant most flowering annuals the following spring to get another show, some species will sprout from seed dropped by last year's plants; some of these plants are named on page 15.

A TRUE ANNUAL

Sweet peas are hardy, true annuals, which means that they perform best in cooler conditions and can survive early or late light frosts. Even so, time sowings to avoid frosts during flowering.

TENDER AND TRUSTY

Zinnias are tender, true annuals with the fortunate habit of covering up old, faded, early-season blooms with new growth and flowers. They are also known as "youth and old age."

CATEGORIZATION

Common foxgloves fall into two main categories: They are both biennials and short-lived perennials, meaning that in some cases they will live for more than two years.

What Is a Biennial?

Biennials have much in common with annuals, but they differ in one major respect: They take two years to complete their life cycle. The first year after sowing, they produce a leaf structure, building energy for the next year. Common garden biennials include honesty *Lunaria annua*, foxglove *Digitalis purpurea* and sweet William *Dianthus barbatus*.

Perennials Grown as Annuals

Besides true annuals, there are a number of perennial plants that are thought of as annuals. These include tender perennials, such as zonal geraniums, or perennials that flower the first season from seed, such as four-o'clocks. These plants live for years in frost-free areas but, like true annuals, they die in freezing temperatures.

SUMMERTIME STAYERS

Zonal geraniums are always grown as annuals, except in frost-free areas. If you live in a cold-winter climate, try potting them up and overwintering indoors. Otherwise, start with new plants or sow seed in spring.

Kinds of Annuals

Annuals are usually further separated into three groups: hardy, half-hardy and tender, based on their cold tolerance. It's useful to know which type of annual you're growing so that you know how soon you can get away with planting it in spring. The catalog, seed packet or plant tag should tell you whether your plant is hardy, half-hardy or tender.

Hardy annuals include forget-me-nots, pansies, snapdragons and other plants that can withstand several degrees of freezing temperatures. Most of these plants perform best during cool weather. They are often planted in early spring by gardeners in cold-winter areas or in autumn by gardeners in warmer areas. Some hardy annuals, such as ornamental kale, are also associated with cool autumn weather.

Half-hardy annuals fit somewhere in the middle of hardy and tender. They will often withstand a touch of frost near the beginning or the end of the gardening season. Many of the most commonly grown annuals fit into this particular category.

A half-hardy classification is like yellow on a traffic signal: You need to use your judgment to decide when you can plant safely. If your spring has been a bit on the warm side and you're itching to plant—even though your average frost-free day has not arrived—you might just get away with planting half-hardy annuals. If you do, though, be

TOUGH ENOUGH

The dainty flowers of forget-me-not don't look particularly robust, yet they are resilient enough to be frost-hardy.

prepared to cover them if cold night temperatures are predicted. Consider hedging your bets by planting out only part of your half-hardy seeds or transplants at one time; then wait a week or two before planting the rest.

Tender annuals, originally from tropical or subtropical climates, can't stand a degree of frost. More than that, they often grow poorly during cool weather and may be stunted in their growth following prolonged exposure to temperatures below 50°F (10°C). For best results, wait until late spring to plant tender annuals, such as love-lies-bleeding *Amaranthus caudatus*, wax begonia *Begonia* spp., browallia *Browallia speciosa* and celosia *Celosia argentea*.

Most of the popular perennials that are grown as annuals fall into the tender category, except for those that are biennial, and will survive only one season. The exception to this is if you live in a mild, frost-free climate.

Dependable Reseeding Annuals and Biennials

Many gardeners count on reseeding annuals and biennials for perennial pleasures. Far from being a nuisance, they delight many gardeners with their perseverance and their ability to pop up in the most unexpected places. Exactly which plants will self-sow depends on your area, but hollyhock, pot marigold, California poppy and morning glory are some of the most dependable.

RELIABLE REPEATER

Cosmos is another reliable reseeding annual that will reappear in your garden every late summer and autumn.

TUBEROUS ROOTS

Ranunculi grow from claw-like tubers. Once spring flowering has finished, the best tubers can be lifted, dried out for a few days (away from the sun), and stored in a cool, dry place.

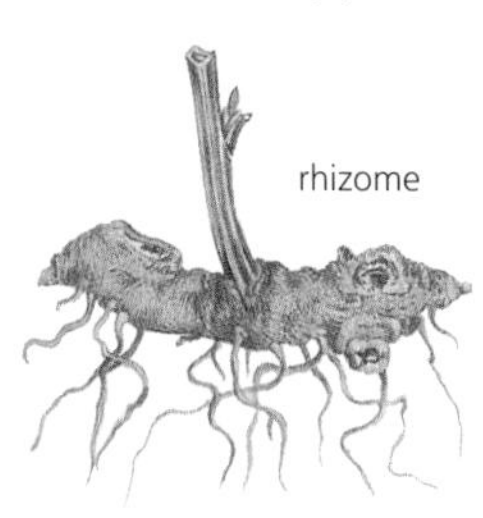

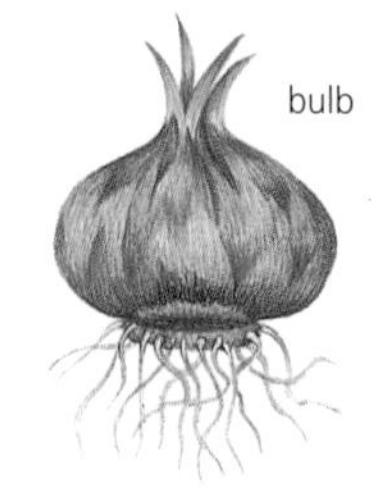

Understanding Bulbs

Many different plants that have underground storage structures are grouped together as "bulbs." But technically, these structures are classified as true bulbs, corms, tubers or rhizomes.

How Bulbs Grow

A bulbous plant stores energy and water below ground in an enlarged root or stem. This storage area allows the plant to grow and flower when the growing conditions are favorable and to ride out unfavorable weather in a dormant state.

Of course, not all bulbous plants behave in the same manner. Some may be stimulated to grow by the return of the rainy season; others respond to warmth. While you don't need to know exactly which conditions encourage a particular bulb to bloom, it's helpful to know that all bulbs go through a cycle of growth and dormancy. The individual entries in the "Plant Directory," starting on page 240, will explain the cycle for each bulb listed, so you'll know when to plant and when to divide or lift and store.

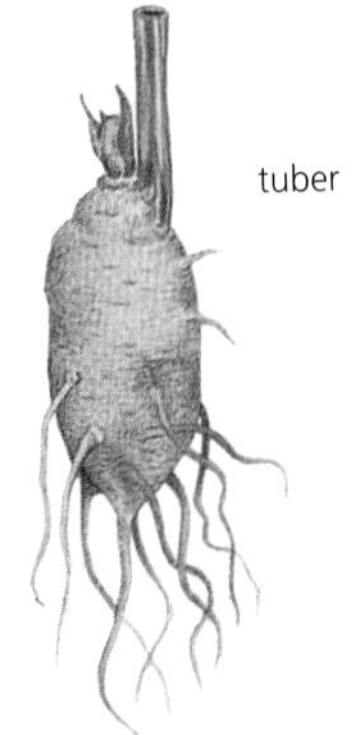

Kinds of Bulbs

True bulbs must reach a particular size before they can flower. With sufficient water, nutrients and light, the bulb will blossom reliably the first year. True bulbs reproduce by seed and by bulblets, produced at the base of the mother bulb.

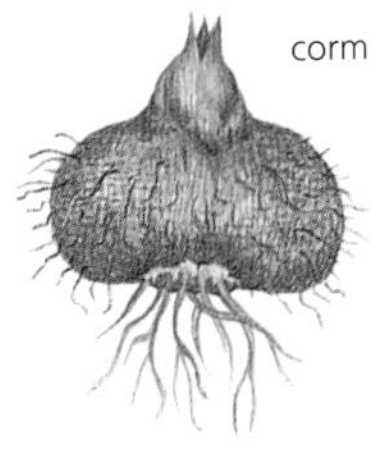

A corm is solid—a reservoir of energy without an embryonic flower inside. As it grows, a corm exhausts its resources and often grows a new corm to replace the old one. Corms also reproduce by forming small new corms, called cormlets or cormels, around the main corm.

Like corms, tubers are solid storage structures. But, unlike corms, tubers can sprout roots from "eyes" (buds) scattered over their surface. They can adapt to most situations as long as they have warmth and moisture. In cold-winter areas, lift them in autumn and store them indoors. Most tubers can be cut or broken to increase stock.

A rhizome is a fleshy, creeping stem that is either visible at ground level or hidden underground. Roots are produced on its underside. Most rhizomes are planted horizontally so the roots can grow down into the soil. To increase rhizomes, cut them into pieces and then replant.

TRUE COLOR

It's hard to beat the pure color power of tulips, which grow from true bulbs. To repeat the show every spring, you may need to replant with new bulbs each autumn.

Annuals and Bulbs in Your Garden

COMPATIBILITY

Madagascar periwinkle, mealy-cup sage and cosmos work well in combination because of the striking color contrasts and the differences in height. All three thrive in a site with full sun.

You could spend a lifetime exploring the rich diversity of annuals and bulbs. If you're looking for exciting ways to enjoy these plants in your garden, here are some ideas to get you started.

Annuals for Garden Challenges

Annuals are ideal for all sorts of gardening challenges. If you have just moved into a new house, you could fill the garden for a year or two while you decide on your long-term landscaping plans. Or, if you rent a home, annuals allow you to enjoy flower gardening without the more permanent investment in perennials. Annuals are great for city gardens, since they can make the most of compact spaces and less-than-ideal sites.

Tall annuals and annual vines are perfect for hiding unsightly views, ugly fences, stumps or neighbors' yards. Annuals also make unbeatable garden accents and fillers in beds and borders.

LONG-LASTING LILIES

True lilies, such as these Asiatic lilies, have blooms that can last for up to a week, unlike daylilies, whose flowers have a 1-day duration. The lovely large flower heads are perfect for adding height to the back of beds and borders.

FANTASTIC FILLERS

Annuals and bulbs, such as these irises, love-in-a-mist and star-of-Persia, are ideal for filling new garden areas until you have the time and the money for permanent plantings. Mixing height, color and flower shapes can create a truly magical effect.

Bulbs for Every Purpose

Like annuals, bulbs are often used in masses in large-scale landscapes for a showy display. But they are just as adaptable for those on a tighter budget or with space restrictions. Well-chosen bulbs can create equally stunning effects in many parts of the home garden.

Bulbs are especially useful in beds and borders when tucked into perennial plantings, since they get the bloom season off to an early start. It's hard to beat them for early color.

Hyacinths, Madonna lilies, tuberoses and many other bulbs offer sweet fragrances that are delightful both outdoors and indoors.

Even without fragrance, many hardy and tender bulbs are excellent for cutting gardens. They also thrive in pots, adding a touch of movable spring color that you can even bring indoors.

Soil and Site Conditions

When you're growing annuals and bulbs in pots, you can adjust the soil mix for each particular plant. But for in-ground gardening, you need to match plants with existing soil and site conditions.

TEXTURE TEST

To see how clayey your soil is, rub a moistened ball of soil about the size of a golf ball between your palms. The goal is to make a "worm" or rope. If you succeed, your soil is more than 15 percent clay; the longer the worm the higher the content of clay.

Testing Your Soil

You can learn a lot about your garden by feeling the soil. To determine your soil type, take a handful of moist (not muddy) soil, squeeze it and open your hand. If the soil crumbles, it's on the sandy side. Sandy soils often drain well but don't hold much water or nutrients. Drought-tolerant annuals, such as California poppy and creeping zinnia, are ideal

MOISTURE LOVER

Common snowdrop thrives in quite moist soil conditions. But, that doesn't mean that it's okay to plant it in soggy or poorly drained soil. It is perfect for planting in drifts or large clumps at the edge of a garden pond.

for sandy sites. Many bulbs also thrive in light, sandy soils.

If the soil forms a clump but breaks apart when you tap it lightly, it's on the loamy side. Loamy soils tend to hold a good balance of water and nutrients, so they can support a variety of annuals and bulbs without much effort on your part.

If the soil stays in a clump even when you tap it, it's probably high in clay. Clays tend to be waterlogged when wet and very hard when dry. While some annuals and bulbs can adapt to heavy, clay soils, it's usually best to dig in lots of organic matter to improve the soil conditions.

You'll find more information about specific annuals and bulbs and the kinds of soil they prefer in the "Plant Directory," starting on page 114. There's also more information about mulching and fertilizing annuals and bulbs to balance soil needs with the type of soil you have in your garden in "Caring for Annuals" on pages 48–51 and "Caring for Bulbs" on pages 80–83.

Building Healthy Soil

If you can see some raw compost, such as leaves or clumpy roots, around the top layer of your soil, it's probably in pretty good shape. If you can't see any at all, it's a good idea to add some. Digging compost into the soil before planting should do the trick. Or, add compost tea to give the soil a quick nutrient boost and to fertilize plants. Soak a shovelful of compost wrapped in a burlap sack in a watering can filled with water. After a few days, drench the soil with the energy-rich liquid.

SITE SELECTION

One of the most important considerations in planning your garden is planting the right plant in the right site. If you have a hot, sunny site with dry or sandy soil, look for drought-tolerant annuals, such as creeping zinnia.

Assessing Your Site

If you've lived in the same house for years, you probably already know which parts of your yard are sunny and which are shady. But if you've just started gardening or if you've recently moved to a new home, figuring this out is your first step to planning a good garden.

COPING WITH SLOPES
Make the most of hillsides and slopes by adapting your garden plan to the lay of the land. On gentle slopes, make shallow basins (top) to trap moisture and minimize erosion. Terraces (bottom) are a better option if you have to handle steep slopes.

Starting today, or the next sunny day, observe how the sun hits your garden. Do you have full sun throughout much of the garden for the entire day? Is the light blocked on one or more sides by buildings, other structures or evergreen trees? Through the seasons, do deciduous trees block more sunlight, or does the changing angle of the sun open some areas up to more sun?

To get the most accurate picture of your garden's sun and shade patterns, you really need to observe your yard

DESIGN POTENTIAL
A terraced bed of stone or timber not only allows you to create a garden on a sloping site, it opens up potential for design interest. The effect of this stone terrace is softened by the color and texture of the petunias and salvias.

SUCCEEDING IN SHADE
Shade-loving browallia is one of the few annuals that will happily thrive out of the sun. It is the perfect choice for filling any dark or neglected parts of the garden with a burst of color.

LIKE MINDS
Bearded irises and daylilies both prefer a site with full sun or partial shade. They also need soil that is moist but not waterlogged.

over a full year. Note which spots are shaded for part of the day during the changing seasons, and which are sunbaked. After a year, you'll have a record to help you plan future plantings.

Of course, this doesn't mean that you can't plant anything until you've watched the garden for a year. Many annuals are surprisingly tolerant of a range of conditions, and they may grow well even if the site turns out to be a little sunnier or shadier than you expected.

Hillsides and slopes are difficult to mow and weed, so the best strategy is to cover them with plants that take care of themselves. Or, if you're willing to invest some time and money, you can build retaining walls or terraced beds that will safely and attractively support a wide range of beautiful annuals and bulbs.

Building a rock garden is another great solution for a sunny, well-drained slope. Place large rocks around at random then half-bury them when they're in position, to stop them washing away.

LIFT AND STORE

In mild-winter areas, gladiolus corms can stay in the ground all year long. In cold climates, though, you'll have to lift them in autumn for winter storage indoors. Keep them in a darkened place that is cool to warm, in a net bag or a basket of dry peat moss.

Climate Considerations

To have healthy, vigorous annuals and bulbs that will grow and thrive with minimal care, it is essential to choose plants that are best adapted to the climate in your area, zonally and locally.

Why Climate Is Important

Knowing about your climate is another important planning tool; it will tell you what you can plant. The three types of climate that you need to consider are your hardiness zone, your local climate and your garden's microclimate.

When you're growing annuals, it is essential that you know the dates of the average first and last frost in your area. These dates will help you decide when it's safe to sow or transplant. They'll also tell you the length of the growing season that you can expect.

Plant Hardiness Zones

Hardiness zones are based on average minimum yearly temperatures. The "Plant Hardiness Zone Maps," on pages 308–311, will help you locate your zone. If you choose plants that are hardy for your zone, you can be fairly confident that they will survive an average winter in your area. You'll find that each bulb entry in the "Plant Directory" gives a range of hardiness zones. If a plant is listed as hardy in Zones 5–8, for example, you could grow it in Zones 5–8; Zones 4 and less would be too cold.

Local Weather Patterns

Hardiness zones help to narrow down your plant choices, but they aren't foolproof guidelines. If you live in a large town or city, your local area may be significantly warmer than the hardiness map would predict. Elevated and open, exposed areas may get colder than other properties in the same zone. In cold areas, consistent snow cover provides insulation and may allow you to grow plants from warmer zones. Gauging local rainfall is also crucial if you want to choose plants that won't need regular watering.

LATE-SEASON STARTERS

Ornamental kale can withstand the frosts of late autumn and often even winter. It looks great in late-season gardens, sometimes right up until early spring.

Microclimates

Each garden might have several unique growing areas which are normally called microclimates. Shady nooks fit into this category. So do hot spots, such as beds that get extra heat from walls or paving.

As you plan your plantings, look for these special spots where particular annuals and bulbs may thrive.

SOME LIKE IT HOT

Most annuals prefer full sun for at least part of the day, but rose moss *Portulaca grandiflora* must have the benefit of full sun all day long. It is adaptable in that it can cope with exposure to windy weather conditions.

SELF-SUFFICIENCY

Nasturtiums pretty much take care of themselves. They don't require any special treatment.

Planning Your Plantings

For a garden to be effective, it has to match your site conditions, your style, the amount of time you can set aside for gardening and the results you want from the garden. It just takes a little planning.

What to Plant

Chances are that you already have some idea of what you want to grow in your garden. As you flip through books, magazines and catalogs for more ideas, it's fun to make a wish list of plants you'd like to try. Along with the names, you'll also want to note the features of each plant, including its light and soil preferences, height, color and season of interest, or bloom time.

If you have already chosen a site for your garden, go through your list and select the plants that are adapted to the site conditions. If you'd like some tips on mixing plants with different heights and colors, "Creative Combinations," on pages 30–31, will help to get you started. If you'd rather grow your annuals and bulbs for a specific purpose, such as for cutting or for fragrance, you'll have to consider the needs of each plant and then find the best spot for it to thrive.

FILLING IN THE GAPS

These tulips are accented beautifully by lower-growing annuals that will cover their maturing leaves.

Where to Plant

The key to successful planning is to always match the plants to the place they are growing. If you have your heart set on growing particular plants, your site choices are probably limited. But if you have an open mind about choosing plants, then you have a lot more freedom in your site selection.

First of all, think about how much sun a particular site gets. Many annuals and bulbs thrive in sun, but some need partial shade or filtered light.

The next thing to think about is your soil's texture. There's an annual and bulb for just about every site, but fairly loose, well-drained soil that isn't too rocky or dry is ideal. If your soil is too clayey, think about excavating and refilling with topsoil, or planting into a raised bed.

Also think about what's growing in the garden now. Clearing out overgrown shrubs is a big task. If the proposed site is currently lawn, you'll need to remove the turf or hire someone to do it for you.

PLAN AHEAD

Not everyone has the space or desire to dedicate a plot of garden just for cutting. Planting masses of tulips in beds and borders overcomes this dilemma: You can enjoy the showy display in your garden and still have plenty of extras for cutting.

HEIGHT AND HABIT

One of the most important considerations in planning a mixed planting is the height and habit of the plants, as well as color combinations. The time you spend planning what to grow will be worth it when your careful groupings of plants bloom.

Putting It on Paper

Sketching garden designs will allow you to try out many different ideas, however unrealistic, without the hassle of physically digging up and moving existing plants. Your plan may simply be the outline of the bed with scrawled notes as to roughly where the plants will go. Or, you may want to invest the time in drawing up a formal scale plan of the bed so you can make sure the garden will have just the right blend of colors, heights and textures, and you'll know just what you need to buy. Some gardeners still prefer to follow their creative urges with plants in hand, designing on the spot. But planning on paper does have one distinct advantage, at least for new gardeners: It can help you figure out how many plants to buy.

The number of plants you need to fill a given space depends on the size of the bed and the spread of the plant. To make a scale plan, measure the final outline of the bed and transfer the dimensions to paper. If your garden is small, you could draw the area right onto your site map. In most cases, though, it's easier to draw each planting area on a separate piece of graph paper—it will give you more room to write. Choose the largest scale that allows your design to fit on one sheet: 1 inch (2.5 cm) on paper to 1 foot (30 cm) of planting area works well for gardens shorter than 10 feet (3 m).

Draw rough outlines on your base plan to show where each plant will go. Check heights to make sure you don't have tall plants at the front, unless the short plants bloom before the tall plants fill out. Also, leave enough room between plants so that each can mature to its full spread. Remember that if you find there are unplanned and unsightly gaps when your plan turns to reality, use more annuals as fillers until you find a more permanent solution.

If you want to make sure your design is just right, make a color map so that you can visualize the color combinations and different seasons.

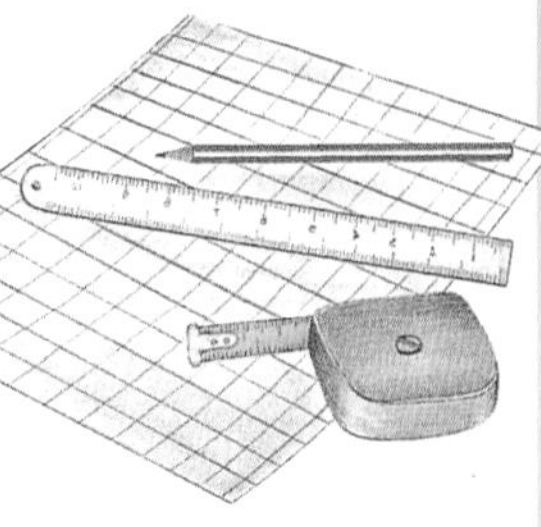

PLAN TO SCALE

The only equipment you need for making a garden plan to scale is graph paper, a ruler, a pencil and a tape measure for determining distances within your garden.

Creative Combinations

When you're a beginner, the idea of planning pleasing combinations may be a little intimidating. But once you start grouping plants with an eye for height, habit and color, you're well on the way.

Choose Compatible Plants

The first step to any good combination is choosing plants that prefer the same conditions. You might think that cornflower *Centaurea cyanus* would look charming with impatiens, but they probably won't grow well together; one needs full sun and the other prefers a shadier position in the garden.

The bloom season is another consideration. Annuals make great companions for bulbs, since the annuals can fill in the space left when the bulbs

CREATIVE CONTAINERS
Don't forget to turn your creative talents toward your container garden. Some of the most striking seasonal color comes from pairing annuals and bulbs, such as these pansies and lilies.

UNDERPLANTING
Low-growing pansies make a charming carpet under these hybrid tulips, and the color combinations are almost endless. Underplanting tall bulbs with low-growing annuals also makes the most of your space.

EYE-CATCHING EFFECTS

Experimenting with color can have surprisingly pleasing results. By grouping together plants with strong contrasting colors, you can create a full look with plenty of interest. Sometimes it takes a leap of faith to see what works.

go dormant. But if you want them to be in flower at the same time, look for those that have similar bloom times.

Unless you're planning on a mass planting of just one type of annual or bulb, it's a good idea to include plants of different sizes. Taller plants generally look best at the back of beds or the center of a bed that is viewed from several vantage points (such as an island bed in the middle of a lawn).

Combining plants with different shapes is another way to add interest to your garden. Some plants and flowers are spiky and rigid (think of hyacinths and snapdragons); some, such as love-in-a-mist and flowering tobacco, are more graceful and loose in habit. Impatiens, marigolds and many other plants have a compact, rounded shape. It's hard to go wrong if you include a variety of plant shapes in your garden.

Experimenting with Color

Colors can be harmonious or contrasting. Some gardeners prefer pastels, while others like primary hues—rich reds, sunny yellows and bright blues.

If you're planning your garden around your favorite color, you'll probably want to use many variations of that color—maybe pale and medium pinks with reds, or cream and yellow flowers with deep gold.

If you plant pastels and bold colors in separate beds, you'll avoid the "explosion in a paint factory" syndrome and learn which combinations please you the most. Go with the hues that you naturally prefer, but leave your options open to try something new and daring.

Part Two

Gardening with Annuals

COVER IT UP

Covering freshly sown seed with plastic bags or plastic wrap will help to keep the soil mix moist and reduce or eliminate the need to water.

Starting from Seed

Growing your own annuals from seed is great fun—and easier than you might think. One packet of seeds can produce dozens of plants for a fraction of the cost of buying transplants.

Sowing Seed Indoors

Starting from seed indoors often gives the best results for annuals, especially tender annuals, such as globe amaranth. Other annuals, such as dwarf morning glory and four-o'clocks, grow equally well indoors or out, but you'll get an earlier bloom if you start them indoors.

Firstly, you need to choose a suitable container to raise your seedlings in. Most pots and trays are fine, but peat pots are great because they can be transplanted into the soil along with the plant. Then pick a growing mix; standard potting mix or a seed-raising mix is best. For good growth, you then need to set your

SENSITIVE SEEDS

Impatiens, including this cultivar, are sensitive to cold weather conditions, so it's best to start them indoors from seed and set them out in the garden after all danger of frost has passed. They also grow well indoors, in pots.

Step-by-step Guide to Planting Seeds

1. Sow seed evenly over the moistened seed-raising mix.

2. Press the seed lightly into the surface with a wooden block.

3. Cover the seed according to packet directions; firm mix lightly.

4. Moisten the top of the seed-raising mix with a fine mist of water.

5. Label the tray or container to remember what you planted.

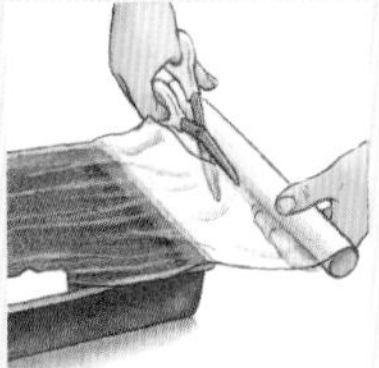

6. Cover the tray with plastic wrap until seeds begin to germinate.

seedlings in the right spot. Most annuals will sprout and grow well at average indoor temperatures (between 60° and 75°F [16° and 24°C]). Finding a spot with enough light can be tricky, so choose a sunny window sill or sunroom, or if you don't have a suitable spot, you'll have to set up a simple light system.

Knowing When to Sow

You can sow most seeds indoors in early spring, about 6–10 weeks before your last frost date, but some need to be started earlier or later. Check the seed packet for sowing times, or entries in the "Plant Directory," starting on page 114.

WAYS TO SOW SEED

The way you plant seed depends on the size of the seed. This one is medium sized, so it can be dropped into a shallow row and then lightly covered with soil.

SEED SIZE

Large seeds, such as those of four-o'clocks, need to be planted into individual holes. Make a hole using a pencil, drop the seed in and cover.

Sowing Seed Outdoors

If you don't have the time or space to raise seedlings indoors, you can still grow a wide variety of annuals from seed. Many popular annuals grow just as well from seed sown outdoors as from that sown indoors. Some even grow better from direct-sown seed because they prefer cool outdoor temperatures or because they don't respond well to transplanting. A few annuals in this easy-to-grow group include morning glories, California poppy and rocket larkspur. To find out if the annuals you want to grow can be direct-sown, check the seed packet or the "Plant Directory" entries, starting on page 114. These sources will tell you the best time for sowing.

Direct-sowing is simple. Sow medium-sized and large seeds individually or scatter them evenly over the surface. Try to space them ½–1 inch (12–25 mm) apart. If you have very small seeds, mix them with a handful of dry sand and distribute them over the seedbed.

Cover most seeds with a thin layer of fine soil or sand. If you're dealing with fine seeds, just pat them into the soil or lightly pat down the area with a board. After sowing, make sure the seedbed stays evenly moist until the seedlings are visible. If rainfall is lacking, water gently with a watering can, sprinkler or fine hose spray. Covering the seedbed with a floating row cover helps to keep the soil moist and protects the seed from drying winds, heavy rain and birds. (Remove the cover once the seedlings emerge.)

Dealing with Damping-off

Damping-off is a disease that can strike young seedlings, killing them just before or after they emerge. Affected seedlings tend to topple over, since their stems are damaged at the soil level. Once a few seedlings are affected, the disease can quickly spread to other seedlings in the same pot or tray.

Preventing damping-off is the best approach: Water in seeds with a fungicide solution just after sowing.

Always use fresh, "sterile" seed-starting mix and knock out the old soil from reused pots. Dip the pots in a 10 percent bleach solution (1 part household bleach to 9 parts water).

Sprinkle a thin layer of sphagnum moss on top of newly planted seeds, and don't sow too closely; damping-off is more likely if seedlings are overcrowded.

Never-fail Seeds

Starting your garden from seed sown directly into the ground is one of the most economical and satisfying ways of getting started. Without a doubt, flowering annuals are one of the best ways to introduce quick color into your garden. Some annuals are naturally easier to start from seed sown outdoors, while others need to be nurtured indoors. The five best seeds for success outdoors are: cosmos, nasturtium, alyssum, sunflower and Mexican sunflower.

HEDGING YOUR BETS

A good way to start your outdoor garden is to set out indoor-grown transplants when the soil is warm enough, then plant direct-sown seeds around them.

Buying Healthy Transplants

In the fun and frenzy of spring plant shopping, it's easy to overlook quality in the quest for getting the "perfect" plant. As you choose, keep in mind that bringing home a diseased plant is a recipe for disaster.

Healthy Plant Checklist

To get the best possible results, follow these guidelines when purchasing plants.

1. Peruse the plant. It should be similar in size and color to other plants of the same type. Avoid plants that look stunted or off-color.

2. Look at the leaves. Avoid plants with yellowed leaves or brown tips (signs of improper watering). Carefully turn over a few leaves and check the undersides for signs of pests. Avoid plants with clusters of small, pear-shaped insects (aphids) or yellow-stippled leaves with tiny webs underneath (caused by spider mites).

3. Check the stems. They should be stocky and evenly colored, with no visible cuts, bruises or pest problems.

4. Inspect the roots. It's okay if a few roots are coming out of the drainage holes in the pot, but masses of tangled roots indicate that a plant is long overdue for transplantation. Overgrown plants can be saved if you loosen matted roots, but it's better to start with younger plants.

CLOSE INSPECTION

Check the top and underside of plant leaves carefully for signs of whitefly (below).

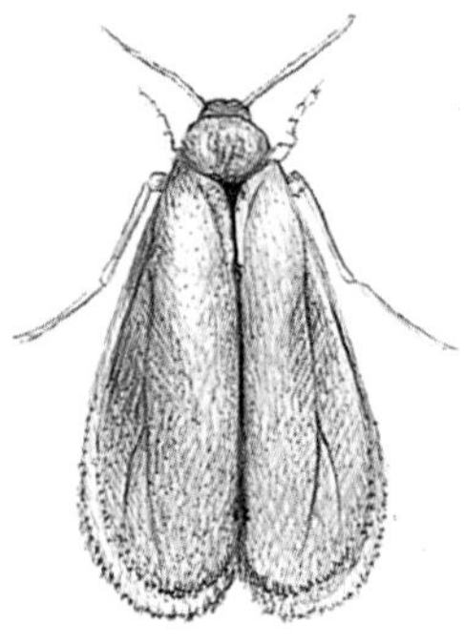

TRANSPLANTS

Try to buy transplants that have healthy leaf growth, as they are quicker to establish.

LEAN CONDITIONS
Unless you're planting annuals that prefer quite lean soil conditions, such as nasturtiums *Tropaeolum majus*, you'll want to work some organic matter into the soil. For nasturtiums, extra nitrogen can promote leaves at the expense of flowers.

DIGGING IN
Most annuals are shallow-rooted. Loosening the top 8–10 inches (20–25 cm) of soil will provide good conditions for root growth. Use a spade or fork to turn the top soil layer, working in any compost you've added.

Preparing the Soil

Along with proper plant selection, preparing a planting bed so that it contains good, crumbly soil is critical to the success of your garden. A careful job will be rewarded with happier plants.

Digging Up Sod

For most gardeners, new flower gardens must be reclaimed from existing lawn areas. You have two options for removing the existing sod—by hand or by machine.

Digging up sod by hand is an option if you have plenty of time or energy, or if you only have a small area to clear. Water the area a day or two before, then use a spade to cut the sod into small squares, about 6 inches (15 cm) on each side. Pull up each block and shake it over the bed to remove excess soil. Then toss the block in a wheelbarrow to go to your compost pile.

Renting a sod-cutting machine is more expensive, but it's also an easier way to clear larger areas for planting.

Adding Amendments to Soil

The ideal time to prepare a planting area is autumn. This will give the amendments a chance to improve soil conditions and allow the soil to settle.

Composted organic matter is the most common amendment added to garden soil. It helps sandy soil hold more water, loosens heavy clay soil and adds a slow-release supply of nutrients to all soils.

If you don't already have a compost pile, think about making one, or simply buy bags of composted manure.

FERTILIZER

Decomposed organic matter, or humus, is rich in nutrients and makes a great fertilizer for boosting flower growth.

HOME-GROWN

A compost mulch may be all most annuals need to produce steady, productive growth. But if your soil is depleted in specific minerals, you may need to supplement with a suitable mineral fertilizer.

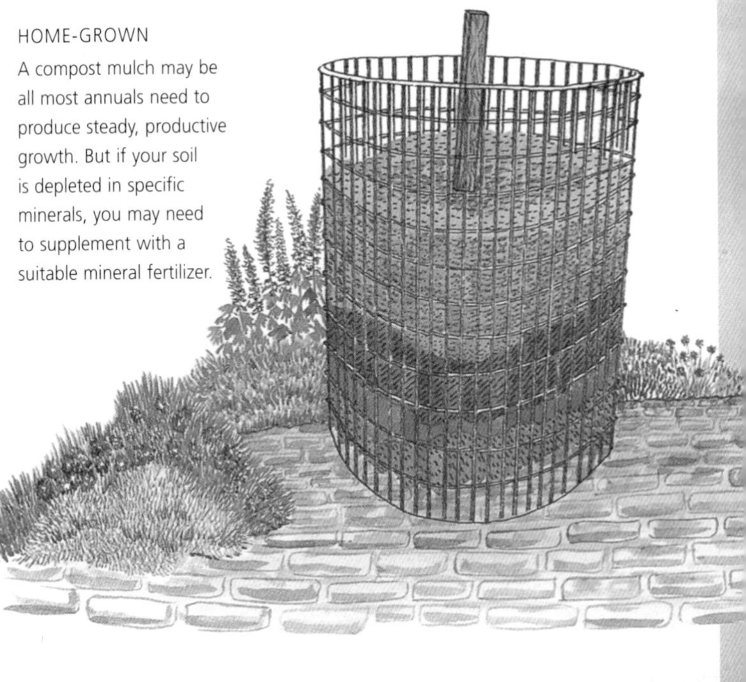

Setting Out Transplants

You have your plants, and you have a place to put them. Now you're ready to plant. The last step is to make sure that your seedlings are "hardened off," or adjusted to the conditions outside.

EARLY STARTERS

Pansies are usually grown as hardy annuals because they can survive early frosts.

Hardening Off

Seedlings will need to be hardened off before transplanting. This involves gradually exposing them to the harsher outdoor conditions: more sunlight, drying winds and varying temperatures.

Start by moving seedlings outdoors on a nice day. Set shade-loving annuals in a sheltered, shady spot for 2 or 3 days before planting. Give sun-loving annuals about 1 hour of full sun, then move them into the shade of a fence or covered porch. (Take them in at night if a frost threatens.) Lengthen the sun time each day, over a period of at least 3 days, until plants can take a full day of sun. Then you can plant them in the garden.

If you don't have a shady spot for hardening off, or if temperatures are unseasonably warm, protect young seedlings under lath fencing or shelter them with sheets of newspaper clipped to stakes or cages.

SEEDLING PREPARATION

Frost-tender nemesia seedlings need to be hardened off before they can be transplanted into your garden.

Using Your Plan

Before planting your annuals, refer back to the notes you made earlier in the season. (See "Planning Your Plantings" on pages 26–29 for details.) Those notes will

MAKING ROOM

If you're going to tuck transplants in around existing plants in beds and borders, you can simply dig an individual hole for each transplant. Otherwise, you'll have to think about spacing them, as appropriate.

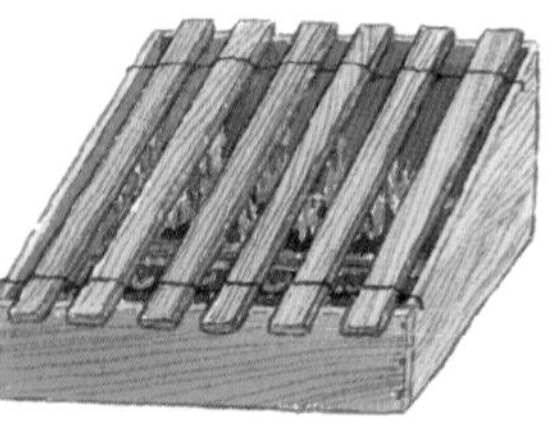

ACCLIMATIZING

Sheltering seedlings beneath sections of lath fencing will give a continuously shifting pattern of sun and shade, giving them time to adjust.

remind you where you wanted the different plants to go and what spacings they need. Check spacing requirements on the back of seed packets, plant labels or entries for individual plants in the "Plant Directory," starting on page 114.

Spacing Transplants

Before you actually plant the annuals, set them in place to see how they look. If you are grouping several of the same kind of plant, mark the outside edge of the planting bed with a hoe or a row of pegs. Then set the plants, still in pots, inside the markers. Move them into a natural-looking arrangement. This approach works particularly well for more mature transplants in flower.

If you live in a hot, dry climate or an area with a short growing season, you may want to set plants a little closer together so they'll shade the soil and fill in faster. In humid climates, use slightly wider spacings to allow good air circulation between plants, which will minimize disease problems.

PICK A COLOR

If you're looking for particular colors, buy plants that have a few blooms, such as these pastel pink petunias. Otherwise, try plants that aren't flowering yet.

Planting Time

Although you may have been anticipating the moment of planting for months, don't rush when it arrives. Planting properly takes time and a lot of bending. Work carefully to save your body.

Getting Ready to Plant

The ideal time to prepare a planting area is in autumn. But, if you don't get a chance to prepare at that time, then early spring is okay, too. It's not a bad idea to do another soil texture test (see page 20 for details) before getting ready to plant, to check whether your hard work has paid off and the soil is ready to support the transplants.

Planting Annuals

Planting time for annuals varies. In cold areas, it is around the average date of the last frost in your area. In tropical and subtropical areas, you can plant many annuals virtually all year round.

To set out plants, use a trowel to dig a hole twice as big as the root mass. Tip the pot on its side, and gently slide the

NURSERY BEDS

You should prepare nursery beds for biennials just as you would any garden area, but site them in out-of-the-way spots so that they don't detract from your garden. Protect the plants by covering the top of the bed.

LOOSENING UP

Large, double types of marigold, such as these, grow best from transplants. More established transplants may need a little bit of extra encouragement to slip out of their plastic pot; try gently sliding a trowel around the edges of the pot.

plant out of its container. Or, if the plant is growing in a peat pot, just tear off the upper rim of the pot and place the whole pot in the hole. Set each plant so that the stem base is at the same level as it was in the pot. Fill around the roots with soil, firm the soil gently and water thoroughly.

Planting Biennials

If you decide to grow biennial plants, such as foxgloves and forget-me-nots, you need a slightly different approach. Most biennials will sprout well when sown outdoors. But if you sow them directly into the garden, their leafy first-year growth will take up room without adding any interest to your flower display.

Consider setting aside a temporary growing area, called a nursery bed, where the plants can grow through summer. Sow seed directly into the bed in spring the first year and thin the seedlings out as necessary. Dig them up in late autumn and move to their final garden spots for flowering the following spring or summer.

COVER UP

Row covers can be very handy for protecting young seedlings from frosts or unwanted animal pests.

HANDLE WITH CARE

Lady's purse *Calceolaria* Herbeohybrida Group is notoriously tender and so best kept for indoor gardens. It can be enjoyed outside in warmer climates, in sheltered sites with filtered light.

Protecting Your Plants

If temperatures are unseasonably warm, your transplants may like a few days of sun protection, especially during the afternoon. Use the lath fencing you used for hardening them off (see "Hardening Off" on page 42 for details), or shelter them with sheets of newspaper clipped to stakes or cages. Mist seedlings occasionally if they wilt, but don't add a lot of extra water to the soil; swampy soil is as bad as dry soil for tender roots.

If late frosts threaten, protect plants through the night with overturned cans, buckets or clay flower pots. Floating row covers (weigh down the edges with rocks or boards) can provide a few degrees of frost protection and also protect young plants from birds and other troublesome animal pests.

Sometimes, soil-dwelling caterpillars, called cutworms, will feed on seedlings at night, eating them off right at ground level. To protect young plants, you can surround them with a metal or cardboard collar. Slip sections of paper towel rolls over seedlings or open-ended soup or juice cans over transplants. Press the collar into the soil, so at least 1 inch (2.5 cm) is below the soil and several inches are left above. Remove after 2 or 3 weeks, or mulch over them and remove at the end of the season; paper collars will break down on their own.

Remember, too, that it isn't just unwanted attention from animal pests or damage from extremes of hot and cold that threaten young plants; spacing them according to their growth habit is also

Step-by-step Guide to Transplanting

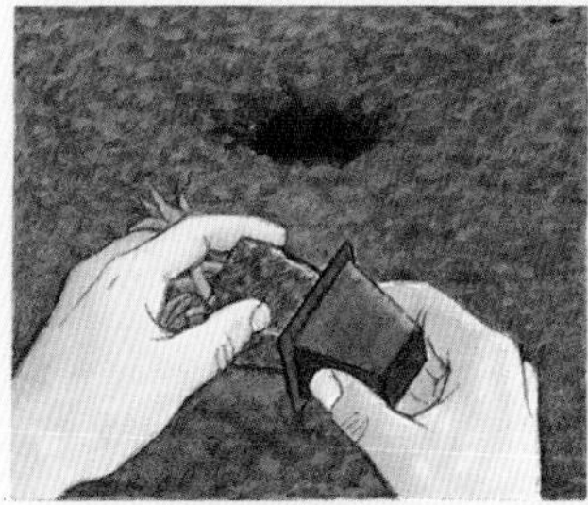

1. Dig a hole, then carefully remove the plant from its temporary container.

2. Set the plant in the hole so the base of the stem is level with the surface of the soil.

3. Gently but firmly, press down the soil around the base of the plant so it is stable.

4. Water the plant thoroughly with a fine spray to wet the soil around the plant's roots.

important. Most annuals grow better when they aren't overcrowded. Crowding leads to competition for water and nutrients and it also makes them more inviting to insect pests. It also interferes with air circulation, providing ideal conditions for diseases to develop (see "Managing Pests and Diseases" on pages 52–55 for more details).

Finally, remember to wet the soil, not the leaves, when you water as this can also lead to problems.

Caring for Annuals

While most annuals can grow just fine without much help from you, providing some basic care through the growing season will keep your flowering plants looking their absolute best.

Mulching

Organic mulches, such as grass clippings, compost, chopped leaves, cocoa shells or shredded bark, help to keep the soil moist, so plants don't need watering as often. Mulch also prevents light from reaching the soil, so weeds are less likely to sprout. And as they break down, organic mulches add a small but steady supply of nutrients to the soil.

Wait until early summer to mulch your garden, when the soil has had a chance to warm up and your seedlings or transplants are at least 4 inches

WATER WISELY

To avoid overwatering your annuals, especially in small-scale plantings or container gardens, try watering with a watering can. It'll most likely encourage you to make a little go a long way, which will ensure the best results. You'll save water, too.

MARVELOUS MULCH

Spreading organic mulches around your flowers is the number-one way to keep other garden maintenance to a minimum. As the mulch breaks down, add more once or twice during the summer to keep it at the right depth.

(10 cm) tall. Then apply a 1–2-inch (2.5–5-cm) layer of mulch over the soil. Keep it at least 1 inch (2.5 cm) from the base of the stems. You can dig it into the soil at the end of the season.

EASY DOES IT

Some reseeders, such as corn cockle, need to be watched carefully, as they have a tendency to become weedy.

Weeding

Controlling weeds is part of caring for any garden. Since the soil in annual gardens gets turned every year, perennial weeds, such as dandelions and thistles, usually don't have much chance to get established. But digging the soil does bring up buried weeds, so annual weeds can be a problem. To catch them early, prepare the soil for planting and let it sit for a week or two. Then hoe out any weeds before planting. Hand weed around the plants in early summer, then mulch.

Saving Annual Seeds

Collecting and saving annual seeds is a fun and easy way to preserve some of your favorite annuals (and save a bit of money, too!). You'll get the best results if you stick with seeds of non-hybrid annuals. These seeds are likely to produce plants that resemble their parents. Seeds of spring-blooming annuals and biennials usually are ready by midsummer; later bloomers can mature their seeds through the first frosts.

Watering

For container gardens, hand watering—either with a hose or a watering can—is the most realistic option. Container gardens tend to dry out quickly, so you may need to water every day (or even twice a day) during hot weather.

For plants in the ground, how often you water depends on how dry the soil is. Before you decide to water, pull back the mulch and feel the soil surface; if it's moist, wait a day or two and test again. If the surface is dry, dig a small hole with a trowel. When you see that the top 2 inches (5 cm) of soil are dry, it's time to water until it's moist again.

Watering by sprinkler isn't very effective and it moistens the plant leaves, making them susceptible to disease.

Fertilizing

Annuals grow quickly, so they need an ample supply of nutrients for good flowering. In spring, scatter a 1–2-inch (2.5–5-cm) layer of compost over the bed, and dig it in as you prepare the bed for planting. Or, if you're tucking annuals around perennials, mix a handful of compost into each planting hole. If you don't have compost, apply a general fertilizer over the soil. Once or twice during the season, pull back the mulch and scatter more compost or fertilizer around the base of each plant; then replace the mulch. For plants that prefer a richer soil, such as wax begonias and sweet peas, a dose of liquid fertilizer can supply the boost they need. Spray the leaves or water the plants with diluted fish emulsion or compost tea (see page 21 for details on compost tea).

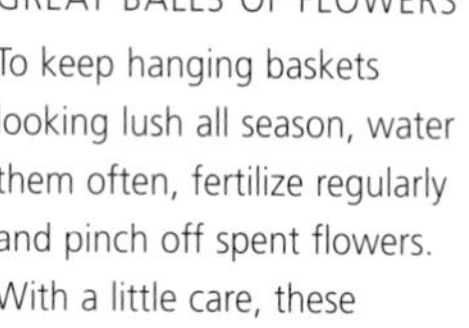

GREAT BALLS OF FLOWERS

To keep hanging baskets looking lush all season, water them often, fertilize regularly and pinch off spent flowers. With a little care, these hanging petunias will remain a solid ball of swirling color summer through autumn.

Staking

Many annuals are bred or selected for compact growth, so staking usually isn't much of a problem. It is useful, though,

IN TRAINING

Tall annuals, such as these sweet peas, need to be staked to train them. Growing vertically instead of horizontally saves space and makes cultivating and cutting easier. It also improves plant health and gives you room to interplant.

for a few plants, such as hollyhocks, tall snapdragons, castor beans and sweet peas. Choose stakes that are about three-quarters of the mature height of the plant. Put them in place early—before planting seed in the garden or as you set out transplants. As the plants grow, attach their stems loosely to the stake with string.

Shorter, thin-stemmed annuals, such as love-in-a-mist and rocket larkspur, can be supported by short pieces of twiggy brush pushed into the soil around them.

CARE AND CAUTION

A bit of moisture is good, but don't overdo it and let water cling to flowers or leaves, as this will provide ideal conditions for diseases to flourish. Some people like to mist their plants directly; just be sure to do it lightly.

Overwintering

Bringing annuals indoors during winter is called overwintering. Strictly speaking, it is tender perennials grown as annuals that can be overwintered. Dig up the plant before the first autumn frost, cut it back by about one-third, then plant it in a pot. Plant out the following spring.

PREVENTION

One way to prevent pest damage is to keep your annuals in great shape. Healthy blooms, such as these pansies, are less attractive to pests.

BENEFICIAL INSECTS

Some ladybug species prefer to eat spider mites, while others may only eat mealybugs. This ladybug is making a feast of aphids.

Managing Pests and Diseases

Most annuals are pretty much trouble-free. If you choose healthy plants that are suited to your growing conditions and care for them properly, you won't have too many pest problems to solve.

Preventing Problems

As always, prevention is better than cure. So with a little thought and planning, problems seldom become serious enough to require action on your part.

Besides spacing plants properly, watering correctly—by wetting the soil, not the leaves—will also prevent disease problems. Ideally, use a soaker hose or irrigation system that will ooze water onto the soil, where it will go right to the roots. If you must water the plants from the top, at least do it in the morning so plants will dry quickly.

Easy Organic Controls and Low-toxicity Commercial Sprays

To catch any problems that slip past your defenses, walk through your garden at least once or twice a week. Look over each planted area and inspect at least two or three plants in each area closely. Check the upper and lower surfaces, the stems and buds or flowers. If you notice any damage or discoloration, match the symptoms to those in "Common Pest and Disease Problems" on pages 54–55.

Sometimes controlling pests is as simple as spraying them with water. This can knock small pests like mites and aphids right off the plants. Pinching or cutting off infected or infested plant parts is another easy way to remove problems. If you're not squeamish, you can even handpick large pests, such as caterpillars, slugs and beetles, and drop them into soap water.

If these measures aren't effective, a simple soap spray will handle many of your pest problems. You can buy commercial insecticidal soap, or you can make your own spray by mixing 1–3 teaspoons of liquid dish soap in 1 gallon (4 l) of water. Soap spray can injure some plants, so test it out before spraying the whole plant. Repeat this treatment 2 or 3 days after the first spraying.

HOSE POWER

A simple, but effective, way to remove pests from foliage is to knock them off with a powerful spray from a garden hose. This one has a hand trigger, which gives you more control.

If pests were a problem in a particular part of your garden last year, spray the plants with insecticide, or dust them every other week with sulfur, starting in early spring.

Of course, there are a multitude of low-toxicity sprays available commercially, too. Most of them come in aerosol spray cans or pump packs for easy use. Check the label on the can to see what pests it is effective against. If you're not sure what treatment option to choose, it's always a good idea to ask for advice at your local garden center.

Common Pest and Disease Problems

WHAT YOU SEE	POSSIBLE CAUSES	SUGGESTED CONTROLS
Leaves or flowers with large, ragged holes	Slugs, snails, beetles, caterpillars	Trap slugs and snails in shallow pans of beer; handpick beetles; spray caterpillars with BT
Leaves curled, puckered or twisted	Aphids, leafhoppers	Spray affected areas with soap solution
Leaves stippled with yellow; look for tiny webs	Spider mites	Spray affected areas with soap solution
Leaves yellow-green; growth stunted	Aster yellows	Destroy infected plants
Leaves or stems speckled or silvery	Thrips	Spray affected areas with soap solution
Leaves yellow; plant weakened; tiny white insects on undersides of leaves	Whiteflies	Spray affected areas with soap solution
Leaves black and sticky or shiny	Sooty mold fungus	Control aphids and other pests causing the mold problem
Leaves and stems with small, hard bumps	Scale insects	Gently scrape bumps off the stem with your fingernail or a dull knife; spray with systemic insecticide
Leaves and stems with white, cottony clusters	Mealybugs	Spray affected areas with soap solution
Leaves with a shiny or sticky coating	Aphids, scale insects, whiteflies, slugs, snaiils	Spray affected areas with soap solution; trap slugs and snails in shallow pans of beer
Leaves or shoots with white spots or patches	Powdery mildew	Pick off badly infected leaves; spray the rest with fungicidal soap

WHAT YOU SEE	POSSIBLE CAUSES	SUGGESTED CONTROLS
Leaves or stems with orange spots	Rust	Dust every 2 weeks with sulfur; destroy badly infected plants
Leaves with brown or black spots	Plant bugs	Handpick pests
Seedlings or young plants cut off at ground level	Cutworms	No control; protect seedling stems with a cardboard or metal collar pressed partway into the soil
Seedlings dying	Damping-off fungus	Water in seeds with a fungicide solution after sowing; allow the soil to dry somewhat before resowing; thin seedlings to reduce crowding
Leaves, stems, buds or flowers with fuzzy gray mold	Botrytis blight	Pick off infected leaves and flowers; thin remaining plants
Leaves curled, webs present	Webworms	Spray with BT
Green part of leaves eaten away, with only veins remaining	Japanese beetles	Handpick beetles; spray with soap solution or all-purpose botanical pesticide
Foliage turns bronze and is unhealthy; flowers become dry	Two-spotted mite	Spray affected areas with soap solution
Plants rot at ground level	Collar rot	Remove affected plants and destroy
Flowers fall before opening	Tarnished bugs	Spray affected areas with botanical pesticide
Plants wither and die; foliage becomes puckered	Broad bean wilt virus	Control aphids and plant later in the season to avoid attack

Annuals for Containers

Annuals make perfect container plants. They grow quickly, flower profusely and provide a long season of good looks. Some also offer distinct foliage, while others perfume the air.

ADDED INTEREST

Start the season early with cold-tolerant primroses and crocuses. Their respective heights and color contrasts complement each other well.

What Plants to Choose

The first step to planning successful container plantings is choosing plants that have similar growth needs. If you have a shady area, impatiens, monkey flower and other shade-lovers are your best bets. Sunny spots can support a wider range of colorful annuals, including treasure flower, mealy-cup sage and narrow-leaved zinnia.

As a rule, try to choose annuals that are about the same height or smaller than the height of the container; otherwise, the planting may look top-heavy.

KEEP THE SHOW GOING

To keep annuals blooming as long as possible, pinch off spent flowers at least once a week. This also stops them from appearing ragged or tired. Also, keep a close eye on soil moisture, as container plants tend to dry out faster.

Window Boxes

Nothing adds country charm to a house like lush window boxes dripping with cascades of colorful flowers and foliage. While the same general principles of container gardening apply here, there are a few tips for keeping them looking great. Position the window box where watering and feeding won't be a problem, and look for flower color and foliage that suit the house and trim.

ADAPTABILITY

We tend to think of showy displays mostly in gardens in the ground, but this container garden works as both a showy display of geraniums and begonias, while it also has the feel of a quaint cottage garden.

While the plants you pick to grow together are up to you, there are some basic guidelines to follow. First, select a "star" plant. Base your container planting around one centerpiece plant—perhaps a bushy marguerite daisy, a free-flowering tuberous begonia or an ornamental cabbage. Then choose a "supporting cast" to complement the star plant and fill out the container. Try one with bold leaves or an upright habit, such as coleus.

Caring for Container Gardens

Container plants share closer quarters than garden plants, so they need some special care to stay lush and lovely. You'll need to first choose a good container. Large pots provide the best conditions for growth, since they hold more soil, nutrients and water, but they are not always practical for your needs.

Fill the container with general potting mix; straight garden soil is not suitable. After making plants sit firmly in the container, water them well and continue to water regularly, perhaps daily when the weather turns warm. Fertilize the plants every 2 weeks for good growth, and don't forget to deadhead, too.

MASS PLANTING
In large groups, marigolds provide a bright, season-long show in beds and borders. The color is unbeatable.

QUAINT AND INFORMAL
This cottage garden is an interesting mixture of informal beds and borders. You can see how colorful annuals complement a mixed perennial planting, too.

BEDS AND BORDERS

Flower beds are traditionally one of the most popular ways to display annuals. Some gardeners like to show their annual flowers in separate beds; others enjoy mixing them with bulbs and other plants.

ANNUALS ALONE

Setting aside separate beds for annual flowers is an easy way to go. Since you start with an empty area each year, spring soil preparation is a snap—just clean up any debris left in the bed, scatter some compost and dig or till to loosen the soil.

One of the decisions facing you before planting out beds and borders is if you want a formal-looking garden or an informal one. The style you choose will determine how many different annuals you'll plant and how you'll arrange them.

FORMAL DISPLAY

The combination of these flowers with dusty miller at the front makes a neat, formal display. Until the plants become established, the border can look a little bare, with soil clearly visible between the plants, but it will fill in beautifully in time.

Formal flower beds tend to have a simple, geometric shape and a limited number of different plants. The simplest may consist of a mass of just one annual, such as marigolds or geraniums. The key to success with formal beds is uniformity: You want the plants to be evenly spaced and evenly developed.

For a more casual look, informal beds and borders may suit you better. They can be any shape you like and they usually include as many different annuals as you like. You aren't limited to planting in masses or rows; set plants out in whatever groupings look good to you.

Annuals with Other Plants

Annuals have a lot to offer in groupings with other plants. In perennial borders, you can use them as a formal or informal edging. While the other plants come in and out of bloom, the annual plants add consistent color throughout most of the season. Annuals and biennials, such as foxgloves and larkspur, are so charming mixed with perennials that they are often thought of as parts of a perennial border. And, shorter, airy annuals blend in well in borders.

TRUSTY STAPLE

Hollyhocks are an old favorite for adding height at the back of beds and borders. Their charming and delicate blooms have long been a staple in cottage gardens.

Annuals as Accents

The dependable color of most flowering annuals makes them perfect for accenting perennial plantings. Their season-long color smooths the way for establishing plants.

EYE-CATCHING COLOR
These bright pink and yellow scabious make a great accent. When perennials are also in flower, the color contrasts are fantastic.

Fillers for Flower Beds

While mulch can suppress weeds, it doesn't add much excitement to a new planting. That's where filler annuals come in handy. A few seed packets of quick-growing annuals can provide welcome color and excitement at minimal cost. Sweet alyssum, flowering tobacco and cornflower are a few great fillers that can quickly cover the soil and deprive weed seeds of the light they need to grow. Self-sowing annuals will provide cover in succeeding years.

If you're looking for annuals to fill in around new perennial plantings, choose those with a similar range of heights and colors as the perennials will have. Select a few short or trailing annuals for the front of the border, a few medium-sized plants for the middle and a few taller ones for the back. While you could sow annual seed directly into the ground around the perennials, it's often easier to start with annual transplants.

Some good filler annuals, such as cleome and cornflower, will drop seed and come back year after year. If your annuals do reseed, thin the seedlings to allow the perennials room to expand.

TEMPORARY SOLUTIONS

In partially completed formal gardens, a colorful display of annuals, such as these zinnias, gives you the time to redesign at leisure. It can act as a temporary filler and ready-made flower bed in one.

GROUNDCOVERS

Try planting a colorful mix of low-growing annuals such as these ice plants, impatiens, petunias and flowering tobacco, around new trees.

Fillers for Groundcovers

Low-growing annuals, such as sweet alyssum and rose moss, make great fillers for young groundcover plantings. Stick with one kind of annual for a uniform effect. In this case, it's just as easy to scatter seed around the groundcover plants, or, if you like, set out transplants in the available spaces instead. While many low-growing annuals will self-sow, you may want to scatter some fresh seed over the planting for the first few springs until the groundcover starts to fill in.

Fillers for Foundation Plantings

New foundation plantings also benefit from annuals for the first few years as they develop. Shrubs and groundcovers may take over their allotted space in a few years, but a carpet of annuals is most welcome in the meantime. A few market packs of favorite annuals will be easy to plant, and the resulting flowers and foliage will provide infinitely more interest than a dull covering of bark chips.

AFFORDABLE OPTION

You don't have to spend a fortune on trellises and supports. These runner beans are trained up a tripod of bamboo cane supports.

Annuals for Screens

While the word "annual" commonly brings to mind compact, small plants, there are some fast-growing annuals that can reach amazing heights of 6 feet (1.8 m) or more in a single season.

Tall Annuals

Grow tall annuals in your yard to block or cover unattractive features, such as dog runs, alleys or clothesline poles. Or plant a row or mass of tall annuals to create a "neighbor-friendly" temporary fence that delineates your property line or separates different areas of your garden. Some top-notch tall annuals include castor bean *Ricinus communis*,

QUICK SOLUTIONS

Morning glory and black-eyed Susan vines are hard-to-beat solutions for creating a shady screen. They are both quick growing and thrive in containers, making them perfect for creating a cozy nook on your patio.

summer cypress *Bassia scoparia* f. *trichophylla*, hollyhocks *Alcea rosea*, sunflowers *Helianthus annuus* and Mexican sunflower *Tithonia rotundifolia*. For more information on growing these high-risers, see their individual entries in the "Plant Directory," starting on page 114.

Annual Vines

A leafy curtain of annual vines is an ideal way to ensure privacy on a porch or patio without appearing to be unneighborly. Flowering vines also add a quaint, old-fashioned touch to an ordinary support. A cloak of morning glories can convert a ho-hum garden shed into a charming garden feature, while a mass of scarlet runner bean will accent an arch or liven up a lamppost.

Most annual vines cover territory in a hurry. You can easily train them to climb a wooden or wire trellis, chain-link fences, lattice work or even strong twine. Tall wooden or bamboo stakes also make effective supports. While annual vines are usually lighter than woody vines (such as wisteria or trumpet creeper), they can put on a lot of growth in one season, so supply a sturdy support. Unlike clinging vines such as ivy, annual vines mostly climb with tendrils or twining stems, so don't expect them to scamper up a bare wall without assistance.

Besides being covered with clusters of colorful blooms, scarlet runner bean has the added bonus of edible beans for summer salads.

Potted Vines

1. Position the support in the container before planting.

2. Firm down the soil and train the vine up the support.

3. Water only the soil of vining plants in containers.

Designing a Color Theme Garden

We all have a favorite color or two, so why not indulge yourself and plant a garden dedicated to your most cherished colors. Color theme gardens are fun to plan, and the results can be delightful.

Hot-color Borders

If knock-your-socks-off color is what you want, consider planning a garden around the hot colors: reds, oranges and yellows. These colors are ideal for accenting outlying areas of your yard, since they tend to catch your eye across long distances. Many annuals are available in these bright hues, including love-lies-bleeding, summer cypress, flowering tobacco and scarlet sage.

GO-BETWEEN

Like cool-color plantings, soft pinks (such as these sweet alyssum), yellows and baby blues planted together tend to have a calm, soothing effect. To keep the garden from looking too washed out, add some spark with bright white flowers or one bright color.

TURN UP THE HEAT

If you're looking for can't-miss color, an all-red border might be the perfect accent you're after. Plant love-lies-bleeding or flowering tobacco in a hot-color border. Reddish brown leaves work with reds, too.

COMPATIBLE COLORS

Blues and purples look best where you can see them up close. Use them to effect by harmonizing the various shades and flower forms.

AN ALL-BLUE GARDEN

Blue theme gardens have a cool, restrained look, but they can be tricky to pull off. Blue and green are such similar colors that blue flowers tend to blend into the background sea of green leaves. Try varying the different kinds of blue, from soft lavender to bright sky blue and deep cobalt-blue. Interplanting with silver-leaved plants, such as dusty miller, is excellent for adding contrasts.

COOL-COLOR BORDERS

If you're not especially adventurous in your color choices, a planting of cool colors may be more to your liking. Blues, violets and greens are best planted where you can see them up close—perhaps along a path or near a deck. If you plant these deep colors in distant beds, they'll tend to fade into the background.

COLORING IN

Forget-me-nots are great for all-blue gardens or as a strong contrast between paler colors.

CREATING ACCENTS USING FOLIAGE

Leaves have lots of color to offer, too. They come in a surprising array of different greens, from the blue-green of California poppy to the yellow-green of summer cypress or the deep green of geraniums. And don't forget to consider the colorful leaves of coleus in your color theme garden. Silver-leaved plants, such as dusty miller, also work well in most garden designs.

CREATING A CUTTING GARDEN

MAIN ATTRACTION
The dried seed heads of wild teasel make an attractive and unusual central focus in mixed, dried arrangements.

If you enjoy having fresh-cut flowers to display indoors but dislike denuding your carefully planned flower beds, consider starting a cutting garden. It doesn't need to be anything fancy.

BEST ANNUALS FOR CUTTING

Keep in mind that some annuals thrive in the heat of summer, while others prefer cooler temperatures. Plan to sow some of each type in your cutting garden to have a steady supply of blooms.

Some of the best annuals for cutting include snapdragon, pot marigold, China aster, celosia, cornflower, rocket larkspur, cosmos, sweet William, sweet pea, sunflower, common stock and zinnia.

HANDLING CUT FLOWERS

The best time to collect cut flowers is in the morning, before it gets too hot. Select blooms that are just opening. Cut the bloom stalks with shears or a sharp knife, taking as much stem as you think you'll need for your arrangement. Put the cut stems immediately into a pail of lukewarm water.

CUTTING FLOWERS
The elegant blooms of Canterbury bells are a must for including in the cutting garden. If you don't have a designated cutting garden, plant extras in a border, such as that pictured opposite, for use in fresh flower arrangements.

DRYING CUT FLOWERS

For best results, pick flowers for drying in the morning, before they are fully open. To keep the stems straight and stiff, separate them into groups of six to eight stems, secure with a rubber band and hang upside-down in a dark, dry place.

Annuals for Fragrance

To some gardeners, having fragrant flowers is just as important as having particular colors or kinds of plants. If you're a fragrance fanatic there are endless scented annuals to choose from.

Scented Blooms

For fragrant flowers, consider sweet William *Dianthus barbatus* or China pinks *D. chinensis*, two carnation relatives noted for their spicy scents. Sweet alyssum *Lobularia maritima* is a common and easy-to-grow annual that's beloved for its fresh, honey-like fragrance. Mignonette *Reseda odorata* is an old-fashioned favorite with small, insignificant flowers but a powerful and delightful fragrance.

A few annuals withhold their scents until the sun sets, then release their sweet perfume on the evening breeze. Night-scented stock *Matthiola longipetala* subsp. *bicornis*, sweet rocket *Hesperis matronalis* and nicotiana *Nicotiana sylvestris* carry remarkably potent night scents.

To get the most pleasure from your fragrant plants, grow them where you will walk, sit or brush by them often. Try them along the path to your front door, around a deck or patio, or in a foundation planting near open windows for indoor enjoyment. Raised beds and

ALL-SEASON SCENT

The distinctive fragrance and almost unlimited color choice make petunias an unbeatable inclusion in any annual garden. They also thrive in containers, so you can enjoy their fragrance indoors or outdoors from summer through frost.

Favorite Aromatic Annuals

Here are a few easy annuals and biennials grown for fragrance:

Wallflower
Erysimum cheiri
Sweet William
Dianthus barbatus
Sweet pea (right)
Lathyrus odoratus
Common stock
Matthiola incana
Four-o'clock
Mirabilis jalapa
Flowering tobacco
Nicotiana alata
Petunia
Petunia x *hybrida*

TRY BEFORE BUYING

Not all flowering tobacco cultivars are scented: Smell the blooms before purchase.

container gardens are especially good spots for scented plants, since they'll be closer to your nose and easier to sniff. Keep in mind that scents are subjective; what's pleasing to one may be offensive to another.

Fragrant Foliage

Of course, flowers aren't the only source of garden scents; some annuals have fragrant leaves as well. Scented geraniums (including *Pelargonium tomentosum*, *P. crispum* and *P. graveolens*) are noted for their aromatic leaves. When you rub them, they release scents resembling those of peppermint, lemons, roses and many other plants. Annual herbs such as basil, anise and dill also offer fragrant foliage.

Edible Annuals

A MIXED BUNCH
Combining taller or upright plants with short or sprawling herbs allows room for each to grow without crowding.

NATURAL DETERRENT
Nasturtiums deter aphids from eating vegetable crops.

Besides adding colorful flowers and foliage to your garden, some annuals also add flavor to your food! Annual herbs and vegetables are easy to grow, and they'll spice up your favorite dishes.

Annual Herbs

What would a cook's garden be without basil? This peppery herb is a traditional part of pestos and tomato dishes. It's also a snappy addition to salads, poultry, pasta, rice, eggs and vegetable dishes. Snip the leaves off as needed. For extra interest, look for purple-leaved basil cultivars; they are ornamental as well as edible.

Coriander is the name commonly used for the seeds of *Coriandrum sativum*, while the leaves are often referred to as cilantro. The leaves have a powerful odor and a flavor that combines sage and citrus. The fresh leaves and roots are popular in many cuisines for use in salads, sauces and relishes. The citrus-flavored seeds are a nice addition to herbal teas or desserts. Pick the leaves as needed; harvest the seeds when they begin to fall from the flower heads.

Grow dill for its lacy green leaves and flavorful seeds. The fresh leaves (often called "dill weed") are a popular addition to fish and vegetable dishes, sauces and salads, and are also used as a pickling spice.

ANNUAL VEGETABLES

Most of the vegetables you'll grow are annuals. Hardy annuals, such as spinach and lettuce, tolerate frost and are able to self-sow. Half-hardy annuals, also known as "winter annuals," need warm soil for germination but can tolerate light frosts. Half-hardy annuals, such as mustard, can be planted in the autumn for harvest the following season. Tender annuals need warm soil for germination and are frost-susceptible. Sweet corn is the best known tender annual vegetable.

Biennials, such as carrots, require 2 years to complete their life cycle, so during the first year they germinate and form a small, compact vegetable plant that remains dormant over winter. Biennials depend on the stored nutrients in their taproots to survive the cold season. In the second year, they bloom and set seed, the same way annuals do.

INTERPLANTING

You'll get twice the harvest variety if you interplant, or mix, your vegetables with flowering annuals and herbs. Interplanting enhances pest prevention, since many insect pests can't locate their favorite plants when scents and sights are mixed.

Part Three

Gardening with Bulbs

CHOOSING HEALTHY BULBS

When you buy bulbs, you get a bag full of promises: a bunch of brown-wrapped packets of plant energy that have the potential to transform themselves into colorful crocuses or delightful daffodils.

REMOVE AND REPLANT
To get the best performance from hybrid tulips, plant new bulbs each autumn.

ROOT OF THE PROBLEM
Lily bulbs may have fleshy roots when you buy them, but other bulbs shouldn't.

WHICH BULBS TO CHOOSE

With bulbs, as with most things, you get what you pay for. High-quality, full-sized bulbs command top dollar, based on the amount of time and labor it takes to produce them, but you can always rely on them for spectacular results. A higher price, however, doesn't always mean that one tulip or daffodil cultivar is better than another. New cultivars are usually more expensive, but the old standbys are still both economical and dependable.

A top-quality bulb is firm to the touch (not soft or squishy) and free of large blemishes or scars. Some bulbs, such as tulips and hyacinths, may have a trace of blue mold on them. A few small mold spots will not harm the bulb, but a noticeable layer may indicate that it was stored improperly before being offered for sale. Look for bulbs that show little or no root or shoot growth, except for a pale growth bud at the top. (Lilies are an exception, since they often have fleshy roots attached.) Shop early in the season so you can buy the bulbs before they dry out from sitting in a store for weeks.

Care of Bulbs Before Planting

If you can't plant right away, store your bulbs in a cool, dark and relatively dry place until you're ready for them. Keep them in the paper or mesh bags they came in. A refrigerator can be handy for storing spring bulbs but is too cold for summer bulbs, such as gladioli or dahlias. Keep summer bulbs in a moderately cool spot—a cupboard or closet in a basement, garage or utility room—until you're ready to start them indoors or plant them outdoors after your last spring frost date.

A GOOD INVESTMENT

Investing in good-quality bulbs will help ensure great results in your garden year after year. Buy generous quantities and plant them in the garden or group them together in container gardens.

Avoiding Wild-collected Bulbs

While much progress has been made in limiting the collection of species bulbs from the wild, some disreputable sources still gather the bulbs they sell from native habitats. Make a point of only buying from dealers that sell cultivated bulbs.

CHOOSE CAREFULLY

Bulbs come in a spectacular array of shapes and sizes. Shop wisely by making sure that you buy only those that are plump and firm to touch. Avoid any shriveled or discolored bulbs that look obviously unhealthy.

Planting Bulbs

TOOLS OF THE TRADE

These hand-held planting tools are all you need if you're only planting a few bulbs. Use them to make individual holes for each bulb.

If you want your bulbs to thrive, it's worth putting some thought into giving them the best conditions possible. Take a little time to prepare a good growing site and plant your bulbs properly.

Preparing the Soil

Many bulbs can grow for years in the same place, so it's worth putting some effort into preparing an ideal planting site. How much work that will take depends on what kind of soil you have.

Bulbs tend to thrive in soil that's on the loamy or sandy side, since good drainage is critical for most bulbs. Very sandy soil, however, can be too dry and infertile. Clayey soil holds a good amount of nutrients, but it can also hold too much water. Loamy soil tends to hold

PLANTING DEPTHS

Different bulbs need to be planted at different depths. The horizontal lines, below the soil surface, indicate the planting depth in inches.

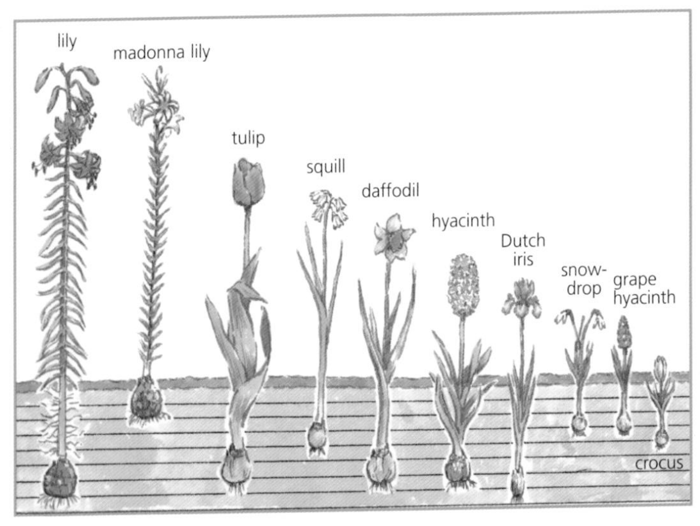

PREPARED BEDS

It's easy to plant bulbs into a prepared garden bed. Simply dig a hole (using a bulb planting tool or a trowel), set in the bulbs (according to the correct depth) and cover them with the soil that you previously removed.

an adequate supply of nutrients and moisture without getting waterlogged.

If your soil isn't naturally loamy, improve its drainage and fertility by adding organic matter before planting.

SHOW STOPPERS

To get a good show of bloom from the first year on, plant your bulbs in clumps rather than as individuals.

Planting in Beds and Borders

Once you've loosened the soil, planting is easy—just dig the hole to the proper depth, pop in the bulb and cover it with soil. The required depth will vary, depending on what bulbs you're growing. A general rule of thumb is that the base of a bulb or corm should be planted at a depth of three to four times the height of the bulb. For example, a crocus corm that measures 1 inch (2.5 cm) high should be planted 3–4 inches (7.5–10 cm) deep; a 2-inch (5-cm) high tulip bulb needs a hole 6–8 inches (15–20 cm) deep. If your soil is a bit sandy, plant a bit deeper.

When to Plant Your Bulbs

NAME	PLANTING TIME	SEASON OF INTEREST
Star-of-Persia	Autumn	Early to midsummer
Giant onion	Early to midautumn	Early to midsummer
Lily leek	Autumn	Late spring or early summer
Naked lady	Late spring to early summer	Late summer through early autumn
Grecian windflower	Late spring through early autumn	Spring
Rue anemone	Early autumn	Spring
Italian arum	Late summer or early autumn	Spring
Hybrid tuberous begonia	Midwinter (indoors)	Summer through autumn
Caladium	Midspring	Late spring until frost
Globe lily	Autumn	Spring through early summer
Mariposa tulip	Autumn	Spring to early summer
Blue camass	Early autumn	Late spring
Common camass	Autumn	Late spring
Canna	Midspring	Mid- through late summer
Himalayan lily	Late autumn, winter or early spring	Late summer
Glory-of-the-snow	Autumn	Early spring to summer
Showy autumn crocus	Mid- to late summer	Late summer through early autumn
Crocosmia	Spring	Summer and early autumn
Snow crocus	Autumn	Late winter to early spring
Showy crocus	Late summer	Early to midautumn
Hardy cyclamen	Summer (tubers); spring or summer (transplants)	Early autumn
Dahlia	Early spring	Midsummer through autumn
Winter aconite	Autumn	Late winter to spring
Dog-tooth violet	Early autumn	Spring
Sierra fawn lily	Early autumn	Late winter to early spring
Crown imperial	Late summer or early autumn	Mid- to late spring
Checkered lily	Early autumn	Midspring

NAME	PLANTING TIME	SEASON OF INTEREST
Common snowdrop	Autumn	Late winter or early spring
Gladiolus	Midspring	Summer to early autumn
Pampas lily	Spring	Summer to early autumn
Daylily	Spring or autumn	Late spring through summer
Hippeastrum	Autumn to winter	Winter to spring in outdoor gardens; spring to summer indoors
Spanish bluebell	Autumn	Late spring
English bluebell	Autumn	Spring
Hyacinth	Autumn	Midspring
Starflower	Autumn	Early spring
Bearded iris	Late summer or spring	Late spring and early summer
Dwarf crested iris	Late summer or autumn	Early spring
Reticulated iris	Autumn	Late winter and early spring
Siberian iris	Autumn	Early summer
Summer snowflake	Early autumn	Mid- to late spring
Spring snowflake	Autumn	Late winter to early spring
Lily	Autumn or early spring	Summer
Magic lily	Midsummer	Late summer to early autumn
Grape hyacinth	Early to midautumn	Early spring
Daffodil	Early to midautumn	Early, mid- or late spring
Guernsey lily	Late summer to autumn	Autumn
Star-of-Bethlehem	Autumn	Spring or summer
Mountain soursop	Early autumn	Winter to summer
Ranunculus	Autumn	Early spring or summer
River lily	Early spring	Summer to late autumn
Peruvian squill	Autumn	Early spring
Siberian squill	Early to midautumn	Early to midspring
Autumn daffodil	Late summer	Autumn
Tiger flower	Late spring	Summer through autumn
Wake robin	Autumn	Spring
Tulip	Mid- to late autumn	Early to midspring
Arum lily	Early autumn	Summer to autumn
Rain lily	Spring	Summer to autumn

YOUR CHOICE

There is no one ideal mulch. Look for the kind that appeals and that you can afford. The straw mulch on these hyacinths is all that they need to thrive.

Caring for Bulbs

Hardy bulbs—including daffodils, crocus and other dependable favorites—are about as close to "no work" as you can get. Plant them once, and with minimal care they return season after season.

Watering

Watering is most important when your bulbs are actively growing. This means autumn and spring for autumn- or spring-blooming bulbs and spring through summer for summer-blooming bulbs. Most bulbs can survive a moderate drought without watering, but they may not bloom well the following year, so water them thoroughly at planting time and then as you would your other plants.

DUAL PURPOSE

Working compost or other organic matter into the soil at planting time and using it as a mulch will provide much of the nutrient supply your bulbs need. Bulbs in pots will need weekly or bimonthly doses of liquid fertilizer.

MULCHING

Mulch helps to hold moisture in the soil and minimize rapid temperature changes, providing ideal rooting conditions. It shades the soil and helps to keep bulbs cool, protecting their shoots from being lured out of the ground too early in spring. It also benefits summer-flowering bulbs, such as lilies, which dislike hot, dry soil. Mulch also discourages weeds from sprouting and prevents rain from splashing soil onto bulb leaves and flowers, keeping your bulb plants clean and discouraging disease problems.

FERTILIZING

A compost mulch is usually all you need to fertilize bulbs, or you could sprinkle commercial organic fertilizer over the soil. Fertilize both spring-blooming and autumn-flowering bulbs in spring. Summer-flowering bulbs usually grow best with several small applications of fertilizer in early to midsummer.

MINIMAL MULCH

Mulch your bulbs after planting in autumn or spring. Apply a 1–2-inch (2.5–5-cm) layer over the soil. Avoid putting on too much, or your bulbs may have trouble poking their shoots up through the mulch.

OUT OF HARM'S WAY

The easiest approach to staking plants is to reduce the need for it. Wherever possible, site your tall bulbs, such as crown imperial, on the sheltered side of fences, hedges or screens, where they'll be protected from the wind and weather.

STAKING

There are two tricks to staking bulbs properly—choosing natural-looking stakes and putting them in early. Don't wait until a stem is fully grown to insert a stake. The results are rarely satisfactory for you or the plant.

Manufacturers sell various metal and wooden stakes, rings and hoops to support plants. Materials painted green or brown tend to be the least noticeable. Some gardeners use twiggy tree or shrub prunings for plant supports. These brushy stakes are nearly invisible when the plants grow up through them.

Select supports that are about three-quarters of the plant's ultimate height. (Allow another 6 inches [15 cm] for the part of the stake that will be underground.) Top-heavy plants

APPROPRIATE SUPPORT

Stake-and-string cages, such as this one, are very useful for supporting the upright habit of gladioli. They provide support without inhibiting the growth of stems.

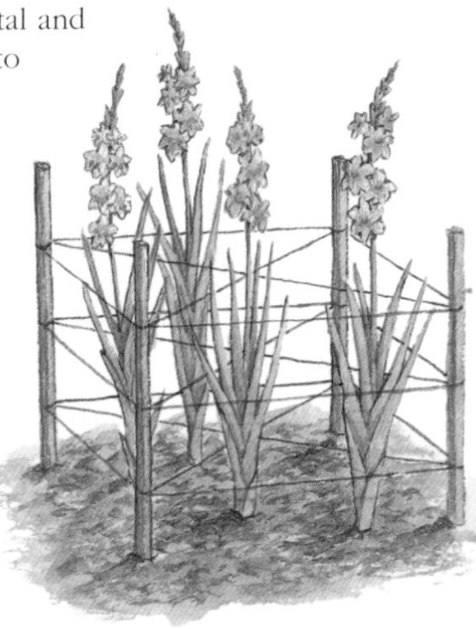

Too Much of a Good Thing

While mulch has many good points in its favor, there are a few disadvantages, too. If your soil tends to be on the clayey side, mulch may hold in too much moisture, promoting bulb rot. It can also provide an ideal hiding place for slugs and snails. If you notice any of these problems, wait until the soil has dried out a little in late autumn or early summer before applying a summer mulch. Over winter, use a light mulch, such as evergreen boughs, to protect emerging bulb shoots without holding extra moisture.

need stakes that are about the same height as the mature height of the plant.

Whatever kind of stake you choose, put it in the ground as soon as the bulb shoots are visible. Place the stake behind the plant so the support is less visible. Insert each stake a few inches away from the shoot to avoid stabbing the bulb. Push the stake at least 6 inches (15 cm) into the soil to steady it. As the bulb shoot grows, attach it to the stake with a flexible tie, such as yarn or string.

Deadheading

Deadheading means removing faded flowers and developing seedpods from plants. Whether or not you decide to deadhead your bulbs is really a matter of personal choice. Some gardeners deadhead large bulbs, such as daffodils, hyacinths and tulips. They claim that this prevents the bulbs from expending energy on seed production, directing all their energy to ripening their leaves and replenishing their food reserves.

LOOKING GOOD

There's another reason to deadhead your bulbs regularly—to keep the garden looking attractive throughout the season. Spent flower heads look messy and may detract from the beauty of healthy blooms.

Controlling Pests and Diseases

ANIMAL DAMAGE

Like other animal pests, squirrels like to feed close to protective cover. Remove brush piles and other debris where they may hide out.

Prevention is the best strategy when considering the pest and disease problems that are likely to affect your bulb garden. Luckily, most bulbs aren't at high risk of attack from pests and diseases.

Diagnosing the Problem

Most bulbs suffer from few pests and diseases. Those insects, animal pests and disease problems that do attack are usually the same as those you find on your other garden plants, such as annuals. Some of the most common problems include aphids, whiteflies, Japanese beetles, spider mites, slugs and snails, thrips, cutworms, botrytis blight and powdery mildew. For more

BEAT THE BURROWERS

Gophers are well known for munching on bulbs, tubers, roots and seeds. The best way to protect your bulbs and other plants from gophers is to line the planting bed or hole with hardware cloth or chicken wire.

information on identifying, diagnosing and controlling these and other problems, see "Common Pest and Disease Problems" on pages 54–55.

INSECT PESTS

Aphids are commonly found on greenhouse plants, but they can also pose a problem for garden plants, such as tulips. The way to control them is to spray the infested plant with an insecticidal soap spray.

Common Pests in Bulb Gardens

Deer, rabbits, mice and other animal pests can also plague bulb gardeners. You can try to discourage pests by planting daffodil bulbs, which are poisonous and usually avoided by animals. Some say that the strong odor of crown imperial *Fritillaria imperialis* bulbs and plants repels voles, mice and squirrels. Pet dogs and cats can be useful for discouraging local wildlife, but they may cause damage, too.

Prevention

It is possible to take preventive measures when planting where mice, voles, shrews and squirrels are especially troublesome. Although it takes some doing, you can fashion bulb crates—similar to lobster traps—out of sturdy wire mesh. Choose mesh with a grid size of about 1 inch (2.5 cm). Small animals can sneak through larger mesh, while your bulb shoots may not be able to poke through smaller mesh. Dig a hole large enough to hold the crate, so the top is just below the soil surface. Place the crate in the hole and backfill with some of the soil you removed. Plant your bulbs in the crate, then fill the rest of the cage with soil and close the lid. Use the remaining soil to cover the lid and fill in around the rest of the cage.

Handling Tender Bulbs

Tender bulbs usually need more work than hardy bulbs, since you may have to dig, or lift, them for winter storage indoors. But, in return, the beautiful blooms make the extra effort worthwhile.

What Is a Tender Bulb?

Whether a bulb is tender or not depends on what climate you live in, but the bulbs that usually come to mind are the ones from tropical and subtropical climates, including dahlias, gladioli, cannas and caladiums. Some tender bulbs can take more cold than others. Cannas, for instance, may survive winters in areas as cold as Zone 7.

Lifting for Storage

When the bulb foliage turns yellow or brown, that's a good sign that the bulb is ready for storage. If the leaves stay green or if you don't have time to dig the bulbs when they are first ready, you can wait

SUMMER BULBS

Most summer bulbs are classified as "tender," with the exception of lilies and ornamental onions. These "hardy" bulbs can survive in the ground from season to season. The key is to plant them early enough so their root systems can establish before warm-weather growth.

Lifting and Storing Tender Bulbs

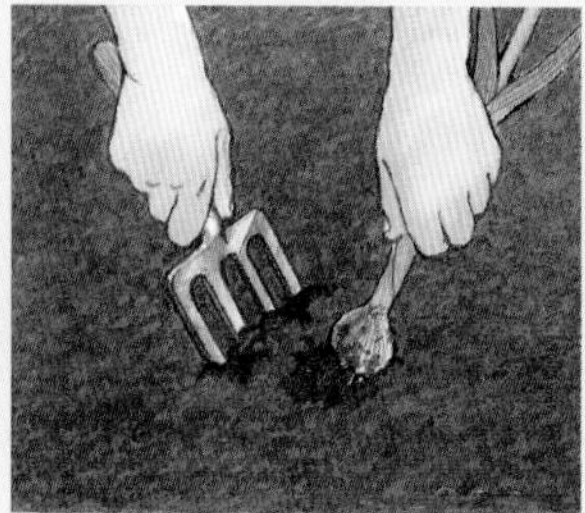

1. Use a garden fork to very carefully lift the bulb out of the ground.

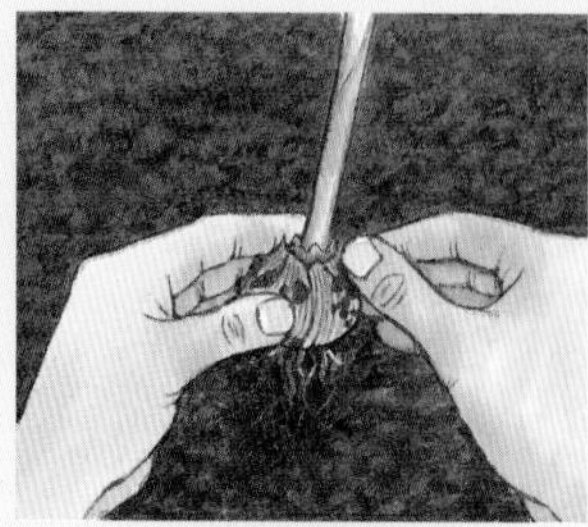

2. Brush off as much soil as you can from around the bulb and its roots.

3. Lay the bulbs out to dry on newspaper in a sheltered spot for a few days.

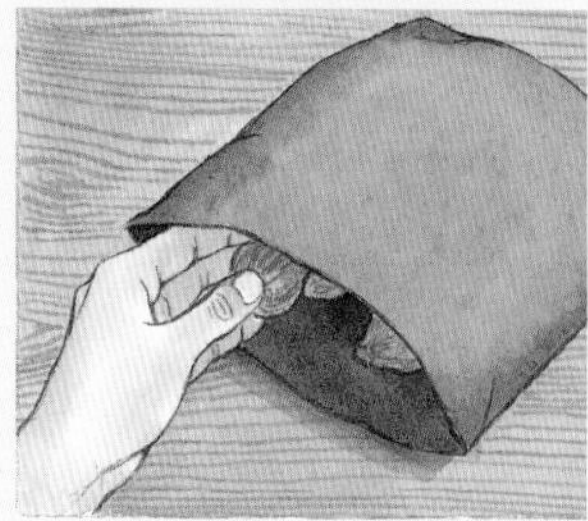

4. Store the bulbs in a paper or mesh bag or a basket and set them in a cool, dark place.

until just after the first frost. The cold temperatures will cause the leaves to turn black, but the bulbs are protected by the soil and should survive a light frost.

Storing Bulbs

Once your bulbs have dried for a few days, you can store them. Some people keep them in mesh bags (like the kind onions come in), or paper bags with a few holes punched in them for better air circulation. Others use boxes filled with damp wood shavings or peat moss to prevent too much drying out over winter.

PROPAGATING BULBS

BEARDED BEAUTIES

Enjoy the orchid-like flowers of bearded irises in early summer and the spiky foliage for the rest of the season.

Once you've had fun growing a few bulbs, it's hard to resist the urge to grow more and more. You can increase your plantings by using division or seeds to propagate the bulbs you already have.

DIVIDING BULBS AND CORMS

Some bulbs, such as tulips and daffodils, form small "bulblets" near their base. With good care, both bulblets and cormels (from parent corms) can grow to full flowering size in a year or two.

To divide spring bulbs, lift the clump with a spade or digging fork after the foliage has died back in late spring. To divide gladiolus corms, lift them in late summer or autumn, as the foliage turns

DIVIDING BULBS

Division is the fastest and easiest way to propagate nearly all bulbs, corms, tubers and rhizomes. It also has another advantage: All new plants will be identical to the parent bulb.

yellow. Separate the bulblets or cormels by gently pulling them away from their parent. Plant the bulblets or cormels in a nursery bed or a corner of the vegetable garden, where they can grow undisturbed for a few years. Water and fertilize them regularly. When the bulbs reach flowering size, move them to their garden position.

Dividing Tubers and Tuberous Roots

Division is also an effective way to increase tuberous plants, such as dahlias and tuberous begonias. The best time to divide is in spring, just after you bring these tender plants out of winter storage. Use a sharp knife to cut begonia tubers into two or three pieces, each with at least one growth bud. On dahlias, cut tuberous roots apart at the stem end, so each root has at least one bud.

Plant each new piece in a pot and set it under lights or in a greenhouse. Keep the temperature between 65° and 75°F (18° and 24°C). Water as needed so the potting soil stays evenly moist, but not wet. (Don't fertilize newly cut bulbs—wait until they're growing in soil.) In a few weeks, you should have healthy new plants that are ready for transplanting into outdoor gardens and containers.

Dividing Rhizomes

Use a sharp knife, a spade (if the clump is really big) or your hands to pull or cut apart the rhizomes. Discard any old, woody pieces from the center of the original clump. Divide canna clumps in spring, just before you plant them in pots or in the garden. Bearded irises prefer to be divided just after they flower.

Tips for Lily Lovers

Lilies, like other bulbs, produce bulblets that you can separate from the parent and grow to full flowering size. There are other techniques you can try to increase your stock. Bulbils are the small, dark minibulbs growing along the underground stems. Twist them off and plant them in pots or a nursery bed. Or remove the outer scales from the parent bulb in autumn and plant them in pots. After a few weeks, bulblets will grow on the base of each scale.

1. Remove bulbils that form along the underground stem.

2. Grow them in pots for a year or two before planting out.

FABULOUS FLOWERS

Dutch crocus bear beautiful chalice-shaped blooms in shades of violet, lavender and white. Some have striking markings on their satiny petals.

CROWNING GLORY

The distinctive flower heads of crown imperial really liven up a spring garden.

Bulbs for Spring

Early-blooming, spring-flowering bulbs signal the return of life to the garden after the rigors of a long, cold winter. These early-season beauties add welcome color and fragrance to any planting.

How Spring Bulbs Grow

Spring-flowering bulbs are best adapted to temperate areas, where they can take advantage of a particular weather "window." These bulbs send up shoots early in the season—sometimes before winter frosts have finished. Melting snow and ample spring rain provide a good supply of moisture as the bulbs send up their buds, hoping to attract the first bees and other insects to ensure pollination. Even though the ground is still cool, the lengthening rays of sunshine provide enough warmth to promote bloom. As summer approaches, the days get longer and the bulbs set seed and ripen their foliage, preparing to end this part of their life cycle.

Early Small Bulbs

Snowdrops *Galanthus nivalis* and spring snowflakes *Leucojum vernum* often arrive first. Their white petals, tinged with green, dangle just a few inches above the warming soil. The flowers of spring snowflake have three separate "petals" that dangle from thin stems, while the flowers on snowdrops resemble tiny, inflated parachutes. Winter aconite *Eranthis hyemalis* blooms at about the same time, with short-stemmed, golden yellow flowers and a collar of frilled leaves. Like the other early bloomers, snow crocus *Crocus chrysanthus* thrives in the brisk weather of late winter and early spring. Its larger cousin, the plump hybrid Dutch crocus *C. vernus*, blooms a few weeks later.

SPRING SPARKLE

Grape hyacinths may produce some leaves in autumn, but spring is the time to enjoy the clustered blooms. The brightly colored flower heads add sparkle to beds and borders. Grape hyacinths naturalize well, too.

Winter Chilling

Winter chilling is an important step in the life of most spring-blooming bulbs. If you live in a warm climate, where winter temperatures generally stay above freezing, you may find that some spring bulbs bloom poorly or don't bloom at all in the years after planting. Hybrid tulips commonly have this problem; some daffodils and crocus also grow poorly without a chilling period.

To have a great show of blooms each year, look for species and cultivars that don't need much chilling. You can also look for "precooled" bulbs, or give new bulbs an artificial cold period by storing them in the vegetable crisper of your refrigerator for 6–8 weeks before planting them in late autumn.

FRAGRANT FAVORITE
Just a few hyacinth blooms are enough to perfume a whole room. Plant them in containers for season-long pleasure indoors or out.

Early Spring Bloomers

The early-spring show sets the stage for the spring-flowering favorites, including daffodils, hyacinths, tulips and crown imperials *Fritillaria imperialis.* And spring just wouldn't be spring without daffodils, which are also referred to as jonquils. With hundreds of species and perhaps thousands of hybrids and cultivars, the variations on the standard yellow, large-cupped daffodil are almost endless. There are types that bear a single flower on each stem and those that produce clusters of blooms. For extra interest, consider the variety of single and double flower forms and the range of colors. You'll see that there's a perfect daffodil for nearly every garden spot. Most daffodils have a light scent, and many have stronger fragrances.

ONE STEP AT A TIME
Keeping spring-blooming potted bulbs in a winter cold frame is a good way to chill them before they bloom. You can also put them in a cool spot, such as the garage, or in the vegetable crisper in your refrigerator.

INDOOR BLOOM

The blooms of potted spring bulbs and primroses will last longer if you keep them in a cool spot. Grouping the pots together will help to keep the humidity level adequate. Just remember that indoor bulbs need more water than those in your garden.

Care of Spring Bulbs

It's easy enough to add spring bulbs to your garden, but it does require a little advance planning.

Water spring bulbs just after planting and again as needed if the soil dries out in winter or spring. Scatter compost or balanced organic fertilizer over the soil when the new shoots appear in spring to provide a nutrient boost for healthy growth and bud formation for next year.

Most spring bulbs thrive in full or partial sun (at least 6 hours of sun a day). They are ideal for planting under deciduous trees, since the bulbs can bloom and ripen their foliage before the tree leaves expand fully and block the sunlight. Unless you plan to plant new bulbs next year, allow the bulb leaves to wither away and die naturally.

LOVELY LILIES

Lilies are grown for their elegant flowers and long stems. They look perfect in informal plantings, combined with ferns and grasses.

Bulbs for Summer

Don't think the bulb season is over when the last spring blossom fades! The tulips may be just a memory, but there are many more beautiful summer blossoms in store for you in your garden.

Early-summer Bloomers

While onions, garlic and leeks are staples of the vegetable garden, ornamental onions are a mainstay of the early-summer flower garden. The most impressive of the ornamental onions is giant onion *Allium giganteum*. Its strong flower stems are topped with grapefruit-sized globes of tightly packed purple flowers in early summer. Persian onion *A. aflatunense* is slightly smaller but also quite showy, with softball-sized clusters of lavender-purple flowers. Other popular early-summer ornamental onions include star-of-Persia *A. christophii* and lily leek *A. moly*. Lily leek offers a rather different look from the other ornamental onions, with small heads of yellow flowers in late spring or early summer.

STAR ATTRACTION

The stunning flower heads of star-of-Persia look wonderful planted beside ornamental grasses, such as Japanese sliver grass or fountain grass.

Mid- to Late-summer Bloomers

Lilies are the stars of the mid- to late-summer garden. True lilies *Lilium* spp. and hybrids grow from a bulb and have straight stems with many short leaves. Although their flower form resembles that of the daylily *Hemerocallis* spp., true lilies have individual blooms that can stay open for more than a week, as opposed to the 1-day duration of a daylily blossom. Hybrid lilies are divided into several broad groups. The three main groups are the Asiatic hybrids, trumpet lilies and oriental hybrids.

Other summer-blooming bulbs include caladiums, which are ideal for accenting the summer shade garden; cannas, the warm-weather favorites; and tuberous begonias, which make great companions in hanging baskets and containers.

DELICATE DAHLIAS

Dahlias are a signature plant of summer gardens. These tender Mexican natives look their best when the weather is hot and moist. The distinctive, showy flowers bloom in an array of colors, sizes and forms.

Care of Summer Bulbs

Some summer bulbs—including lilies and ornamental onions—can live from year to year, so you'll plant them once and enjoy their blooms for years to come. These "hardy" bulbs are usually planted in autumn for bloom the following summer, although lilies can also adapt to early-spring planting. The key is to plant early enough so the root system can get established before warm weather promotes lush topgrowth.

Other summer bloomers are classified as "tender" bulbs. These cold-sensitive beauties may not be able to survive the winter in your area. Unless you live in a warm climate (roughly Zones 8 and above), you'll need to plant gladioli, cannas, dahlias and other tender bulbs in spring to early summer and dig them up in the autumn for winter storage indoors. For more information on lifting and storing, see "Handling Tender Bulbs" on pages 86–87.

Bulbs for Autumn

The end of summer doesn't spell the end of the bulb season. The charm of autumn-blooming bulbs is in the grace and freshness they add to the late-season garden as the weather starts to cool down.

Tall Autumn Bloomers

If you're looking to add some excitement to your late-season plantings, consider adding a few magic lilies *Lycoris squamigera* or naked ladies *Amaryllis belladonna* to your flower beds. Magic lilies, also known as surprise lilies, seem to appear out of nowhere in late summer to early autumn. The infamous naked lady has a similar habit and look but is less cold-hardy. Both plants produce leaves in spring and early summer, which wither away a month or two before the flowering stems appear.

Italian arum *Arum italicum* is another dramatic addition to the garden. It is especially showy in autumn, when it produces round, reddish orange berries in clusters atop thick stems.

LATE-SEASON PLEASERS
Naked ladies ripen their leaves in spring but the unusual and elegant blooms don't appear until autumn.

Small Late-autumn Bloomers

Start with some of the autumn-blooming crocus, such as showy crocus *Crocus speciosus* and saffron crocus *C. sativus.* Showy crocus braves the coolest weather of autumn, opening its flowers during sunny days. Showy crocus leaves appear in spring and go dormant in summer. Saffron crocus, on the other hand,

blooms with its leaves, which persist through winter and die back in spring. The flowers of saffron crocus are similar in height and color to those of showy crocus. Slightly larger than the true crocus, showy autumn crocus *Colchicum speciosum* emerges from the soil in spring. Many gardeners prize the late show of hardy cyclamen *Cyclamen hederifolium,* especially since it thrives in shady spots and brings a touch of springlike beauty to woodlands.

A CARPET OF FLOWERS
If you can find them, plant hardy cyclamen as transplants rather than as tubers; plants tend to establish more quickly. Their dainty pink flowers look great with yellow crocus.

Care of Autumn Bulbs

Like other bulbs, autumn bloomers need to ripen their leaves fully to store enough food for good flowering. So live with their leaves until they wither away—don't cut or pull them off before they turn yellow. If you naturalize autumn bulbs in grassy areas, you'll need to stop mowing as soon as you see the first flower buds emerging in late summer to early autumn.

MAIN ATTRACTION
Striking winter leaves, interesting spring flowers and showy autumn fruit give Italian arum a multiseason interest. Its hooded, white spring flowers are attractive but not nearly as spectacular as the reddish orange berries.

Growing Bulbs Indoors

WATER GARDEN
Use hyacinth glasses to grow bulbs in water.

There's nothing more heartwarming to a gardener than a pot of flowering bulbs on the window sill in the depths of winter. Luckily, it's easy to convince most spring bulbs to rush the season a bit.

Which Bulbs Are Suitable?

Most spring bulbs can be forced, but some perform better in pots than others. Forcing simply means providing a condensed version of winter that the bulbs would otherwise get when growing in the ground outdoors.

Spring-blooming crocus, Siberian squill *Scilla sibirica*, glory-of-the-snow *Chionodoxa luciliae* and reticulated iris

INDOOR CHALLENGE
The stunning flowers of florist's cyclamen *Cyclamen persicum* certainly brighten dull winter days, but it can be tricky to get plants to bloom again the following year. If you buy cyclamen in flower, you don't need to fertilize it.

Iris reticulata are very easy to chill and bring into bloom. Daffodils and some tulips are also gratifyingly easy to force.

The best time to plant bulbs for forcing is in mid- to late autumn. Set the bulbs shoulder to shoulder in clay or plastic pots in ordinary, well-drained potting soil. The "nose" of the bulb should just peek above the soil surface. Label the pot with the name of the bulb and the date, water it thoroughly and then stash it in its winter quarters for chilling.

UP CLOSE AND PERSONAL

To get a good show, you can plant many bulbs close together in a container; it's not going to be a problem if the bulbs touch each other.

Chilling

Your bulbs need a cool, dark place while they're producing roots. The ideal temperatures for forcing bulbs are between 33° and 45°F (1° and 7°C). Some people use an unheated garage or basement; others set their bulbs in a potting shed or a cold frame. You may need to protect the bulbs with a heavy layer of straw, newspapers or even old blankets to keep them from getting too cold. Refrigerators can work well for chilling if your outdoor winter temperatures don't get cold enough for proper chilling.

Your bulbs will signal they're ready to grow in two ways: Tiny white roots will be visible in the drainage holes of the pot, and new shoots will appear at the top of the bulbs. When the shoots are an inch or two (2.5–5 cm) tall, place them in a cool, bright spot and lightly fertilize each time you water—about once a week.

Bulbs and Companions

Whether you enjoy growing bulbs in formal displays or more natural-looking plantings, you can add extra interest by choosing compatible companion plants that enhance the flowering bulbs.

Bulbs and Annuals

Showy bulbs, such as tulips and hyacinths, can make a dramatic feature when planted in rows or blocks. But it's even more exciting when you fill in between the bulbs with a pretty carpet of early-blooming annual flowers rather than leaving the soil bare or mulched.

SEASONAL DISPLAY
Mix bulbs with annuals and perennials to create beautiful color theme plantings, such as this elegant white garden. The low-growing sweet alyssum and the green and white leaves of the hostas complement the taller tulips.

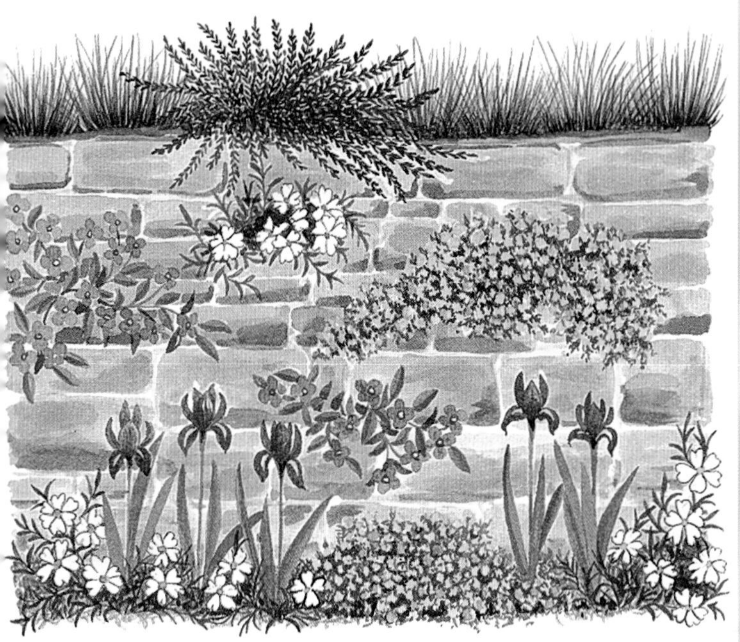

PLAN YOUR PLANTING
Planting bulbs and perennials along walls (and even in the wall, if possible) will soften the look of the hard edges. These irises add color and height interest to the mixed perennial planting: You can solve problems and improve the design at the same time.

Good choices for planting under bulbs include pansies, English daisies and forget-me-nots. As summer-blooming annuals grow, they cover the bare soil and disguise the maturing bulb leaves. Self-sowing annuals are ideal for this.

Bulbs and Perennials

Tall bulbs, including lilies, ornamental onions and crown imperial, usually look best near the middle or back of a bed or border. Planting them in between clumps of slightly shorter perennials makes attractive combinations, especially if the perennials bloom at the same time as the bulbs. For instance, Asiatic lilies are especially pretty with shasta daisies and coral bells at their feet. You can also combine bulbs with taller perennials, such as delphiniums and meadow rues.

GROUNDCOVERS

Combine showy autumn crocus with groundcovers, such as leadwort *Ceratostigma plumbaginoides*, to help support the blooms and to keep them clean.

Bulbs and Groundcovers

Combining bulbs with groundcovers is a great way to go. The groundcover provides a pretty backdrop for the bulbs' flowers and then remains to add interest when the bulbs go dormant. Most bulbs have no trouble poking their flowers through a carpet of creeping stems and leaves. Many low-growing, spreading perennials, including thyme, sedums, creeping baby's breath and sun rose, can be used as groundcovers. In shady areas, try common periwinkle, creeping Jenny, English ivy and self-heal.

Bulbs and Shrubs

You can create stunning garden scenes by grouping flowering shrubs and bulbs with similar bloom times and colors. Forsythia creates a golden glow behind a mass of daffodils, while lilac beautifully echoes the colors of ornamental onions. The arching branches and fragrance of old-fashioned roses make them a classic companion for lilies. Viburnums, mock oranges, hydrangeas and azaleas are some other flowering shrubs that look great with spring bulbs. Evergreen shrubs, such as junipers and yews, complement flowering bulbs throughout the year. White or pink tulips can create a soothing scene against the blue-gray cast of a juniper.

WOODY COMPANIONS

There are thousands of tulip cultivars to choose from. Opposite, tulips have been planted with daffodils under deciduous trees. Bulbs and trees look good together in woodland gardens.

Bulbs and Trees

Spring bulbs are especially well suited for growing under deciduous trees, since they can get the sunlight they need before the leaves shade the ground. Spring-flowering bulbs that perform well under trees include crocus, squills, snowdrops and daffodils.

Bulbs for Containers

Pots filled with bright flowers add a colorful touch to decks, patios and entryways. As you plan your container plantings, don't stop with geraniums and petunias; liven them up with some bulbs.

LAYERING

Different bulbs need to be planted at different depths, so in mixed plantings in a single container, layer them as appropriate for each bulb.

Planting Bulbs in Pots

For best results, choose a large pot that can hold plenty of potting mix. Large pots will provide ample rooting room for your annuals and bulbs, and they tend to dry out less quickly than small pots. For lilies, choose a pot at least 10 inches (25 cm) wide and deep. Smaller bulbs can grow in slightly smaller pots, but they'll also do well in large containers. Big plants, such as cannas and dahlias, need plenty of room.

BRILLIANT COLOR

By growing hyacinths in containers, you can make the most of their explosive color and scent to brighten up an indoor or outdoor area.

Fill the bottom of the container with a well-drained commercial potting mix. Adjust the thickness of this layer to match the needs of the bulbs you're planting. Lily bulbs should have 5–6 inches (12.5–15 cm) of potting mix over their tops; set smaller bulbs so they're covered with 3–4 inches (7.5–10 cm) of mix. Fill the container with potting mix to within 1–2 inches (2.5–5 cm) of the rim. Plant young annuals into the container as you normally would, firming them in well and watering thoroughly. If you're growing warmth-loving summer bulbs, you can get a head start on the season by starting them indoors. Plant them

inside in 6–8-inch (15–20-cm) pots, 6–8 weeks before night temperatures hit 50°F (10°C). Grow them under lights, in a greenhouse or on a sunny porch or window sill while you wait for the weather to warm up. When you're ready to set them out, remove the bulbs from their pot and plant them at the same depth they were growing. Then plant annuals around the sides, being careful not to damage the bulb shoots.

POTTED COLOR
Tulips thrive in containers. Grow them close together for mutual support of the stems.

Mixing Annuals and Bulbs

Bulbs make excellent companions for annuals in pots, since the annuals usually root in the top soil layer while the bulbs are planted much deeper. The bulbs also benefit from the covering of annuals, which shade the soil and pot to some extent, keeping the bulbs cool. Some bulbs provide beautiful blooms; others provide eye-catching foliage. And there's a bulb for almost every exposure, from bright sunshine to dappled shade.

Caring for Container Bulbs

Through the season, keep a close eye on your containers to make sure the soil doesn't dry out completely. In hot, dry weather, you may need to water every day, especially for small containers. Fertilize several times during the summer to keep the plants growing vigorously. At the end of the season, lift the bulbs or tubers of tender bulbs for winter storage. Shake off the soil and let the bulbs air dry for several days. Store them in labeled paper or mesh bags, or peat moss to prevent the bulbs from drying out.

Bulbs for Naturalizing

Naturalizing means planting bulbs in random, natural-looking drifts under trees, in woodlands or in grassy areas. The results look better every year as the bulbs multiply, producing more and more blooms.

LOW MAINTENANCE

Try planting crocus in low-maintenance spots where you can put off the mowing for a while. You'll know it's safe to start again when the leaves have died off.

Where to Plant

Naturalized bulbs often work best in low-maintenance areas, where you can enjoy the blooms all season long but not be bothered by the sight of the ripening leaves. Very early flowering bulbs, such as spring crocus, are sometimes naturalized in lawns to provide color. You may have to put off the first spring

GRASSY AREAS

Naturalize grape hyacinths and daffodils under a spring-flowering tree. To plant bulbs in grass, especially large bulbs such as daffodils, use a hand-held bulb planter or trowel to make individual holes for each bulb.

NATURAL BEAUTY
Naturalized tulips, daffodils and grape hyacinths create a wonderful carpet of color in this woodland setting. It's easy to naturalize bulbs that are suitable, and every year they multiply to produce a display of more blooms than before.

mowing for a week or two to let the bulb foliage turn yellow, but after that you can mow as usual. Autumn bloomers can also look good in grassy areas, but you'll have to stop mowing in late summer, as soon as you see the flower buds sprouting from the soil.

Thick grass may be too competitive for some bulbs, but a sparse lawn—especially under deciduous trees—is just the right environment to help bulbs take hold. They get plenty of spring sun and moisture before the trees leaf out, and the flowers add cheerful spring and/or autumn color to otherwise drab areas. If you have many trees in your garden, you can combine sweeps of naturalized bulbs with shade-loving annuals, perennials and shrubs to create a charming woodland garden with four-season interest. Groundcovers also make great companions for naturalized bulbs.

Step-by-step Guide to Planting Small Bulbs in Grass

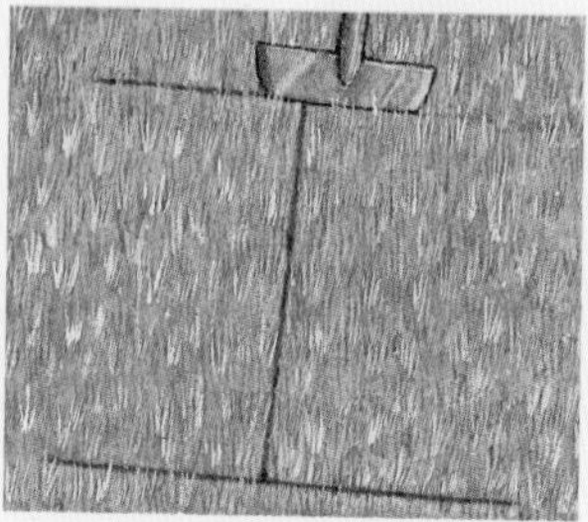

1. Use a spade or edging tool to cut an "H" shape into the top layer of the grass.

2. Slip the blade of the spade under the grass to allow you to pull back the flaps.

3. Loosen the exposed soil, then set your bulbs in, pressing them into the soil.

4. Replace the turf flaps and carefully press them down; then water area thoroughly.

How to Plant

The key to naturalizing is planting bulbs in random-looking arrangements rather than in straight rows or patterns. It's usually best to place them over the planting area by hand until the arrangement looks right to you. Don't just toss out handfuls of bulbs from a standing position; they may get bruised or damaged and become prone to pest or disease problems. A narrow trowel is the easiest tool to use for planting small bulbs. Insert the trowel into the ground at an angle, lift up a flap of sod, tuck the

HAPPY COMPANIONS

Small bulbs, such as glory-of-the-snow (planted here with Polyanthus primroses), are ideal for growing under trees; they'll bloom and go dormant before the trees begin to leaf out.

Best Bulbs for Naturalizing

Small bulbs tend to be best for naturalizing: They are dependable bloomers, and they're easy to plant. Best of all, they're relatively inexpensive. Here are some of the all-time favorites:

Lily leek *Allium moly*
Grecian windflower *Anemone blanda*
Showy autumn crocus *Colchicum speciosum*
Common snowdrop *Galanthus nivalis*
Grape hyacinth *Muscari armeniacum*
Daffodil *Narcissus* hybrids

ALL-ROUNDERS

Daffodils are a big favorite for all garden situations. They are often sold in bargain mixtures for naturalizing.

bulb into the soil and replace the flap. Or you can plant bulbs in groups by lifting up larger sections of sod, pressing the bulbs into the soil and replacing the sod. (This technique works best with smaller bulbs, such as crocus.)

Avoiding Animal Pests

One drawback to naturalizing bulbs is that various animals find them to be a tasty snack. This problem is often worse in wooded areas, where deer and various rodents may feast on both the flowers and the bulbs themselves.

Unfortunately, there are no easy answers for dealing with these animal pests, short of fencing them out of your garden. If you've had problems in the past, make a few test plantings of different bulbs before you invest time and money in setting out large quantities. Once you see which bulbs tend to be left alone, you can start planting more of those kinds. Some bulbs tend to be naturally less attractive to hungry animal pests, so you may want to try those first; they include daffodils, starflower *Ipheion uniflorum* and montbretia *Crocosmia* spp.

Designing a Cutting Garden

The qualities that make bulbs great garden plants—their spectacular, long-lasting blooms and lovely scents—make them ideal cut flowers as well. Plant bulbs in a cutting garden for taking indoors.

SURE BETS

Tulips, daylilies and gladioli all make wonderful cut flowers. They are all also available in a wide variety of colors and flower forms.

Planning Where to Put It

You can start planning your cutting garden any time of year, although summer is usually the best time; that will give you plenty of time to prepare the soil and place your bulb orders for autumn planting.

Bulbs for cutting need the same conditions as those growing in ornamental gardens. A sunny area with fertile, well-drained soil suits most bulbs. If you have extra room in your vegetable garden, that's usually an ideal site to add

AUTUMN BLOOM

Dahlias make excellent cut flowers. Stake the plants of tall types, such as these, to keep the stems growing straight. Grow a variety of cultivars so that you can enjoy different colors and forms in a single arrangement.

TAKE PRECAUTION

Lilies have the unfortunate habit of leaving a nasty yellow pollen stain on clothes when you brush by them. To avoid a fashion disaster and to protect soft furnishings, simply snip the offending bright yellow anthers from the center of each flower.

a few blocks or rows of flowers for cutting. Otherwise, you'll need to remove the grass and weeds from your chosen site, dig the soil to loosen the top 8–10 inches (20–25 cm) and work in liberal amounts of organic matter to provide ideal rooting conditions.

Planting and Maintenance

Plant hardy bulbs in autumn and tender ones in spring after the soil has warmed sufficiently. During the growing season, water as needed to keep the soil evenly moist. Mulch regularly to keep the roots cool, maintain steady soil moisture and keep the flowers clean. Stake tall plants, such as dahlias and gladioli, to keep the stems straight.

When to Collect Cut Flowers

The best time to collect cut flowers is when the buds are just opening, not when they are in full bloom. If you are picking from bulbs that produce many flowers on a single stem, such as lilies or gladioli, cut them when the first few flowers at the bottom are opening. Cut blooms during the cool part of the day.

BORDER BULBS

A bulb border of Grecian windflowers, bright blue hyacinths and daffodils works well if you plan to take flowers for cutting only once or twice during flowering.

Part Four

Plant Directory ~ Annuals

BEST SITE
Full sun to partial shade; average, well-drained soil. A site with morning sun and afternoon shade is best for plants in warm- to hot-summer climates.

HEIGHT
6–12 inches (15–30 cm)

SPREAD
6–8 inches (15–20 cm)

FLOWERING TIME
Early summer through frost.

AGERATUM

NATIVE TO MEXICO, AGERATUMS ARE LOW-GROWING ANNUALS THAT NEED LITTLE CARE; JUST WATER DURING DRY SPELLS. THEY ARE ALSO COMMONLY KNOWN AS FLOSS FLOWERS.

Description A half-hardy annual that forms tidy clumps of hairy, medium green, roughly triangular leaves. From early summer until frost, the leaves are nearly covered by clusters of ¼–½-inch (6–12-mm), puffy flower heads in shades of lavender-blue, deep blue, pink and white.

Growing guidelines Buy transplants in spring for earliest color, or start them from seed sown indoors 6–8 weeks before your last frost date. Sow seed on the surface, press it in lightly and put the pots in plastic bags until seedlings appear. Set out young plants after the last frost. Space compact cultivars 6–8 inches (15–20 cm) apart; allow 1 foot (30 cm) between plants of tall cultivars. If the plants stop producing new blooms, cut them back by about half; water and fertilize to promote new growth.

Pest and disease prevention Treat aphids or whiteflies with pyrethrins or an insecticidal soap.

Landscape uses Compact cultivars are ideal for edging flower beds. Use tall-stemmed types as accents in perennial borders.

Agrostemma githago CARYOPHYLLACEAE

BEST SITE
Grows best in a wind-protected site with full sun and well-drained, rocky or gravelly soil.

HEIGHT
1–3 feet (30–90 cm)

SPREAD
1⅓ feet (40 cm)

FLOWERING TIME
Late spring through summer.

CORN COCKLE

CORN COCKLE IS A SHOWY ANNUAL WITH DAINTY PINK OR CERISE FLOWERS. ITS SWOLLEN SEED CAPSULE LOOKS LIKE A CHINESE LANTERN ENCASED BY 10 RIBS.

Description Corn cockle is a fast-growing, frost-hardy annual. The petals are 1–2½ inches (2.5–6 cm) wide and have distinctive veins; behind them are longer, narrow, green sepals. The flower heads are borne one per stem. The seed capsule is inflated, with the sepals at the top. The very small, dark brown seeds are poisonous. The stems grow from a shallow taproot.

Growing guidelines Propagate from seed sown in early spring or autumn. If grown in exposed areas, young plants may need to be thinned and staked lightly to support the plant's willowy habit. Once flowering is finished, dig the plants out to prevent reseeding as corn cockle has a tendency to become weedy.

Pest and disease prevention No specific problems.

Landscape uses Corn cockle is ideal for planting at the back of borders, or in massed plantings, spaced closely for mutual support of the stems.

BEST SITE
Full sun; average, well-drained soil.

HEIGHT
3–6 feet (90–180 cm)

SPREAD
2 feet (60 cm)

FLOWERING TIME
Midsummer until autumn.

HOLLYHOCK

HOLLYHOCKS ARE A STAPLE IN COTTAGE GARDENS AS THEY ADD BOTH HEIGHT AND COLOR INTEREST. PLANT THEM BEHIND OR BETWEEN SMALLER SHRUBS TO HARMONIZE YOUR GARDEN DESIGN.

Description Hollyhocks are perennials usually grown as annuals or biennials, which form large clumps of rounded leaves and thick bloom stalks. Plump flower buds produce bowl-shaped, single or double blooms up to 5 inches (12.5 cm) wide. The crinkled petals usually bloom in white or shades of red, pink and yellow.

Growing guidelines For bloom the same year, sow seed indoors 8 weeks before your last frost date. Sow 1/4 inch (6 mm) deep in individual pots. After risk of frost has passed, set plants out 1½–2 feet (45–60 cm) apart. For earlier bloom the following year, sow outdoors in spring or early summer. Move the young plants to their garden position in autumn. Stake hollyhocks growing in exposed sites to keep stems upright.

Pest and disease prevention Hollyhocks are prone to rust, a fungal disease that produces orange spots on leaves. Pull affected plants out after bloom.

Landscape uses Use hollyhocks as accents in a flower border, with shrubs, or along a wall or fence.

BEST SITE
Full sun; average, well-drained to dry soil. Make sure the soil has some organic matter added to it.

HEIGHT
3–5 feet (90–150 cm)

SPREAD
2 feet (60 cm)

FLOWERING TIME
Midsummer until frost.

LOVE-LIES-BLEEDING

TRY PLANTING LOVE-LIES-BLEEDING AT THE EDGE OF A RAISED BED, SO THE SHOWY, DROOPING FLOWERS CAN TRAIL FREELY.

Description This unusual tender annual produces thick, sturdy, branched stems with large, oval, pale green leaves. Long clusters of tightly packed, deep crimson flowers dangle from the stem tips. The ropy, tassel-like clusters can grow to 1½ feet (45 cm) long.

Growing guidelines Sow seed indoors, ⅛ inch (3 mm) deep, 4–6 weeks before your last frost date. Set plants out 1½ feet (45 cm) apart when the weather is warm, 2–3 weeks after the last frost date. Seed also germinates quickly in warm soil, so you could also sow it in the garden in late spring.

Pest and disease prevention No specific problems.

Landscape uses Makes a striking accent in flower beds and borders and in cottage gardens. It also makes a great cut flower in fresh or dried arrangements.

BEST SITE
Full sun; fertile, well-drained soil.

HEIGHT
3 feet (90 cm)

SPREAD
1½ feet (45 cm)

FLOWERING TIME
Summer through late autumn.

JOSEPH'S COAT

JOSEPH'S COAT IS APTLY NAMED FOR ITS MANY-COLORED LEAVES. THE BRILLIANT FOLIAGE MAKES A DRAMATIC AND UNUSUAL BACKDROP FOR ANNUAL BEDS AND BORDERS.

Description Joseph's coat is a fast-growing, hardy annual with striking variegated leaves that come in red, gold, bronze and orange, often with deep green at the base of the plant. The leaves are about 8 inches (20 cm) long.

Growing guidelines Prepare soil for planting by adding manure or other organic matter about 1 week in advance. Sow seed in spring in warmer climates, or when the danger of frost is past. You can continue planting until early summer. Transplant clumps of seedlings about 1⅓ feet (40 cm) apart. Thin out seedlings and pull out paler plants; water well until established. Mulch during hot spells to prevent drying out. Fertilize mature plants every week or so.

Pest and disease prevention No specific problems.

Landscape uses Because of its size, Joseph's coat is well suited to large gardens or as a background plant in summer beds.

BEST SITE
Thrives in full sun; average, well-drained, light soil.

HEIGHT
1⅓ feet (40 cm)

SPREAD
1⅓ feet (40 cm)

FLOWERING TIME
Early summer to late autumn.

CAPE FORGET-ME-NOT

CAPE FORGET-ME-NOT'S BOTANIC NAME COMES FROM ANCHUSIN, THE RED DYE FOUND IN THE PLANT'S ROOTS, WHICH IS USED COMMERCIALLY IN MAKING ROUGE AND FOR DYING WOOL.

Description A biennial in cooler climates, Cape forget-me-not has vivid ultramarine-blue flowers with a white center. The stunning flower heads grow from hairy side stems sprouting along the length of the upright central stem. The small, thin, green leaves are a minor feature of the plant.

Growing guidelines Cape forget-me-not can be sown from seed very early in spring in warm-temperate climates, or when all danger of frost is past. Space plants approximately 10–12 inches (25–30 cm) apart. If you're transplanting seedlings, do it as early as possible to allow the plants' taproot to mature and establish in the ground. Water mature plants well and cut flower stalks back after flowering to extend bloom season. Stake taller cultivars.

Pest and disease prevention No specific problems.

Landscape uses Works well in most garden situations, including rock gardens. Its spreading habit makes it perfect for growing over stepping stones or terraced garden beds, or in drifts in borders. It's also suitable for pots and planters.

Best site
Full sun to light shade (especially in hot-summer areas); average, well-drained soil.

Height
Ranges from 1 foot (30 cm) for dwarf types, up to 4 feet (1.2 m) for taller types.

Spread
8–18 inches (20–45 cm)

Flowering time
Summer.

Snapdragon

SNAPDRAGONS ARE A MUST IN THE CUTTING GARDEN AS THEY MAKE GREAT FRESH ARRANGEMENTS. IF YOU LEAVE A FEW SPIKES TO SET SEED NEAR THE END OF THE SEASON, THEY MAY SELF-SOW.

Description Tender perennials usually grown as hardy or half-hardy annuals, snapdragons may be low and mound-forming or tall and spiky. The slender stems carry narrow, bright green leaves topped with spikes of tubular flowers that resemble puckered lips. The 1½-inch (3.5-cm), velvety flowers bloom in nearly every color.

Growing guidelines Buy transplants in spring, or start your own by planting seed indoors 6–8 weeks before your last frost date. Set out seedlings after the last frost date or sow them directly into prepared garden soil. Set or thin dwarf-type plants 8 inches (20 cm) apart, intermediates 10 inches (25 cm) apart and tall types 1½ feet (45 cm) apart. Water during dry spells to keep the soil evenly moist.

Pest and disease prevention Snapdragons are prone to rust, a fungal disease that shows up as brownish spots on leaves. Grow snapdragons as annuals and pull affected plants out in autumn.

Landscape uses Use the low-growing cultivars in masses or as edging plants for annual beds.

Argyranthemum frutescens ASTERACEAE

BEST SITE
Full sun; well-drained, moist soil with compost added.

HEIGHT
3 feet (90 cm)

SPREAD
3 feet (90 cm)

FLOWERING TIME
Spring through autumn.

MARGUERITE

MARGUERITES OFFER FERNY FOLIAGE COVERED WITH DAINTY, DAISY-TYPE BLOOMS PRACTICALLY ALL SUMMER. THEY ARE PERENNIAL IN WARMER CLIMATES; GROW THEM AS ANNUALS NORTH OF ZONE 9.

Description This shallow-rooted, shrubby plant has bright green or bluish leaves. The abundant, daisy-type, 2-inch (5-cm) blooms flower in white, pink or yellow.

Growing guidelines Marguerites are propagated from seed or cuttings, which can be taken at any time. Plant in a well-drained soil after the last frost. Fertilize regularly during the growing season and keep the soil evenly moist. Prune plants lightly every month or two for best flowering. Large-flowered types are not as prolific as those with small blooms. You can bring marguerites indoors for overwintering and move them back outdoors the following spring.

Pest and disease prevention No specific problems.

Landscape uses Marguerites make a lovely display in flower beds or cottage gardens. They also make a good cut flower.

BEST SITE
Full sun; prefers gravelly, well-drained soil.

HEIGHT
1 foot (30 cm)

SPREAD
2 feet (60 cm)

FLOWERING TIME
Spring and summer.

WOODRUFF

A NATIVE OF TURKEY, WOODRUFF IS A SHOWY ANNUAL THAT MAKES A GREAT CUT FLOWER; THE FRAGRANCE OFTEN DEVELOPS AS THE CUT FOLIAGE DRIES.

Description Woodruff is a half-hardy annual with very slender, small, green leaves on fine stems that are topped by dense clusters of tiny, delicate, lilac flower heads.

Growing guidelines If you want to raise woodruff from seed, sow indoors in individual pots about 6 weeks before your last frost date. Transplant seedlings or sow seed directly into the garden when all danger of frost has past; if you live in a cooler climate it's best to wait until late spring or early summer, since these plants prefer warmer conditions. Space plants or thin seedlings to stand 6–8 inches (15–20 cm) apart. Mulch lightly around the base of plants to discourage weeds.

Pest and disease prevention No specific problems.

Landscape uses Rock gardens are the perfect place to plant woodruff because it loves gritty, well-drained soil. It's also a good choice for cutting and cottage gardens.

Bassia scoparia f. *trichophylla*

CHENOPODIACEAE

BEST SITE
Full sun; average, well-drained soil.

HEIGHT
3–4 feet (90–120 cm)

SPREAD
2 feet (60 cm)

FLOWERING TIME
Autumn.

SUMMER CYPRESS

THE LOW-GROWING BUSHINESS OF SUMMER CYPRESS MAKES IT A PERFECT BORDER PLANT. IT PROVIDES AN INTERESTING CONTRAST WITH THE MORE DELICATE FLOWERING ANNUALS IN YOUR GARDEN.

Description This half-hardy annual is grown for its compact, shrubby clumps of foliage and attractive autumn color. Plants form feathery, oval or rounded mounds of narrow, spring green leaves 1–2 inches (2.5–5 cm) long, that take on purplish red tints when cool weather arrives. Tiny petal-less flowers bloom along the stems in early autumn.

Growing guidelines Sow seed indoors 4–6 weeks before your last frost date. Press it lightly into the soil and enclose the pot in a plastic bag until seedlings appear. Set plants out or sow seed directly into the garden after the last frost date. Set transplants or thin seedlings to stand 2 feet (60 cm) apart. (If you're growing summer cypress as a hedge, space plants 10–12 inches [25–30 cm] apart.) Stake young plants in exposed sites.

Pest and disease prevention No specific problems.

Landscape uses A great filler for the back of beds or borders, or use single plants as shrubby accents. Summer cypress also makes a good temporary hedge.

Best site
Partial shade to sun; evenly moist soil with added organic matter.

Height
6–8 inches (15–20 cm)

Spread
6–8 inches (15–20 cm)

Flowering time
Early summer until frost.

Wax begonia

MOST WAX BEGONIAS PREFER A POSITION WITH MORNING SUN AND AFTERNOON SHADE, BUT THE BROWN-LEAVED TYPES TEND TO BE MORE HEAT- AND SUN-TOLERANT.

Description These tender perennials are grown as tender annuals. The succulent stems bear shiny, rounded, green or reddish brown leaves. The mounded plants are covered with single or double, 1½-inch (3.5-cm) flowers in red, pink or white.

Growing guidelines They are easiest to grow from purchased transplants in spring. If you want to try raising them yourself, sow the dustlike seed at least 12 weeks before your last frost date. Don't cover the seed; just press it lightly into the soil and place the pot in a plastic bag until seedlings appear. Set transplants out after the last frost date, when temperatures stay above 50°F (10°C) at night. Space plants 6–8 inches (15–20 cm) apart. Wax begonias require little or no care during the season. Pull them out after frost, or cut them back by one-third after frost and pot them up for indoor bloom in winter.

Pest and disease prevention Watch out for mildew in warm, humid areas.

Landscape uses Ideal as edging plants for flower beds. They also look great in pots, window boxes and hanging baskets.

Bellis perennis ASTERACEAE

BEST SITE
Full sun to partial shade; average, well-drained soil with added organic matter.

HEIGHT
6 inches (15 cm)

SPREAD
6–8 inches (15–20 cm)

FLOWERING TIME
Spring to early summer.

ENGLISH DAISY

THESE EASY-TO-GROW, SHORT-LIVED PERENNIALS ARE USUALLY GROWN AS HARDY ANNUALS OR BIENNIALS. ENGLISH DAISIES ARE SUPER FOR SPRING COLOR IN FLOWER BEDS AND WINDOW BOXES.

Description Plants form rosettes of oval, green leaves. Short, thick stems are topped with 1–2-inch (2.5–5-cm) flowers. The daisy- or pompon-like blooms may be white, pink or red.

Growing guidelines If your area has cool summers, you can start seed indoors in midwinter and set plants out in midspring for bloom the same year. In hot-summer areas, or for earliest spring bloom elsewhere, grow English daisies as biennials. Sow seed in pots indoors or outdoors in early summer; cover lightly. Transplant seedlings in autumn. Space plants 6 inches (15 cm) apart. Protect large-flowered types with a light mulch, such as straw or pine needles, over winter. Pinch off the spent flower stems at the base to prolong bloom and prevent reseeding. Pull out plants after bloom and start new ones for next year.

Pest and disease prevention No specific problems.

Landscape uses They look great edging a walk, or in beds and borders with spring-flowering bulbs and forget-me-nots *Myosotis sylvatica*.

Best site
Full sun or partial shade; fairly rich, moist, well-drained soil.

Height
1½–2 feet (45–60 cm)

Spread
1½ feet (45 cm)

Flowering time
Midsummer through first frost.

Borage

This robust and bristly annual contrasts nicely with dark greens in the garden. The drooping clusters of blossoms attract honeybees, and the leaves have a cucumber flavor.

Description The blooms are star-shaped circles of pink, purple, lavender or blue, with black centers. The broad, hairy leaves arise from a central stalk.

Growing guidelines Sow seed ½ inch (12 mm) deep outdoors after danger of hard frost has passed. Indoors, plant in tall pots with a small diameter and try to avoid disturbing the sensitive taproot when transplanting. Mulch with light materials, such as straw, to keep the foliage off the soil and prevent rotting. Mulching also prevents weeds from coming up and competing for moisture. If you want to promote blooming, don't overdo the nitrogen supplementation. Borage is a reliable self-sower. Tall plants may need to be staked for support.

Pest and disease prevention No specific problems.

Landscape uses Borage is a must for cottage, herb and cutting gardens. As useful as it is attractive, borage can be harvested summer through autumn for use in salads, or cooked with vegetables. The pretty blooms are also suitable for drying.

Best site
Full sun; average, well-drained soil with added organic matter.

Height
1 foot (30 cm)

Spread
1½ feet (45 cm)

Flowering time
Midsummer until frost.

Swan River daisy

For earliest bloom, buy transplants and set them out after your last frost date. Shear Swan River daisy back after each flowering flush to encourage more flowers to form.

Description This half-hardy annual forms bushy mounds of thin stems and lacy, finely cut leaves. Plants bear many 1-inch (2.5-cm), rounded, daisy-like flowers in shades of blue, purple, pink and white. The delicately scented blooms may have a black or yellow center.

Growing guidelines You can either buy transplants or start Swan River daisy from seed planted indoors or outdoors. Sow seed indoors 6–8 weeks before your last frost date. Scatter the seed over the surface, lightly press it into the soil and enclose the pot in a plastic bag until seedlings appear. Set plants out after the last frost date. Or sow directly into the garden in late spring. Space plants 8–10 inches (20–25 cm) apart to form a solid, even carpet.

Pest and disease prevention No specific problems.

Landscape uses Swan River daisy makes an unusual edging for beds and borders. Its trailing habit is ideal for window boxes and hanging baskets.

Bracteantha bracteata ASTERACEAE

BEST SITE
Full sun; average, well-drained soil.

HEIGHT
2–4 feet (60–120 cm)

SPREAD
1 foot (30 cm)

FLOWERING TIME
Midsummer until frost.

STRAWFLOWER

GROW AN AMPLE SUPPLY OF STRAWFLOWERS IN THE CUTTING GARDEN FOR DRYING. IF YOU PICK THE FLOWERS WHEN THE FLOWER HEADS ARE ABOUT THREE-QUARTERS CLOSED, THEY'LL OPEN MORE AS THEY DRY.

Description This half-hardy annual is a bushy plant displaying long, narrow, green leaves and daisy-like flower heads with stiff, papery, petal-like bracts. The flower heads bloom in white, pink, rose, red, orange or yellow. Fully open flower heads are 1–2 inches (2.5–5 cm) wide and have yellow centers.

Growing guidelines Sow seed indoors 6–8 weeks before your last frost date. Press the seed lightly into the surface and enclose the pot in a plastic bag until seedlings appear. Set plants out 2 weeks after the last frost date, or sow seed directly into the garden after the last frost date. Set transplants or thin seedlings to stand 10–12 inches (25–30 cm) apart. Cutting strawflowers for fresh arrangements or drying will promote branching and prolong the bloom season.

Pest and disease prevention No specific problems.

Landscape uses Strawflowers are most often grown as a cutting flower. After harvesting, the dried stems tend to be brittle, so remove them and insert a piece of floral wire into the base of the flower head.

Best site
Full sun to light shade; average, well-drained soil.

Height
1–1½ feet (30–45 cm)

Spread
1½ feet (45 cm)

Flowering time
Autumn to early spring.

Ornamental cabbage

Also known as flowering cabbages, ornamental cabbages add a showy accent to late-season gardens. They may even continue to bloom through several frosts.

Description This biennial is grown as a frost-hardy annual for its rosettes of colorful autumn foliage. The smooth, glossy, blue-green leaves are marked with pink, purple, cream or white. As temperatures drop in autumn, the leaves in the center of the rosette become much more colorful, to the point where they are green only around the edge. Ornamental kale is very similar, but its leaves are more frilly or finely cut.

Growing guidelines In hot-summer areas, sow seed indoors; elsewhere, sow outdoors in pots or a nursery bed. Plant seed ¼ inch (6 mm) deep in midsummer. Move plants to garden in autumn. Set in holes 1 foot (30 cm) apart, deep enough to cover stem to lowest leaves.

Pest and disease prevention If caterpillars damage the leaves, pick them off by hand or spray with BT, a microbial insecticide.

Landscape uses Ornamental cabbage adds color to autumn flower beds and borders as other annuals are finishing for the season. It is also attractive in containers or large window boxes.

BEST SITE
Partial shade; average to moist soil with added organic matter.

HEIGHT
Ranging from 8–18 inches (20–45 cm), depending on the cultivar.

SPREAD
8–18 inches (20–45 cm)

FLOWERING TIME
Summer until frost.

BROWALLIA

SHADE-LOVING BROWALLIAS ARE IDEAL COMPANIONS FOR WAX BEGONIAS, FERNS, HOSTAS OR OTHER PLANTS THAT PREFER A SHADY OR SEMI-SHADY POSITION.

Description This tender perennial is usually grown as a tender annual. The bushy plants have lance-shaped, green leaves and 2-inch (5-cm) wide, starry flowers, which are purple, blue or white.

Growing guidelines Buy plants in spring, or start your own by planting seed indoors 8 weeks before your last frost date. Don't cover the seed; just lightly press it into the soil. Enclose the pot in a plastic bag until seedlings appear. Set plants out after the last frost. Space compact cultivars 10–12 inches (25–30 cm) apart; allow 1½ feet (45 cm) between tall types. Pinch off the stem tips of young plants once or twice to promote compact, branching growth. For winter bloom, dig plants before frost, pot them up and bring them indoors.

Pest and disease prevention No specific problems.

Landscape uses Browallia's star-shaped flowers brighten up shady beds and borders, hanging baskets, window boxes and container gardens.

Calceolaria Herbeohybrida Group SCROPHULARIACEAE

BEST SITE
Best suited to growing indoors or in a warm, semi-shaded position in the garden.

HEIGHT
From 6 inches (15 cm) to 1–1½ feet (30–45 cm), depending on the cultivar.

SPREAD
10 inches (25 cm)

FLOWERING TIME
Late winter through spring.

LADY'S PURSE

THE STUNNING FLOWERS OF LADY'S PURSE ARE SO NAMED BECAUSE THEY FORM LITTLE POUCHES. THIS PLANT IS BEST SUITED TO GROWING INDOORS.

Description This tender annual is marginally frost hardy. Lady's purse has oval, hairy leaves and pouched flowers that come in a variety of colors from bright red, orange and yellow, to tan and cream. Some cultivars have veined or splotched coloring, while others are plain.

Growing guidelines It's best to buy lady's purse as seedlings, as it is very difficult to raise from seed. Pot up in a well-drained potting mix and keep indoors in bright, indirect light, away from windows. If you are intent on a challenge, lightly scatter the very fine seeds on the top of seed-raising mix, then leave uncovered in a warm, shaded position. Pot up seedlings individually when the plants are about 1–2 inches (2.5–5 cm) high. Fertilize when the seedlings are in individual pots and then about once a week while flowering.

Pest and disease prevention Be careful not to overwater these plants as the soft stems will rot.

Landscape uses Grow lady's purse indoors or in summer flower beds, but make sure the plants are not exposed to very hot, dry conditions.

BEST SITE
Full sun; average, well-drained soil.

HEIGHT
1–2 feet (30–60 cm)

SPREAD
1 foot (30 cm)

FLOWERING TIME
Summer to autumn.

POT MARIGOLD

IN HOT-SUMMER AREAS, YOU CAN GROW POT MARIGOLDS FOR LATE-WINTER TO LATE-SPRING COLOR. THEY ARE LIKELY TO SELF-SOW IF YOU LET SOME SEEDS FORM AT THE END OF THE SEASON.

Description Also known as calendula, pot marigold is an easy-to-grow, hardy annual. The clumps of lance-shaped, bright to pale green, aromatic leaves are topped with single or double, daisy-like flowers in orange or yellow. The yellow- or brown-centered, 2–4-inch (5–10-cm) wide flowers tend to close during cloudy weather and at night.

Growing guidelines For summer and autumn bloom, sow seed indoors 6–8 weeks before your last frost date or outdoors in early to late spring. Set plants out around the last frost date. In hot-summer areas, sow seed directly into the garden in midautumn for late-winter bloom. Plant seed ¼ inch (6 mm) deep. Space plants or thin seedlings to stand 8–12 inches (20–30 cm) apart. Shear off spent flowers to promote later rebloom.

Pest and disease prevention To prevent problems with rust on self-sown seedlings, water only the base of the plants at the end of the day.

Landscape uses They make sunny accents for flower beds, borders and containers; their strong-stemmed blooms also make great cut flowers.

Callistephus chinensis ASTERACEAE

BEST SITE
Full sun; average, well-drained soil with added organic matter.

HEIGHT
1–2 feet (30–60 cm)

SPREAD
1–1½ feet (30–45 cm)

FLOWERING TIME
Late summer to frost.

CHINA ASTER

CHINA ASTERS GROW IN JUST ABOUT ANY CLIMATE, BUT REPLANT THEM IN A DIFFERENT SPOT IN YOUR GARDEN EACH YEAR TO GUARD AGAINST ASTER WILT.

Description This tender annual is grown for its showy white, cream, pink, red, purple or blue blooms. The stems carry broadly oval, toothed, green leaves and are topped with daisy-like or puffy, single or double flowers up to 5 inches (12.5 cm) wide.

Growing guidelines For late-summer bloom, buy transplants in spring or sow seed indoors, ⅛ inch (3 mm) deep, 6 weeks before your last frost date. Set plants out 2–3 weeks after the last frost date. For autumn bloom, sow seed directly into the garden after the last frost date. Space plants or thin seedlings to stand 10–12 inches (25–30 cm) apart; leave 1½ feet (45 cm) between tall-stemmed, staked cultivars. Pinch off stem tips once in early summer to promote branching.

Pest and disease prevention Aster wilt is a soilborne disease that causes plants to droop; destroy infected plants. Aster yellows causes yellowed, stunted growth; prevent it by controlling aphids with soap spray, or destroy infected plants.

Landscape uses Grow in masses or with other plants in beds, borders and planters for late-season color.

BEST SITE
Full sun; average, well-drained soil.

HEIGHT
1½–3 feet (45–90 cm)

SPREAD
1 foot (30 cm)

FLOWERING TIME
Spring to early summer.

CANTERBURY BELLS

CANTERBURY BELLS ARE NATURALS FOR COTTAGE GARDENS; THE PINKISH PURPLE FLOWERS HARMONIZE BEAUTIFULLY WITH MOST OTHER COLORS IN YOUR GARDEN.

Description Canterbury bells are slow-growing biennials that form leafy rosettes of toothed, lance-shaped leaves during their first year. In the second year, they send up slender stalks topped with loose spikes of bell-shaped blooms in white, pink or purple-blue. The flowers may be single or surrounded by a larger, colored cup.

Growing guidelines Sow seed outdoors in summer in pots or a nursery bed. Cover the seed lightly and keep the soil moist until seedlings appear. Move plants to their flowering positions in autumn or early spring. Space plants 1 foot (30 cm) apart. Pinch off spent blooms to prolong flowering and pull out plants that have finished blooming.

Pest and disease prevention No specific problems.

Landscape uses Grow Canterbury bells in small clumps in beds and borders with later-blooming annuals and perennials that can fill in the space left when you remove spent plants in midsummer. Try them in containers and cutting gardens, too.

Best site
Full sun; fertile, well-drained soil.

Height
2–3 feet (60–90 cm)

Spread
2 feet (60 cm)

Flowering time
Summer.

Safflower

FROST-HARDY SAFFLOWER IS BOTH ATTRACTIVE AND USEFUL IN THE GARDEN. THE DRIED FLOWERS ARE A SOURCE OF RED AND YELLOW DYES USED IN COOKING FOR FOOD COLORING.

Description Safflower is a fast-growing annual thistle with upright stems that branch at the top. Its leaves are spiny and oblong shaped, running down the stems. The flower heads are bright yellow to orange florets sitting atop a ring of spiny bracts.

Growing guidelines Safflower transplants poorly, so it's best to sow seed directly into your garden. Sow seed ¼ inch (6 mm) deep outdoors in spring; thin seedlings to stand 6 inches (15 cm) apart. Fertilize mature plants regularly.

Pest and disease prevention Hand-pick snails and slugs from seedlings.

Landscape uses Plant safflower in a cottage garden or at the back of flower beds. Collect flowers when fully opened and dry on paper in the shade.

Best site
Full sun; average, well-drained soil. Tolerates heat, pollution and drought.

Height
1–1½ feet (30–45 cm); grows bigger in frost-free climates.

Spread
1–1½ feet (30–45 cm)

Flowering time
Early summer until frost.

Madagascar periwinkle

MADAGASCAR PERIWINKLE ADAPTS WELL TO MOST GARDEN SITUATIONS, ESPECIALLY MASSED PLANTINGS, AS IT FLOWERS MOST OF THE YEAR IN FROST-FREE AREAS.

Description A tender perennial commonly grown as a tender annual, Madagascar periwinkle forms compact, bushy clumps of glossy, dark green leaves with white central veins. Stems are topped with flat, five-petaled, white, rose or pink flowers up to 2 inches (5 cm) wide.

Growing guidelines For best results, buy transplants in spring; it grows slowly from seed. If you want to try raising your own, sow seed ¼ inch (6 mm) deep indoors 10–12 weeks before your last frost date. Keep pots in an especially warm place (75–80°F [24–27°C]) until seedlings appear, then move pots to regular room temperature. Set transplants out 2–3 weeks after the last frost date, when the soil is warm. Space plants 6–12 inches (15–30 cm) apart. Pinch off stem tips in early summer to promote compact growth and more flowers.

Pest and disease prevention No specific problems.

Landscape uses Madagascar periwinkle is a beautiful, easy-care annual for edging flower beds, borders and walkways. It also adapts well to life in containers.

Celosia argentea Plumosa Group

AMARANTHACEAE

Best site
Full sun; average, well-drained soil with added organic matter.

Height
1–2 feet (30–60 cm)

Spread
1 foot (30 cm)

Flowering time
Summer until frost.

Celosia

Celosias can be tricky to get started but are easy once established. If plants are inadvertently disturbed during transplanting, later growth may be slow and stunted.

Description These tender perennials are grown as tender annuals. Their sturdy stems carry oval to narrow, pointed leaves that are green or tinted with bronze. The feathery flower spikes bloom in shades of fiery red, pink, orange or yellow.

Growing guidelines For best results, sow seed directly into the garden after the last frost date, or buy small transplants. Alternatively, sow seed indoors about 4 weeks before your last frost date. Plant seed 1/8 inch (3 mm) deep in individual pots. Set transplants out 2–3 weeks after the last frost date, when the soil is warm. Space compact types 6–8 inches (15–20 cm) apart; allow 1–2 feet (30–60 cm) between tall cultivars. Height and spread can vary widely, depending on the cultivar.

Pest and disease prevention No specific problems.

Landscape uses Grow in groups or masses to show off the unusual flowers. Use compact types to edge beds and walkways and to accent container gardens and window boxes. Include celosia in the cutting garden, too.

Celosia spicata AMARANTHACEAE

BEST SITE
Full sun; rich, well-drained soil.

HEIGHT
2–4 feet (60–120 cm)

SPREAD
10 inches (25 cm)

FLOWERING TIME
Summer.

WHEAT CELOSIA

WHEAT CELOSIA HAS GAINED POPULARITY IN RECENT YEARS AS A CUT FLOWER BECAUSE THE BLOOMS LAST WELL WHEN DRIED CAREFULLY.

Description Wheat celosia produces short, dense flower spikes on top of tall stems. The blooms start out as purplish pink buds and gradually age to a paler pink as the spikes elongate in late summer. There are many cultivars available, so ask your local nursery for details of those that are of interest to you.

Growing guidelines Propagate from seed sown in spring in warmer climates. In colder areas, wheat celosia is treated as a conservatory plant, so raise seedlings under glass in a warm position. Prepare the soil by adding organic matter. Plant out in late spring or early summer in cooler areas.

Pest and disease prevention No specific problems.

Landscape uses Wheat celosia is an obvious choice for a cutting garden, or as a bedding annual. To dry the flowers, harvest stems as soon as the flower heads reach the size you want, then hang them upside-down in a dark, dry place.

BEST SITE
Full sun; average, well-drained soil.

HEIGHT
1–2½ feet (30–75 cm)

SPREAD
1 foot (30 cm)

FLOWERING TIME
Late spring and summer (cooler areas).

CORNFLOWER

INTERPLANTING CORNFLOWERS AMONG LATE-SEASON BLOOMERS WILL COMPENSATE FOR THEIR RELATIVELY SHORT DISPLAY.

Description This is a dependable, easy-care, hardy annual. The bushy plants have narrow, lance-shaped, silvery green leaves and thin stems topped with fluffy flower heads. The 1–2-inch (2.5–5-cm) flowers bloom in white or shades of blue, purple, pink or red.

Growing guidelines Grows easily from seed sown directly into the garden in early autumn (in mild-winter areas) or early spring. Plant seed ⅛ inch (3 mm) deep. To extend the flowering season from an early-spring planting, sow again every 2–4 weeks until midsummer. Alternatively, buy transplants in spring or start the seed indoors about 8 weeks before your last frost date. Set plants outdoors about 2 weeks before the last frost date. Space or thin plants to stand 8–12 inches (20–30 cm) apart. Stick brushy prunings into the ground around young cornflower plants to support the stems as they grow.

Pest and disease prevention Aphids can be a problem in dry spring weather; treat with insecticide.

Landscape uses Cornflowers look great in meadow gardens, cutting gardens and flower beds. Try compact cultivars in container gardens.

Cirsium occidentale

ASTERACEAE

BEST SITE
Full sun; average, well-drained soil.

HEIGHT
2–5 feet (60–150 cm)

SPREAD
Up to 3 feet (90 cm) or more

FLOWERING TIME
Spring through summer.

COBWEB THISTLE

A NATIVE OF CENTRAL WESTERN AND SOUTHWESTERN CALIFORNIA, COBWEB THISTLE IS ONE OF THE MORE UNUSUAL CHOICES FOR AN ANNUAL GARDEN.

Description This hardy biennial is a spiky plant with a basal leaf rosette and branched stems that bear spiny, clustered flower heads. White, woolly bracts enclose the flower heads and the scarlet florets contrast with the deeply divided, hairy leaves that bear spikes along the sides and at the tip.

Growing guidelines Cobweb thistle is easy to grow from seed sown directly in your garden from early spring or after your last frost date. Thin seedlings to stand 8–12 inches (20–30 cm) apart. Cobweb thistle is a prolific self-sower, so care must be taken to prevent setting seed in surrounding gardens. Dig out the plants after flowering to control reseeding, but be sure to protect your hands from the spikes by wearing gardening gloves.

Pest and disease prevention No specific problems.

Landscape uses This plant has a tendency to become weedy, but with some care it can be enjoyed as a unique accent in beds and borders or in cottage and meadow gardens.

Clarkia amoena syn. *C. grandiflora* ONAGRACEAE

BEST SITE
Full sun; moist, well-drained soil.

HEIGHT
1–2½ feet (30–75 cm)

SPREAD
1 foot (30 cm)

FLOWERING TIME
Mid- to late spring; early summer in cooler areas.

FAREWELL-TO-SPRING

APTLY NAMED, FAREWELL-TO-SPRING IS THE LAST OF THE SPRING ANNUALS TO COME INTO FLOWER; ITS ATTRACTIVE BLOOMS MAKE A SHOWY END TO THE SEASON.

Description Farewell-to-spring is a fast-growing, hardy annual with a bushy habit and an abundance of open, cup-shaped, red, white, pink or pale purple flowers. The leaves are narrow and lanceolate, and the distinctively silky flowers sit atop tall, thin, upright stems.

Growing guidelines Sow seed directly into your garden or in individual pots in autumn. Cover seed with a light layer of soil. Transplant seedlings after your last frost date, about 8–12 inches (20–30 cm) apart. Once established, water only when the soil has dried somewhat, as overwatering results in rotting and death of the plant. Remove any end-of-season plants when they start to look untidy.

Pest and disease prevention Watch out for signs of botrytis; pick off any infected leaves or flowers and thin remaining plants.

Landscape uses A must for the cutting garden, farewell-to-spring lasts for up to a week in water. It also works well in massed plantings.

BEST SITE
Full sun to light shade; average, well-drained soil with added organic matter.

HEIGHT
4–6 feet (1.2–1.8 m)

SPREAD
3–4 feet (90–120 cm)

FLOWERING TIME
Midsummer until midautumn.

CLEOME

ALSO KNOWN AS SPIDER FLOWER, THE WISTFUL, ELEGANT BLOOMS OF CLEOME CREATE A WONDERFUL EFFECT IN COTTAGE GARDENS AND INFORMAL PLANTINGS.

Description Cleome is a fast-growing, half-hardy annual. Its tall, sturdy stems and palmlike leaves are slightly sticky and have a musky (some say skunklike) odor. The stems are topped with globes of four-petaled flowers with long stamens protruding from them, giving a spidery look. The white, pink or rosy lavender blooms are followed by long, narrow seedpods.

Growing guidelines Sow seed directly in the garden in mid- to late spring. For earlier bloom, buy transplants or start your own by sowing seed indoors about 4 weeks before your last frost date. Lightly press the seed into the surface, then enclose the pot in a plastic bag until seedlings appear. Set plants out around the last frost date. Space transplants or thin seedlings to stand 3 feet (90 cm) apart. Cleome usually self-sows prolifically. Pinching off seedpods regularly can reduce or eliminate self-sown seedlings.

Pest and disease prevention Aphids can sometimes be a problem.

Landscape uses A must for butterfly gardens. Try it in the back of flower beds and borders in large groupings to show off the spidery flowers.

BEST SITE
Full sun (or afternoon shade in hot-summer areas); average to moist, well-drained soil with added organic matter.

HEIGHT
Can grow to 10 feet (3 m) or more, depending on the size of its support.

SPREAD
10 feet (3 m)

FLOWERING TIME
Late summer until frost.

CUP-AND-SAUCER VINE

CUP-AND-SAUCER VINE IS USUALLY GROWN AS AN ANNUAL BECAUSE IT TENDS TO BECOME A LITTLE RAGGED BY WINTER TIME.

Description This vigorous, tender perennial climber is grown as a half-hardy annual. It has compound leaves, as well as tendrils that help the stems climb. Inflated buds on long stalks open to 2-inch (5-cm) long, bell-shaped flowers. Short, green, petal-like bracts surround the base of each bell. The flowers open light green and age to purple or white; mature flowers have a sweet, honey-like fragrance.

Growing guidelines Before planting, make sure you have a sturdy support in place for the vines to climb on. Sow seed indoors 8–10 weeks before your last frost date. Soak the flat seeds in warm water overnight, then plant them on their edge in peat pots. Sow two or three seeds ¼ inch (6 mm) deep in each pot. Once seedlings emerge, clip off extras to leave one per pot. Set plants out 6 feet (1.8 m) apart after the last frost date.

Pest and disease prevention No specific problems.

Landscape uses Cup-and-saucer vine makes a super screening plant for quick shade or privacy. It also makes a wonderful background plant for cottage gardens.

Consolida ajacis RANUNCULACEAE

BEST SITE
Full sun; average, well-drained soil with added organic matter.

HEIGHT
Up to 1 foot (30 cm) for dwarf types and 4 feet (1.2 m) for tall cultivars.

SPREAD
1 foot (30 cm)

FLOWERING TIME
Late spring through summer.

ROCKET LARKSPUR

THE COLORFUL AND ATTRACTIVE BLOOMS OF ROCKET LARKSPUR MIX WELL WITH PERENNIALS IN YOUR GARDEN; THEY MAKE GREAT CUT FLOWERS, TOO.

Description This hardy annual is grown for its showy flowers. The plants produce tall stems with finely divided, bright green leaves. Spikes of purple-blue, rose, pink or white flowers bloom atop the stems. There is a curving spur on the back of each flower. Rocket larkspur is also listed in seed catalogs as *C. ambigua*, *Delphinium ajacis* and *D. consolida*.

Growing guidelines Grows best from seed sown directly into the garden. Plant seed ¼ inch (6 mm) deep in autumn or early spring. Sow seed indoors in individual peat pots 6–8 weeks before your last frost date. Set seedlings out in mid- to late spring. Thin or space plants to stand 8–12 inches (20–30 cm) apart. Tall cultivars of rocket larkspur may need support to stay upright. Push pieces of twiggy brush into the ground around young plants to support them as they grow.

Pest and disease prevention No specific problems.

Landscape uses Use the spiky flowers of rocket larkspur to add height and color to flower beds, borders and cottage gardens.

Convolvulus tricolor

CONVOLVULACEAE

BEST SITE
Full sun to light shade; average, well-drained soil.

HEIGHT
1 foot (30 cm)

SPREAD
8–18 inches (20–45 cm)

FLOWERING TIME
Midsummer through early autumn.

DWARF MORNING GLORY

DWARF MORNING GLORY IS A VIGOROUS VINE THAT WILL COVER WALLS, FENCES AND TERRACED BEDS IN NO TIME.

Description This compact, easy-to-grow, hardy annual forms bushy, spreading mounds of oval to narrow green leaves topped with showy, trumpet-shaped blooms. The 1½-inch (3.5-cm) wide flowers are deep purple-blue on the outside, with a starry white center and a bright yellow throat.

Growing guidelines For earliest flowering, sow seed indoors 6 weeks before your last frost date. Soak seed overnight, then plant it ¼ inch (6 mm) deep in individual peat pots. Dwarf morning glory also grows easily from seed sown directly into the garden after the last frost date. Set transplants or thin seedlings to stand 8 inches (20 cm) apart. Stick short pieces of twiggy brush into the soil around young plants to support the stems. Water during dry spells. Pinch off spent flowers to prolong bloom.

Pest and disease prevention No specific problems.

Landscape uses Grow near the front of flower beds and borders or in container gardens. Dwarf morning glory looks especially charming cascading out of window boxes and hanging baskets.

Coreopsis tinctoria ASTERACEAE

BEST SITE
Full sun; average, well-drained soil.

HEIGHT
Up to 2–3 feet (60–90 cm), depending on the cultivar.

SPREAD
1 foot (30 cm)

FLOWERING TIME
Midsummer until frost.

CALLIOPSIS

YOU CAN ALWAYS DEPEND ON CALLIOPSIS FOR ADDING FAST, NO-FUSS COLOR TO BEDS AND BORDERS IN MOST GARDEN DESIGNS.

Description Calliopsis is a colorful, fast-growing, hardy annual. Its wiry stems carry narrow, green leaves and 1–2-inch (2.5–5-cm) wide, single or double, daisy-like flowers. The flowers are usually golden yellow with maroon centers but may also be found in all-yellow or all-orange varieties.

Growing guidelines Grows quickly from seed sown directly into the garden in early to midspring. You can also sow seed ⅛ inch (3 mm) deep indoors about 6 weeks before your last frost date. Set plants out around the last frost date. Space transplants or thin seedlings to stand about 8 inches (20 cm) apart. Push twiggy brush into the soil around young plants of tall-growing cultivars to support the stems as they grow. Shearing the plants back by one-third in mid- to late summer can prolong the bloom season.

Pest and disease prevention No specific problems.

Landscape uses Calliopsis looks wonderful in meadow gardens and informal plantings. Grow some in the cutting garden for fresh arrangements. Try the compact cultivars in containers.

BEST SITE
Full sun is best, although plants can take partial shade; average to moist, well-drained soil.

HEIGHT
3–4 feet (90–120 cm)

SPREAD
1½ feet (45 cm)

FLOWERING TIME
Late summer through autumn.

COSMOS

COSMOS IS A VERY POPULAR HALF-HARDY ANNUAL THAT IS GROWN FOR ITS COLORFUL BLOOMS OVER A LONG SEASON.

Description Cosmos is a bushy plant bearing many finely cut, green leaves. The stems are topped with white, pink or rosy red flowers. The single or semidouble, daisy-like blooms can grow up to 4 inches (10 cm) across.

Growing guidelines For earliest blooms, buy transplants in spring or start seed indoors 3–4 weeks before your last frost date. Plant seed ¼ inch (6 mm) deep. Set plants out 2–3 weeks after the last frost date. You can also sow seed directly into the garden around the last frost date. Space transplants or thin seedlings to stand 6–12 inches (15–30 cm) apart. Pinch off stem tips in early summer to promote branching and more flowers. Push sturdy pieces of twiggy brush into the soil around young plants to support the stems as they grow, or stake individual stems as needed. Or just let the plants sprawl; they'll send up more flowering stems. Deadhead regularly to promote bloom.

Pest and disease prevention No specific problems.

Landscape uses Cosmos adds height and color to flower beds, borders and meadows. Use it to fill spaces left by early-blooming annuals.

BEST SITE
Full sun; average, well-drained soil.

HEIGHT
2–3 feet (60–90 cm)

SPREAD
1½ feet (45 cm)

FLOWERING TIME
Late summer until frost.

YELLOW COSMOS

YELLOW COSMOS IS HARD TO BEAT FOR BRIGHT, LATE-SEASON COLOR IN FLOWER BEDS, BORDERS AND CONTAINER GARDENS.

Description Yellow, or Klondike, cosmos is a half-hardy annual that forms bushy mounds of deeply lobed, dark green leaves. The thin stems carry showy, single or semidouble, daisy-like flowers. The yellow, orange or red blooms are 1–2 inches (2.5–5 cm) wide.

Growing guidelines To get the earliest flowers, start seed indoors 4–6 weeks before your last frost date. Plant seed ¼ inch (6 mm) deep. Set plants out after the last frost date. Yellow cosmos also grows easily from seed sown directly into the garden around the last frost date. Set plants or thin seedlings to stand about 1 foot (30 cm) apart. Pinching off spent flowers can prolong the bloom season. If you leave a few flowers to mature at the end of the season, plants will self-sow.

Pest and disease prevention No specific problems.

Landscape uses These bushy plants make great fillers for any spaces left by spring-blooming annuals and perennials.

Cynoglossum amabile BORAGINACEAE

BEST SITE
Full sun; fertile, well-drained soil.

HEIGHT
1¼–2 feet (40–60 cm)

SPREAD
1 foot (30 cm)

FLOWERING TIME
Spring and early summer.

CHINESE FORGET-ME-NOT

CHINESE FORGET-ME-NOT IS A DEPENDABLE SELF-SOWER THAT MAKES A GOOD CHOICE FOR AN ALL-BLUE GARDEN.

Description Chinese forget-me-not is a frost-hardy annual or biennial. It has dull, green, hairy lanceolate leaves. The flowers are produced in racemes and although generally blue, some cultivars come in pink or white.

Growing guidelines Sow seed directly into your garden in autumn or spring. Thin seedlings or space transplants to stand about 1 foot (30 cm) apart. When established, fertilize and mulch around the plant stems, but don't overdo it, as Chinese forget-me-nots tend to flop over when overnourished. Remove spent flowers regularly to extend the bloom time.

Pest and disease prevention No specific problems.

Landscape uses These plants are a trusty staple in bed and border plantings and in container gardens. Their long flowering period ensures an attractive show all season.

BEST SITE
Full sun to partial shade; average, well-drained soil.

HEIGHT
1–1½ feet (30–45 cm)

SPREAD
8–12 inches (20–30 cm)

FLOWERING TIME
Early to midsummer.

SWEET WILLIAM

SWEET WILLIAM IS RELATED TO THE CARNATION FAMILY AND ITS FRAGRANT BLOOMS LOOK JUST AS WONDERFUL IN FRESH ARRANGEMENTS.

Description This short-lived perennial is grown as a hardy biennial or annual. An old favorite, it forms clumps of narrow, lance-shaped, green leaves. The stems are topped with dense, slightly rounded clusters of five-petaled flowers. Each fragrant bloom is ½–¾ inch (12–18 mm) wide. Red, pink and white are the most common colors; some flowers have eyes, or zones, of contrasting colors.

Growing guidelines For earliest bloom, grow as a biennial: Sow seed outdoors in pots or in a nursery bed in summer, then move plants to their garden position in autumn. For bloom the same year, sow seed indoors (just barely cover it) about 8 weeks before your last frost date. Set plants out 2–3 weeks before the last frost date. Space transplants 8–10 inches (20–25 cm) apart. Sweet William will self-sow if you leave a few flowers to form seeds.

Pest and disease prevention No specific problems.

Landscape uses Sweet William looks super as an early-summer filler for beds and borders. Plant some in the cutting garden, too.

Dianthus chinensis CARYOPHYLLACEAE

Best site
Full sun (afternoon shade in hot-summer areas); average, well-drained soil.

Height
8–12 inches (20–30 cm)

Spread
8–12 inches (20–30 cm)

Flowering time
Summer.

China pink

China pinks are biennials or short-lived perennials that are more commonly grown as annuals.

Description These plants form tufts of narrow, green leaves. The upright stems bear 1-inch (2.5-cm) wide, flat flowers with broad white, pink or red petals that are fringed at the tips. China pinks have also been hybridized to produce more colorful and larger flowers over a longer season.

Growing guidelines Buy plants in spring, or start seed indoors (just barely cover it) 6–8 weeks before your last frost date. You can also sow seed directly into the garden 2–3 weeks before the last frost date. Thin seedlings or set transplants to stand 6–10 inches (15–25 cm) apart. Pinch off spent flowers to prolong the bloom season.

Pest and disease prevention No specific problems.

Landscape uses China pinks are a natural choice for cottage gardens. They also make colorful edgings for flower beds and walkways. Try a few in container gardens, too.

Best site
Full sun to partial shade (afternoon shade in hot-summer areas); average, well-drained soil with added organic matter.

Height
3–5 feet (90–150 cm)

Spread
2 feet (60 cm)

Flowering time
Early to midsummer of following year.

Common foxglove

All parts of common foxglove are poisonous, especially the leaves, so always be sure to wear protective gloves when handling them.

Description This beautiful biennial or short-lived perennial is grown for its showy blooms. During the first year, plants form mounds of broad, velvety, grayish green leaves. During the second season, the rosettes send up long, graceful spikes topped with thimble-shaped flowers. The 2–3-inch (5–7.5-cm) blooms may be white, cream, pink or pinkish purple and often have contrasting spots on the inside.

Growing guidelines Grow most foxgloves as biennials by sowing outdoors in pots or in a nursery bed in late summer. Sow seed on the soil surface, press it in lightly and keep the soil moist until seedlings appear. Move plants to their garden positions in autumn. Space them about 1½ feet (45 cm) apart. Tall cultivars may need staking.

Pest and disease prevention No specific problems.

Landscape uses Grow them in the back of borders where other plants will fill the space left in midsummer. The tall spires also look stunning in masses in lightly shaded woodlands.

BEST SITE
Full sun; fertile, well-drained soil.

HEIGHT
8–12 inches (20–30 cm)

SPREAD
8–12 inches (20–30 cm)

FLOWERING TIME
Late winter and spring.

RAIN DAISY

THESE COLORFUL DAISIES ONLY OPEN IN SUNSHINE, SO BE SURE TO POSITION THEM IN A SITE WITH FULL SUN.

Description Rain daisy is a low-growing annual that produces small, colorful flower heads that are pure white on top and purple on the underside of the petals. The center of each flower is a striking brownish purple color.

Growing guidelines Sow seed outdoors in spring, after the last frost. Fertilize regularly during the growing season and keep the soil evenly moist. Prune lightly after flowering to prolong the bloom season. You can bring rain daisy indoors for overwintering and move it outdoors again the following spring.

Pest and disease prevention Watch out for fungal diseases in high rainfall areas.

Landscape uses Rain daisy is a bedding annual that is perfect for rock gardens and borders. It also grows well in container gardens and window boxes.

Dipsacus fullonum DIPSACACEAE

BEST SITE
Full sun or part shade; fertile, well-drained soil.

HEIGHT
5–6 feet (1.5–1.8 m)

SPREAD
2–3 feet (60–90 cm)

FLOWERING TIME
Midsummer through late autumn.

WILD TEASEL

IT'S EASY TO IDENTIFY WILD TEASEL BY ITS DISTINCTIVE SEED HEADS. THESE SPIKY STRUCTURES ARE DRAMATIC IN WILDFLOWER ARRANGEMENTS AND OTHER NATURE CRAFTS.

Description Wild teasel is a biennial that produces a rosette of leaves at ground level the first year and a coarse, prickly, upright stem the second year. The long, pointed, prickly, toothed leaves attach in pairs directly to the stem. The white or purple, four-petaled flowers bloom in an egg-shaped head that becomes a prickly seed head.

Growing guidelines Sow seed directly into your garden after the last frost. Thin seedlings to stand 2–3 feet (60–90 cm) apart. Wild teasel self-sows freely, so mulch to prevent existing seeds from sprouting. Dig or pull larger plants before they set seed (make sure to get the deep taproot, too).

Pest and disease prevention No specific problems.

Landscape uses Wild teasel makes a great cut flower for dried arrangements, so plant some in the cutting garden or at the back of flower beds.

Dorotheanthus bellidiformis AIZOACEAE

BEST SITE
Full sun; sandy, well-drained soil.

HEIGHT
6 inches (15 cm)

SPREAD
1 foot (30 cm)

FLOWERING TIME
Late spring through summer.

ICE PLANT

ICE PLANT'S LOW-GROWING HABIT AND COLORFUL BLOOMS MAKE IT A WINNING FILLER IN ANNUAL BEDS AND BORDERS.

Description A marginally frost-hardy, succulent annual, ice plant bears masses of bright flowers in shades of white, yellow, pink, red and sometimes bicolored blooms with dark centers. The flowers only open in direct sunlight. Its succulent, midgreen leaves are narrow and pointed.

Growing guidelines Sow seed directly into your garden after the last frost date, or indoors 6–8 weeks before the last frost date. Plant out when danger of frost has passed. No special soil preparation is required, but plants must be in a site with good drainage, otherwise they will rot and die. Pinch out dead flower heads for appearance and to promote longer bloom time.

Pest and disease prevention No specific problems.

Landscape uses Ice plant is perfect in massed plantings, borders, rock gardens or simply growing in the cracks between paving stones. Try it in hanging baskets for something different.

Erysimum cheiri

BRASSICACEAE

BEST SITE
Full sun to partial shade; average to moist, well-drained soil, ideally with a neutral to slightly alkaline pH.

HEIGHT
1–2 feet (30–60 cm)

SPREAD
1 foot (30 cm)

FLOWERING TIME
Midspring to early summer.

WALLFLOWER

WALLFLOWER IS A BUSHY PLANT THAT HAS BEEN A COTTAGE GARDEN FAVORITE FOR MANY YEARS. THE FLOWERS ARE IDEAL FOR SPRING ARRANGEMENTS.

Description This perennial is commonly grown as a half-hardy annual or biennial for spring color. The bushy clumps of slender green leaves are topped with clusters of 1-inch (2.5-cm) wide, four-petaled flowers.

Growing guidelines To grow as an annual, sow seed outdoors in early spring or indoors about 8 weeks before your last frost date. Plant seed ¼ inch (6 mm) deep. Set plants out 8–12 inches (20–30 cm) apart around the last frost date. In frost-free areas, grow wallflower as a biennial. Sow seed in pots or in a nursery bed in early summer; move plants to their flowering position in early autumn. Water during dry spells to keep the soil evenly moist. Pull out plants when they have finished blooming.

Pest and disease prevention No specific problems.

Landscape uses Grow in masses or in flower beds for spots of early color. One classic combination is orange wallflowers underplanted with blue forget-me-nots *Myosotis sylvatica*. Wallflowers also combine beautifully with tulips.

BEST SITE
Full sun; average to sandy, well-drained soil.

HEIGHT
1–1½ feet (30–45 cm)

SPREAD
1–1½ feet (30–45 cm)

FLOWERING TIME
Early summer through early autumn.

CALIFORNIA POPPY

CALIFORNIA POPPY WAS NAMED BY GERMAN BOTANIST AND POET ADALBERT VON CHAMISSO, IN RECOGNITION OF HIS FRIEND JOHAN FRIEDRICH ESCHSCHOLZ.

Description This tender perennial is usually grown as a hardy annual. Plants form loose clumps of deeply cut, blue-green leaves. The thin stems are topped with pointed buds that unfurl into single, semidouble or double flowers up to 3 inches (7.5 cm) across. The silky-looking petals are usually orange or yellow, but they can also bloom in white, pink or red.

Growing guidelines California poppy transplants poorly, so it's usually not worth starting seed indoors. Plants will grow quickly from seed sown directly into the garden in very early spring (or even in autumn in frost-free areas). Scatter the seed over the soil surface and rake it in lightly. Thin seedlings to stand 10 inches (25 cm) apart. If blooms are sparse by midsummer, cut plants back by about one-third to encourage a new flush of flowers. Plants usually self-sow in mild-winter areas.

Pest and disease prevention No specific problems.

Landscape uses California poppies are colorful, easy-to-grow fillers for flower beds and borders. They're also excellent in meadow gardens.

BEST SITE
Full sun; average, well-drained soil.

HEIGHT
2–4 feet (60–120 cm)

SPREAD
1–1½ feet (30–45 cm)

FLOWERING TIME
Summer.

SNOW-ON-THE-MOUNTAIN

ALSO KNOWN AS GHOSTWEED, THIS SHRUBBY ANNUAL MAKES A WONDERFUL CONTRAST FOR THE MORE BRIGHTLY COLORED FLOWERS IN BEDS AND BORDERS.

Description Snow-on-the-mountain forms showy clumps of white-marked leaves. This half-hardy annual is grown for its attractive foliage. Young plants produce upright stems with oblong to pointed, green leaves. In mid- to late summer, the stems begin to branch more, and the leaves produced on the upper parts of the branches are edged with white. At the branch tips, clusters of tiny flowers are surrounded by pure white, petal-like bracts.

Growing guidelines For earliest color, start seed ½ inch (12 mm) deep indoors 4–6 weeks before your last frost date. Set plants out after the last frost date. Or sow seed directly into the garden around the last frost date. Thin seedlings or space transplants to stand 1 foot (30 cm) apart. Plants may lean or flop by late summer; prevent this by staking them in early to midsummer, while they're still young. Plants often self-sow.

Pest and disease prevention No specific problems.

Landscape uses Use this old-fashioned favorite as a filler or accent plant in beds and borders.

Eustoma grandiflorum

GENTIANACEAE

Best site
Full sun to partial shade; average, well-drained soil.

Height
1–2 feet (30–60 cm)

Spread
1 foot (30 cm)

Flowering time
Summer.

Prairie Gentian

PRAIRIE GENTIAN IS A BEAUTIFUL BUT SLOW-GROWING BIENNIAL THAT IS MORE OFTEN GROWN AS A HALF-HARDY ANNUAL.

Description The slender, upright stems of prairie gentian carry oblong, gray-green leaves and are topped with pointed buds. The buds unfurl to produce long-lasting, single or double flowers that resemble poppies or roses. The 2–3-inch (5–7.5-cm) flowers bloom in white and shades of cream, pink, rose and purple-blue.

Growing guidelines You'll get the quickest results by buying transplants in spring. If you want to try raising your own, sow seed indoors in midwinter. Scatter the seed over the surface of the soil, press it in lightly and enclose the pot in a plastic bag until seedlings appear. Set transplants out 12 weeks after your last frost date. Space them about 10 inches (25 cm) apart in clumps of three or more plants. Pinching off stem tips once or twice in early summer will promote branching and more blooms. Remove the spent blooms to prolong flowering.

Pest and disease prevention No specific problems.

Landscape uses Prairie gentian looks stunning planted in masses with shrubs or alone in a container.

Best site
Full sun; fertile, moist, well-drained soil.

Height
8–12 inches (20–30 cm)

Spread
8–12 inches (20–30 cm)

Flowering time
Summer.

Persian violet

PERSIAN VIOLET IS A SHOWY MINIATURE THAT CAN ONLY BE GROWN OUTDOORS IN A WARM, FROST-FREE CLIMATE.

Description Persian violet is a biennial usually grown as a tender annual. It has shiny, oval leaves and an abundance of small, five-petaled, rounded, purple-blue flowers with bright yellow stamens.

Growing guidelines Sow seed indoors or outdoors after all danger of frost has passed; sow into pots or directly into the position where you want the plants to grow. Transplant toward the end of spring into prepared soil. Space plants to stand about 10 inches (25 cm) apart. Indoor plants need to be kept in a warm position with diffused sunlight and a night temperature that does not go below 50°F (10°C).

Pest and disease prevention No specific problems.

Landscape uses Persian violet is most often grown as an indoor plant or as a neat filler in beds and borders.

Best site
Full sun; fertile, well-drained, gravelly soil.

Height
1⅔ feet (50 cm)

Spread
1⅔ feet (50 cm)

Flowering time
Late spring to autumn (warmer areas).

Blue daisy

A native of South Africa, blue daisy is a firm favorite in color-theme, cottage and fragrance gardens.

Description Marginally frost-hardy, blue daisy is a dome-shaped, spreading annual with grayish green, lance-shaped leaves. The single blue flower heads perch atop long, thin stems.

Growing guidelines Sow seed directly into your garden in midspring, or indoors 6–8 weeks before your last frost date. Set out transplants or thin seedlings in late spring to stand 1½ feet (45 cm) apart. Deadhead spent flowers to prolong the bloom time. Prune ragged shoots regularly.

Pest and disease prevention No specific problems.

Landscape uses Blue daisy grows well in rock gardens, beds and borders. Its mat-forming habit also makes it a good groundcover in big or small-scale plantings.

Gaillardia pulchella ASTERACEAE

BEST SITE
Full sun; average, well-drained to dry soil.

HEIGHT
1–2 feet (30–60 cm)

SPREAD
1–2 feet (30–60 cm)

FLOWERING TIME
Summer.

BLANKET FLOWER

BLANKET FLOWERS ARE WELL SUITED TO HOT, DRY AREAS AS THEY ARE HEAT- AND DROUGHT-TOLERANT.

Description Blanket flower is a fast-growing, hardy annual. Plants produce clumps of narrow, hairy, gray-green leaves highlighted by orange-red flowers with yellow tips, which may also be red, yellow or orange around a reddish purple center. The single or double, daisy-like blooms may be up to 3 inches (7.5 cm) wide, with toothed petals that give a fringed appearance around the edge.

Growing guidelines In most areas, you'll get best results by sowing seed directly into the garden. Plant seed ⅛ inch (3 mm) deep in spring around your last frost date (or even in autumn in mild-winter areas). If your summers are short and cool, get an early start by sowing seed indoors 4–6 weeks before the last frost date. Space transplants or thin seedlings to stand 1 foot (30 cm) apart. Support the stems of young plants. Plants will self-sow if you allow a few flowers to set seed.

Pest and disease prevention No specific problems.

Landscape uses Blanket flowers add loads of summer color to flower beds and borders. Grow a few in the cutting garden for fresh flowers.

BEST SITE
Full sun; average, well-drained soil.

HEIGHT
8–12 inches (20–30 cm)

SPREAD
1 foot (30 cm)

FLOWERING TIME
Midsummer until frost.

TREASURE FLOWER

TREASURE FLOWER'S MAT-FORMING HABIT MAKES IT A PERFECT CHOICE FOR GROWING BETWEEN PAVING STONES IN YOUR GARDEN.

Description This eye-catching tender perennial is grown as a half-hardy annual. Plants form low mats of narrow-lobed, green leaves that are silvery underneath. These plants are topped with brilliantly colored daisy-like flowers to 3 inches (7.5 cm) across. Treasure flowers usually bloom in red, orange or yellow but can also be pink, purplish or white. They close up at night and during cloudy weather. The petals may have a contrasting center stripe and usually have a dark brown or green spot at the base.

Growing guidelines Buy transplants or start seed indoors 6–8 weeks before your last frost date. Plant seed ⅛ inch (3 mm) deep. Set transplants out after the last frost date. Or sow seed directly into the garden 12 weeks after the last frost date for late-summer bloom. Thin seedlings or set transplants to stand 10 inches (25 cm) apart. Pinch off spent flowers to prolong the bloom season. Dig up a few plants before frost and bring them indoors for winter bloom.

Pest and disease prevention No specific problems.

Landscape uses Use it as an edging plant, or grow it in masses for an eye-opening annual groundcover.

BEST SITE
Full sun; prefers cool, wet winters and hot summers, and well-drained soil.

HEIGHT
2 feet (60 cm)

SPREAD
8 inches (20 cm)

FLOWERING TIME
Summer and early autumn.

QUEEN ANNE'S THIMBLES

QUEEN ANNE'S THIMBLES ARE NATIVE TO THE WEST COASTAL RANGES OF CANADA, USA AND MEXICO. THEY ARE ALSO KNOWN AS BLUE THIMBLE FLOWERS.

Description This is an erect, branching annual that is moderately to very frost hardy. It has midgreen, feathery leaves that are finely divided and grow from long, thin stems with small, lavender-blue flowers at the tip. The flowers form a pincushion-like ball.

Growing guidelines Sow seed directly into the garden in mid- to late spring, when the soil has warmed up. Thin seedlings to stand 6–8 inches (15–20 cm) apart. Water lightly and regularly, as these plants tend to wilt rapidly in drought conditions. You may need to stake young plants lightly in windy or exposed sites to protect their stems.

Pest and disease prevention No specific problems.

Landscape uses Queen Anne's thimbles work best in borders and cutting gardens.

Gomphrena globosa

AMARANTHACEAE

BEST SITE
Full sun; average, well-drained to dry soil.

HEIGHT
8–18 inches (20–45 cm)

SPREAD
8–12 inches (20–30 cm)

FLOWERING TIME
Midsummer until frost.

GLOBE AMARANTH

GLOBE AMARANTH IS POPULAR AS A DRIED FLOWER BECAUSE THE FLOWER HEADS KEEP THEIR COLOR WELL WHEN AIR-DRIED.

Description This tender annual is grown for its long-lasting flower heads. The oblong to elliptical, green leaves grow in pairs along the sturdy stems; both the stems and the leaves are covered with fine hairs. Tiny, yellow flowers peek out from between layers of colorful, papery bracts that make up the clover-like flower heads. The magenta, pink or white flower heads are 1 inch (2.5 cm) wide.

Growing guidelines Buy transplants in spring, or start your own by sowing seed indoors 4–6 weeks before your last frost date. Sow seed ⅛–¼ inch (3–6 mm) deep. For quickest germination, place the pots in a warm place (about 75°F [24°C]), until seedlings appear; then move them back to normal room temperature. Set transplants out 2–3 weeks after the last frost date. In warmer climates, you can also sow seed directly into the garden after the last frost date, when the soil is warm. Space transplants or thin seedlings to stand 8–10 inches (20–25 cm) apart.

Pest and disease prevention No specific problems.

Landscape uses Try the compact cultivars as edgings or in containers.

BEST SITE
Full sun (or afternoon shade in hot-summer areas); average, well-drained soil.

HEIGHT
1½–2 feet (45–60 cm)

SPREAD
1 foot (30 cm)

FLOWERING TIME
Up to 2 months in spring and early summer.

ANNUAL BABY'S BREATH

THIS HARDY ANNUAL IS GROWN FOR ITS AIRY SPRAYS OF DAINTY FLOWERS, WHICH ARE OFTEN USED IN FRESH ARRANGEMENTS.

Description Annual baby's breath forms loose clumps of slender stems with pairs of narrow, gray-green leaves. Loose clusters of many five-petaled flowers bloom atop the stems. The ¼–½-inch (6–12-mm) wide flowers are usually white or light pink; some cultivars have deeper pink flowers.

Growing guidelines Plant seed directly into the garden where you want plants to grow; cover it with ⅛ inch (3 mm) of soil. Sow seed in early spring (or in autumn in mild-winter areas). Thin seedlings to stand 10 inches (25 cm) apart. Push twiggy brush into the soil around young plants to support the stems as they grow. Sowing the seed of annual baby's breath every 2–3 weeks from early to late spring can extend the bloom season well into summer. Pull out plants after flowering.

Pest and disease prevention No specific problems.

Landscape uses Makes a nice filler for flower beds and borders in late spring and early summer. It looks especially charming in masses with other cool-loving annuals, such as rocket larkspur *Consolida ajacis* and sweet peas *Lathyrus odoratus*.

Helianthus annuus ASTERACEAE

Best site
Full sun; average, well-drained soil.

Height
2–8 feet (60–240 cm)

Spread
1½–2½ feet (45–75 cm)

Flowering time
Midsummer through midautumn.

Common sunflower

Common sunflowers are much-loved hardy annuals grown for their large, showy blooms (and often for their tasty seeds as well).

Description This easy-to-grow plant produces large, sturdy stalks with coarse, heart-shaped leaves. The stems are topped with flat, daisy-like flower heads to 1 foot (30 cm) wide or more. The flower heads normally have a purple-brown center, with yellow, bronze, mahogany, red or orange petals.

Growing guidelines Common sunflowers grow so quickly that it's easiest to sow seed directly into the garden after your last frost date. Plant seed ½ inch (12 mm) deep. Thin seedlings to stand 1½ feet (45 cm) apart. Unless you're growing plants for the edible seeds, remove spent flowers to prolong the bloom season.

Pest and disease prevention No specific problems.

Landscape uses Sunflowers tend to drop their leaves along the bottom half of their stem, so place them in the middle or back of the border where other plants will hide their bare ankles. Small-flowered types are excellent as cut flowers. The seed-producing types are best left in the vegetable garden, since they aren't especially showy after bloom.

BEST SITE
Full sun, though well-adapted to shade and tolerates dry conditions; sandy, well-drained soil.

HEIGHT
2 feet (60 cm)

SPREAD
4 feet (1.2 m)

FLOWERING TIME
Summer.

LICORICE PLANT

LICORICE PLANT HAS SOFT, SILVERY LEAVES THAT COMPLEMENT BOTH PALE PASTELS AND BOLD, BRIGHT HUES. IT'S A PERFECT CHOICE FOR CASCADING OVER THE EDGES OF BORDERS, BANKS AND CONTAINERS.

Description Licorice plant is a perennial that is more often grown as an annual in colder climates. It has a shrubby form that's partly upright and partly trailing. The woody stems carry oval, felted, white-green-gray foliage. Small, yellow-white blooms may appear.

Growing guidelines Sow seed indoors or outdoors in late spring or early summer. Take cuttings during the growing season. When planting, space the plants well to allow for spread and allow the soil to dry somewhat between waterings. Pinch off the shoot tips every few weeks to encourage bushy growth and to avoid the stems becoming leggy. This plant makes a good summer container plant in cold climates; bring it indoors for overwintering.

Pest and disease prevention No specific problems.

Landscape uses Licorice plant combines well with almost any colorful companion. It's especially good with dark-leaved plants. Use licorice plant in flower beds, on slopes or in containers.

Heliotropium arborescens BORAGINACEAE

BEST SITE
Full sun (to afternoon shade in hot-summer climates); average, well-drained soil with added organic matter.

HEIGHT
2–3 feet (60–90 cm)

SPREAD
1–2 feet (30–60 cm)

FLOWERING TIME
Summer until frost.

COMMON HELIOTROPE

THE VIOLET, PURPLE-BLUE OR WHITE FLOWERS OF COMMON HELIOTROPE MAY HAVE A VANILLA- OR CHERRY-LIKE SCENT. SNIFF THE FLOWERS BEFORE YOU BUY TO FIND THE MOST FRAGRANT ONES.

Description This tender perennial is usually grown as a tender annual. Plants produce shrubby clumps of sturdy stems and hairy, deep to medium green, heavily veined, oval leaves. Clusters of ¼-inch (6-mm) wide, tubular flowers bloom atop the stems.

Growing guidelines Easiest to start from nursery-grown or overwintered plants. If you want to grow your own, sow seed indoors 10–12 weeks before your last frost date. Seed may take several weeks to germinate. Set plants out about 1½ feet (45 cm) apart, 2–3 weeks after the last frost date. Pinch off the stem tips in early summer to promote branching and more flowers. Remove spent flower clusters. To overwinter plants, cut them back, then dig and pot them up before the first frost; or take stem cuttings in late summer.

Pest and disease prevention No specific problems.

Landscape uses Grow common heliotrope in flower beds and borders, or as part of an outdoor container garden.

BEST SITE
Full sun; moist, well-drained, neutral to alkaline, not-too-fertile soil.

HEIGHT
2–3 feet (60–90 cm)

SPREAD
2 feet (60 cm)

FLOWERING TIME
Summer.

DAME'S ROCKET

DAME'S ROCKET IS GROWN FOR ITS SHOWY BLOOMS THAT, ON HUMID EVENINGS, GIVE OFF A WONDERFUL FRAGRANCE.

Description This upright, frost-hardy biennial has smooth, slim, oval leaves and branching flower heads that come in delicate shades from white to pale lilac.

Growing guidelines Dame's rocket is easy to grow from seed sown indoors or directly into the garden. Sow seed or set out transplants after the last frost date. Thin seedlings to stand about 1½ feet (45 cm) apart and water plants regularly but don't allow the soil to become too moist. In warmer areas, dame's rocket will naturalize. Plants tend to lose their vigor after a few seasons and are best renewed every 2 years.

Pest and disease prevention Check regularly for mildew and signs of snail and slug damage.

Landscape uses A must for a fragrance or cutting garden. It also looks good in cottage gardens.

BEST SITE
Full sun to partial shade; average, well-drained soil.

HEIGHT
8–12 inches (20–30 cm)

SPREAD
8–10 inches (20–25 cm)

FLOWERING TIME
Late spring through midsummer.

ANNUAL CANDYTUFT

IN HOT-SUMMER AREAS, PULL OUT ANNUAL CANDYTUFT AFTER FLOWERING AND REPLACE IT WITH SUMMER-BLOOMING ANNUALS.

Description This dependable, hardy annual forms mounds of narrow, green leaves on many-branched stems. The mounds are covered with dense, slightly rounded flower clusters approximately 2 inches (5 cm) across. Each cluster contains many ¼–½-inch (6–12-mm) wide, four-petaled blooms in white, pink, pinkish purple, rose or red.

Growing guidelines For the earliest flowers, sow seed indoors 6–8 weeks before your last frost date. Plant seed ¼ inch (6 mm) deep. Set plants out around the last frost date. Annual candytuft also grows easily from seed sown directly into the garden. Make the first sowing in early to midspring. Sowing again every 3–4 weeks until early summer can extend the bloom season until autumn if your summer temperatures don't get much above 90°F (32°C). Thin seedlings or space plants 6–8 inches (15–20 cm) apart. Tends to self-sow freely.

Pest and disease prevention No specific problems.

Landscape uses Annual candytuft makes a colorful edging or filler for flower beds and borders.

Best site
Full sun to partial shade; average to moist, well-drained soil with added organic matter.

Height
2–2½ feet (60–75 cm)

Spread
1½ feet (45 cm)

Flowering time
Midsummer until frost.

Garden Balsam

The bright flowers of garden balsam bloom near the tops of the stems, among the lance-shaped, green leaves. This old-fashioned favorite can grow in full sun if the soil is kept moist.

Description This tender annual has a bushy, upright habit. The 1–2-inch (2.5–5-cm) wide, single or double flowers bloom in white or shades of pink, purple-pink, rose or red.

Growing guidelines Garden balsam is sometimes sold as transplants, but it is also easy to start from seed. To grow your own transplants, sow seed indoors 6–8 weeks before your last frost date. Press the seed lightly into the soil surface and enclose the pot in a plastic bag until seedlings appear. Set plants out 2–3 weeks after the last frost date. You can also sow seed directly into the garden after the last frost date. Plant seed ⅛ inch (3 mm) deep and keep the soil moist until seedlings appear. Thin seedlings or space transplants 1–1⅓ feet (30–40 cm) apart. Water during dry spells. Plants often self-sow freely.

Pest and disease prevention No specific problems.

Landscape uses The lovely flowers and foliage of garden balsam add height and color to shady beds and borders. For the best show, set out three or more plants in each area to form lush clumps.

Impatiens New Guinea hybrids

Best site
Full sun to partial shade; average to moist, well-drained soil with added organic matter.

Height
1–2 feet (30–60 cm)

Spread
1–1½ feet (30–45 cm)

Flowering time
Early summer until frost.

New Guinea impatiens

If you want a particular flower or leaf color, buy New Guinea impatiens as plants in spring. You can also start some types from seed.

Description These tender perennials are usually grown as tender annuals. The bushy, well-branched plants have large, pointed, green or reddish bronze leaves, which are sometimes striped with pink, red or yellow. Vibrant pink, red, orange, purple or white flowers to 3 inches (7.5 cm) across bloom atop the plants during flowering.

Growing guidelines Most New Guinea impatiens are grown from cuttings, so you can buy plants with the colors you like best in spring. Some are available from seed; sow indoors (just barely cover with soil) 6–8 weeks before your last frost date. Set plants out 1–1½ feet (30–45 cm) apart 2–3 weeks after your last frost date. Plants are sometimes difficult to overwinter indoors, but if you want to keep a particular plant, try taking stem cuttings in summer. Pot up rooted cuttings and keep them on a sunny window until the following spring.

Pest and disease prevention No specific problems.

Landscape uses Enjoy the showy leaves and jewel-like flowers in beds, borders and containers.

Best site
Partial to full shade; average to moist, well-drained soil with added organic matter.

Height
Ranging from 6–24 inches (15–60 cm), depending on the cultivar.

Spread
6–24 inches (15–60 cm)

Flowering time
Early summer until frost.

Impatiens

Impatiens are tender perennials usually grown as tender annuals. They make a colorful annual groundcover under trees and shrubs.

Description Impatiens form neat shrubby mounds of well-branched, succulent stems; the lance-shaped, green or bronze-brown leaves have slightly scalloped edges. The plants are covered with flat, spurred flowers up to 2 inches (5 cm) wide. The single or double blooms may be white, pink, red, orange or lavender; some have an eye, or swirls of contrasting colors. The flowers are followed by swollen, ribbed seedpods that burst open when ripe, spreading seeds.

Growing guidelines Sow seed indoors 8–10 weeks before your last frost date. Don't cover the seed; press it lightly into the soil surface. Enclose the pot in a plastic bag and keep it in a warm place until seedlings appear. Set transplants out about 2 weeks after your last frost date. Space compact types 6–8 inches (15–20 cm) apart and tall cultivars 1–1½ feet (30–45 cm) apart.

Pest and disease prevention No specific problems.

Landscape uses Grow them alone in masses under trees and large shrubs. Impatiens also perform well in pots, window boxes and hanging baskets.

BEST SITE
Full sun; average, well-drained soil.

HEIGHT
Up to 10 feet (3 m) or more; ultimate height and spread depend on the size of the support the vine is climbing on.

SPREAD
10 feet (3 m)

FLOWERING TIME
Summer.

MOONFLOWER

BEFORE PLANTING MOONFLOWER, SET UP SOME KIND OF CLIMBING SUPPORT, SUCH AS VERTICAL WIRES OR A TRELLIS.

Description This tender perennial vine is usually grown as a tender annual. The twining stems produce heart-shaped leaves and pointed buds that unfurl into funnel-shaped to flat, white blooms up to 6 inches (15 cm) across. The fragrant flowers open in the evening and may stay open through the next morning. Moonflower is also listed in seed catalogs as *Calonyction aculeatum*.

Growing guidelines Start seed indoors 4–6 weeks before your last frost date. Soak seed in warm water overnight, then plant it 1 inch (2.5 cm) deep in peat pots (two or three seeds per pot). When seedlings appear, keep the strongest one in each pot and cut off the others at the soil surface. Set plants out 2–3 weeks after the last frost date. In warmer areas, sow seed directly into the garden after the last frost date, when the soil is warm. Set plants or thin seedlings to stand 6 feet (1.8 m) apart.

Pest and disease prevention No specific problems.

Landscape uses Use it as a fast-growing screen for shade. Moonflower's night-blooming habit makes it an excellent choice for planting around decks and patios.

BEST SITE
Full sun; average, well-drained soil.

HEIGHT
Up to 8 feet (2.4 m) or more; ultimate height and spread depend on the size of the support.

SPREAD
8 feet (2.4 m)

FLOWERING TIME
Summer.

MORNING GLORY

MORNING GLORY GROWS SLOWLY AT FIRST, THEN REALLY TAKES OFF WHEN THE WEATHER HEATS UP IN MIDSUMMER.

Description Morning glory is a fast-growing, tender perennial vine grown as a tender annual. It has twining stems and heart-shaped, green leaves. The pointed buds open in early morning to reveal showy, trumpet-shaped flowers up to 5 inches (12.5 cm) across. Each flower lasts for only a day, but new buds open every day during bloom.

Growing guidelines Before planting, make sure you have a support for the vines to climb up. For earliest flowers, sow seed indoors 4 weeks before your last frost date. Soak seed in warm water overnight, then sow it ½ inch (12 mm) deep in peat pots. Plant two or three seeds in each pot, then thin to one seedling per pot. Set plants out 2 weeks after the last frost date. You can also start morning glory from seed sown directly into the garden after the last frost. Set plants or thin seedlings to stand 6 feet (1.8 m) apart.

Pest and disease prevention No specific problems.

Landscape uses Morning glory makes a good quick-growing screen for shade or privacy. It also looks great climbing through large shrubs or roses, or on a trellis or wall behind a cottage garden.

Lablab purpureus PAPILIONACEAE

BEST SITE
Full sun; average, well-drained soil.

HEIGHT
Up to 15 feet (4.5 m), depending on the size of the support.

SPREAD
15 feet (4.5 m)

FLOWERING TIME
Summer.

HYACINTH BEAN

HYACINTH BEAN MAKES AN EYE-CATCHING ACCENT WHEN TRAINED UP A TRELLIS OR A TRIPOD OF STAKES IN A BORDER.

Description This tender perennial climber is grown as a tender annual. The twining stems carry green or purplish leaves, each with three leaflets. The pinkish purple or white flowers are ¾ inch (18 mm) long and bloom in spiky clusters. The scented flowers are followed by glossy, deep purple seedpods.

Growing guidelines Before planting, install a support for the vine to climb. Sow seed directly into the garden 2 weeks after the last frost date, when the soil is warm. Plant the seed ½ inch (12 mm) deep, with the white eye facing down. Soaking seed in water overnight before planting can help speed up germination. You can get an earlier start in cool-summer areas by sowing indoors 4–6 weeks before your last frost date. Plant two or three seeds in each pot, then thin seedlings to one per pot. Set plants out after the last frost date. Space transplants or thin seedlings to stand 6 feet (1.8 m) apart.

Pest and disease prevention No specific problems.

Landscape uses Use this fast-growing vine for quick shade or privacy, or as a backdrop for a flower bed along a wall or arbor.

BEST SITE
Full sun (or afternoon shade in hot-summer areas); loose, evenly moist soil enriched with ample amounts of organic matter.

HEIGHT
4–6 feet (1.2–1.8 m)

SPREAD
6–12 inches (15–30 cm)

FLOWERING TIME
Midspring into summer.

SWEET PEA

DOZENS OF SWEET PEA CULTIVARS ARE AVAILABLE IN A RANGE OF HEIGHTS AND COLORS, ALTHOUGH MANY MODERN CULTIVARS AREN'T PARTICULARLY FRAGRANT.

Description These old-fashioned hardy annuals are grown for their charming flowers. Plants produce leafy vines that climb by tendrils. Dainty, pea-type flowers to 2 inches (5 cm) long bloom on long, slender flower stems. Flower colors are usually white, or bright or pastel shades of pink, red or purple. The flowers often have crimped or ruffled petals.

Growing guidelines Before planting, set up some sort of string or netting trellis for the vines to climb. Start seed indoors 6–8 weeks before your last frost date. Soak seed in warm water overnight, then plant ½ inch (12 mm) deep in peat pots. Set plants out in midspring, after danger of heavy frost. Or sow seed directly into the garden in early spring. Set transplants or thin seedlings to stand 4–6 inches (10–15 cm) apart. Mulch plants to keep the roots cool and moist. Pull out the vines when they stop blooming in summer.

Pest and disease prevention No specific problems.

Landscape uses Train sweet peas to climb a tripod of stakes as an early-season accent for beds, borders and cottage gardens.

BEST SITE
Full sun; average, well-drained soil.

HEIGHT
1–2 feet (30–60 cm)

SPREAD
1 foot (30 cm)

FLOWERING TIME
Summer.

ANNUAL STATICE

ANNUAL STATICE IS A NATURAL FOR FRESH OR DRIED ARRANGEMENTS. TO DRY IT, PICK STEMS WHEN THE CLUSTERS ARE ABOUT THREE-FOURTHS OPEN, THEN HANG THEM IN A DARK, AIRY PLACE.

Description This biennial or tender perennial is usually grown as a half-hardy annual. Plants form low rosettes of wavy-edged, green leaves that send up sturdy, winged stems during bloom. The loosely branched stems are topped with flattened clusters of ¼-inch (6-mm) wide white, pink, peach, red, orange, yellow, purple or blue flowers, each surrounded by a papery, tubular calyx—the colorful part of the flower head.

Growing guidelines Buy transplants in spring, or sow seed indoors 6–8 weeks before your last frost date. Plant the seed ¼ inch (6 mm) deep; move seedlings to individual pots when they have two or three sets of leaves. Plant them in the garden around the last frost date, or sow seed directly into the garden after the last frost date. Space transplants or thin seedlings to stand 8–10 inches (20–25 cm) apart.

Pest and disease prevention No specific problems.

Landscape uses Annual statice is an unusual and attractive filler for flower beds and borders. Try the compact types in container gardens.

BEST SITE
Full sun; moderately fertile, well-drained soil.

HEIGHT
1–2 feet (30–60 cm)

SPREAD
1 foot (30 cm)

FLOWERING TIME
Late summer and early autumn.

STAR DAISY

ORIGINALLY FROM THE LIMESTONE SOILS OF TEXAS, STAR DAISY IS A NATURAL CHOICE FOR COTTAGE GARDENS.

Description This frost-hardy, fast-growing annual is the only species in this genus. It is primarily grown for its charming daisy-like, bright yellow flowers that sit atop erect, branching stems that are covered in fine hairs. The leaves are oval and slightly pointy, with serrated, hairy surfaces. The bright green leaves hide the seed heads.

Growing guidelines Grows best from seed sown directly into the garden in mid- to late spring, when the soil is warm. Thin seedlings to stand 8–10 inches (20–25 cm) apart. Water during dry spells and mulch lightly to prevent reseeding.

Pest and disease prevention No specific problems.

Landscape uses Star daisy is a must for the cutting garden, or in beds and borders in cottage gardens and informal plantings. The sunny yellow flowers look especially good teamed up with blue summer-flowering annuals, such as baby-blue-eyes *Nemophila menziesii*.

Lobelia erinus CAMPANULACEAE

BEST SITE
Full sun to partial shade (especially in hot-summer areas); average, well-drained soil with added organic matter.

HEIGHT
6–8 inches (15–20 cm)

SPREAD
6–10 inches (15–25 cm)

FLOWERING TIME
Late spring through frost.

EDGING LOBELIA

IF YOU GROW EDGING LOBELIA FROM SEED OR BUY SEEDLINGS IN TRAYS, TRANSPLANT THEM IN CLUMPS (RATHER THAN SEPARATING THEM INTO INDIVIDUAL PLANTS) TO AVOID DAMAGING THE STEMS.

Description This tender perennial is usually grown as a half-hardy annual. Plants form trailing or mounding clumps of slender stems with small, narrow, green leaves. Plants are covered with ¼–½-inch (6–12-mm) wide flowers. The five-petaled flowers bloom in white and shades of blue, purple and pink.

Growing guidelines Buy transplants in spring, or start your own by sowing seed indoors 8–10 weeks before your last frost date. Don't cover the seed; just press it lightly into the soil and enclose the pot in a plastic bag until seedlings appear. Set plants out 6–8 inches (15–20 cm) apart after the last frost date. Water during dry spells. Shear plants back by half after each flush of bloom and fertilize to promote rebloom.

Pest and disease prevention No specific problems.

Landscape uses Looks great along the front of beds and borders or as a filler among taller plants. Cascading types make attractive fillers for container gardens, window boxes and hanging baskets until bushier plants fill in.

Lobularia maritima BRASSICACEAE

BEST SITE
Full sun to partial shade (especially in hot-summer areas); average, well-drained soil.

HEIGHT
4–8 inches (10–20 cm)

SPREAD
10–12 inches (25–30 cm)

FLOWERING TIME
Summer and autumn.

SWEET ALYSSUM

SWEET ALYSSUM MAY STOP BLOOMING DURING SUMMER HEAT BUT WILL START AGAIN WHEN COOL WEATHER RETURNS.

Description Sweet alyssum is a tender perennial grown as a hardy annual. Plants form low mounds of many-branched stems and narrow, green leaves. Domed clusters of many ¼-inch (6-mm) blooms cover the plants. The sweetly scented, four-petaled flowers bloom in white and shades of pink and purple. Sweet alyssum is also listed in seed catalogs as *Alyssum maritimum*.

Growing guidelines Buy transplants in spring, or start your own by sowing seed indoors 6–8 weeks before your last frost date. Just barely cover the seed with soil. Set plants out around the last frost date. Sweet alyssum also grows easily from seed sown directly into the garden in mid- to late spring. Space transplants or thin seedlings to stand 6 inches (15 cm) apart. Plants usually self-sow.

Pest and disease prevention No specific problems.

Landscape uses Grow sweet alyssum as an edging or filler in flower beds and borders or as a groundcover under roses and shrubs. This plant also grows happily in container gardens and window boxes.

Lunaria annua BRASSICACEAE

BEST SITE
Partial shade; average, well-drained soil (added organic matter is a plus).

HEIGHT
1½–3 feet (45–90 cm)

SPREAD
1 foot (30 cm)

FLOWERING TIME
Spring.

HONESTY

HONESTY IS A HARDY BIENNIAL GROWN FOR ITS FLOWERS AND SHOWY DRIED SEEDPODS. LEAVE A FEW PLANTS IN TO SELF-SOW AND HARVEST THE REST FOR ARRANGEMENTS.

Description In the first year, honesty plants form clumps of coarse, heart-shaped, hairy, green leaves. The following spring, the clumps send up loosely branched stems topped with elongated clusters of ½-inch (12-mm) wide, four-petaled flowers. The lightly fragrant, purple-pink blooms are followed by flat, circular seedpods with papery outer skins and a white central disk.

Growing guidelines Buy and set out nursery-grown plants in early spring for bloom the same year, or start your own from seed for bloom next year. Sow seed directly into the garden, ⅛–¼ inch (3–6 mm) deep, in spring or late summer. Set transplants or thin seedlings to stand about 1 foot (30 cm) apart.

Pest and disease prevention No specific problems.

Landscape uses The white-flowered forms look especially nice in woodland gardens. Honesty is also a traditional favorite in cutting gardens for its dried seedpods. When the seedpods turn beige, cut the stems off at ground level and bring them indoors. Once seedpods feel dry, gently peel off the outer skins to reveal the silvery center membrane.

Best site
Full sun; well-drained, fertile, slightly acidic, sandy soil. Prefers cool, wet winters and long, dry summers.

Height
2½ feet (75 cm)

Spread
1⅓ feet (40 cm)

Flowering time
Late winter, spring and early summer.

Hairy lupin

Remember to pinch off the spent flowers of hairy lupin to prolong the plant's life and to prevent reseeding.

Description Hairy lupin is a compact, fast-growing annual that is easy to grow. It has dark green, hairy leaves and slim spikes of flowers that bloom in shades of blue, white or pink.

Growing guidelines For best results, sow seed directly into prepared garden soil in autumn. Thin seedlings to stand 8–12 inches (20–30 cm) apart. Water well after sowing; wait until seedlings appear before watering again, unless conditions have been dry or windy. Digging in healthy plants when they are finished for the season will give your soil a nitrogen boost.

Pest and disease prevention Watch out for slug and snail damage. Earth mites and viral infections may cause problems; remove affected plants.

Landscape uses Hairy lupins look good in almost any garden display. Include some in the cutting garden; harvest them when the buds are showing some color and scald the stem tips to prolong their life in fresh arrangements.

Lupinus texensis PAPILIONACEAE

BEST SITE
Full sun; thrives in poor soil, as long as it is well drained.

HEIGHT
1 foot (30 cm)

SPREAD
10 inches (25 cm)

FLOWERING TIME
Late spring.

TEXAS BLUE BONNET

TEXAS BLUE BONNET IS THE STATE FLOWER OF TEXAS, WHICH IS THE ONLY PLACE WHERE THIS PRETTY ANNUAL GROWS WILD.

Description This bushy annual has bright green leaves that are divided into five smaller leaves, known as leaflets, which are covered in fine hairs on their underside. The plant bears striking dark blue and white flowers that are borne along a central stem.

Growing guidelines Sow seed directly into the garden in autumn. The soil does not require any special preparation before sowing, but water well afterward until the seedlings appear. Thin seedlings to stand 6–8 inches (15–20 cm) apart.

Pest and disease prevention No specific problems.

Landscape uses Texas blue bonnet is a natural for cottage gardens and informal beds and borders. Try growing it in containers, or as part of a meadow garden.

BEST SITE
Full sun to partial shade (in hot-summer areas); average, well-drained soil.

HEIGHT
6–8 inches (15–20 cm)

SPREAD
4 inches (10 cm)

FLOWERING TIME
Summer until frost.

VIRGINIA STOCK

VIRGINIA STOCK IS THE PERFECT STOPGAP AS IT CAN GROW FROM SEED TO FLOWERING PLANT IN JUST A COUPLE OF WEEKS.

Description The upright, branching stems of this fast-growing hardy annual carry small, pointed, grayish green leaves. Flat, four-petaled, lightly fragrant flowers bloom in loose clusters atop the stems. The purple, pink or white flowers are ¼–½ inch (6–12 mm) wide.

Growing guidelines Grows best from seed sown directly into the garden. For the longest bloom season, sow at 3–4 week intervals from early spring through midsummer. (In mild-winter areas, you can sow in autumn for even earlier spring bloom.) Rake the seedbed to cover the seed lightly, then keep the soil moist until seedlings appear. Thin seedlings to stand 3–4 inches (7.5–10 cm) apart. Plants may self-sow freely.

Pest and disease prevention No specific problems.

Landscape uses Virginia stock makes a nice filler or edging for annual flower beds and borders. The flowers are very popular with bees. They also look great as companions for potted spring bulbs.

BEST SITE
Full sun; well-drained, light sandy soil.

HEIGHT
2 feet (60 cm)

SPREAD
1½ feet (45 cm)

FLOWERING TIME
Summer and autumn.

GERMAN CHAMOMILE

GERMAN CHAMOMILE IS AN AROMATIC ANNUAL HERB THAT IS HIGHLY VALUED FOR ITS TRADITIONAL MEDICINAL PROPERTIES. IT IS ALSO OFTEN ENJOYED AS A HERBAL TEA.

Description German chamomile has upright stems with finely divided, light green leaves attached along their length. Each stem has beautiful, white, daisy-like flowers borne at the tip.

Growing guidelines Fully frost-hardy, German chamomile is easy to grow from seed. Sow seed directly into the garden in summer; keep soil evenly moist until seedlings appear. Pinch out spent flowers to prolong bloom season. Dig out plants once flowering ends.

Pest and disease prevention No specific problems.

Landscape uses Grow in a rockery, herb garden or as a border edging. German chamomile is also a good choice for cottage gardens. The fully opened flowers can be dried and used as herbal tea. After steeping the flowers in boiling water to make tea, deposit the flower heads on the compost pile to stimulate decomposition.

Matthiola incana BRASSICACEAE

Best site
Full sun; average, well-drained soil with added organic matter.

Height
1–2 feet (30–60 cm)

Spread
1 foot (30 cm)

Flowering time
Summer.

Common stock

THE FRAGRANT, SINGLE OR DOUBLE FLOWERS OF COMMON STOCK BLOOM IN WHITE AND SHADES OF PINK, RED AND MAUVE.

Description This biennial or short-lived perennial is usually grown as a hardy annual. The fast-growing, bushy plants have upright stems and lance-shaped, grayish leaves. The stems are topped with spikes of four-petaled, 1-inch (2.5-cm) wide flowers.

Growing guidelines Grows easily from seed sown directly into the garden. Make the first sowing about a month before your last frost date. To extend the bloom season, make another sowing in late spring or early summer. (In mild-winter areas, you can also sow in late summer for winter and early-spring bloom.) Scatter seed on the soil surface, then rake lightly to just cover the seed. Keep the seedbed moist until seedlings appear. Thin seedlings to stand 6–8 inches (15–20 cm) apart. Mulch plants to keep the roots cool and moist. Water during dry spells.

Pest and disease prevention Root rot can become a problem if plants are overwatered.

Landscape uses Use as a filler in beds and borders near your house or outdoor sitting areas, where you can enjoy the fragrance. Common stock also makes an excellent cut flower for fresh arrangements.

BEST SITE
Part or full shade, sheltered from wind; moist, fertile soil.

HEIGHT
1–1½ feet (30–45 cm)

SPREAD
1 foot (30 cm)

FLOWERING TIME
Midspring to autumn.

WELSH POPPY

ALTHOUGH ITS SEASON OF INTEREST IS RELATIVELY SHORT, WELSH POPPY SELF-SEEDS READILY, MAKING IT A WORTHWHILE INVESTMENT FOR YOUR GARDEN.

Description This moderately frost-hardy annual poppy has slightly hairy, deeply divided, midgreen leaves that make up a basal rosette. The flowers come in shades of light yellow and dark orange.

Growing guidelines For best results, prepare the soil about 2 weeks before planting by adding nutrient-rich compost and working it into the garden bed. Sow seed directly into the garden; keep soil evenly moist until seedlings appear. Thin seedlings to stand 10–12 inches (25–30 cm) apart. Provide shelter from strong winds.

Pest and disease prevention No specific problems.

Landscape uses Plant Welsh poppy in beds and borders with summer-flowering bulbs.

BEST SITE
Partial shade; moist soil. Plants can take full sun if they have evenly moist soil.

HEIGHT
6–12 inches (15–30 cm)

SPREAD
6–12 inches (15–30 cm)

FLOWERING TIME
Summer.

MONKEY FLOWER

YOU CAN OVERWINTER MONKEY FLOWER INDOORS BY DIGGING AND POTTING UP PLANTS BEFORE FROST OR BY ROOTING STEM CUTTINGS IN LATE SUMMER; GROW THEM IN A COOL, SUNNY ROOM.

Description This tender perennial is grown as a half-hardy annual. Plants form clumps of green to reddish stems with oval, light green leaves that have toothed edges. Velvety, tubular flowers with flat faces bloom atop the plants. The 1–2-inch (2.5–5-cm) flowers are usually yellow, orange or red and are often dotted or splashed with other colors in the center.

Growing guidelines Start seed indoors 8–10 weeks before your last frost date. Scatter the dustlike seed over the soil surface, but don't cover it. Just press the seed lightly into the soil and enclose the pot in a plastic bag until seedlings appear. Set transplants out 8 inches (20 cm) apart after the last frost date. Water during dry spells. If plants stop blooming in hot weather, cutting them back halfway and watering thoroughly may promote rebloom.

Pest and disease prevention No specific problems.

Landscape uses Monkey flowers add glowing color to moist-soil beds and borders. Try them as a groundcover in wet spots to fill in after spring-blooming primroses.

BEST SITE
Full sun to partial shade; average, well-drained soil.

HEIGHT
2–3 feet (60–90 cm)

SPREAD
2 feet (60 cm)

FLOWERING TIME
Midsummer until frost.

FOUR-O'CLOCK

FOUR-O'CLOCKS HAVE FRAGRANT FLOWERS THAT OPEN IN THE LATE AFTERNOON. THEY TEND TO CLOSE THE NEXT MORNING, UNLESS THE WEATHER IS CLOUDY. GROW THEM IN THE GARDEN OR IN POTS.

Description These tender perennials are usually grown as half-hardy annuals. The bushy, fast-growing plants have branching stems and oval to lance-shaped, deep green leaves. Trumpet-shaped, 1-inch (2.5-cm) wide flowers bloom in white or shades of pink, magenta, red and yellow; sometimes different colors appear on the same plant.

Growing guidelines Four-o'clocks are gratifyingly easy to grow from seed. For earliest bloom, start them indoors 4–6 weeks before your last frost date. Soak the seed in warm water overnight, then plant it ¼–½ inch (6–12 mm) deep in peat pots. Transplant seedlings to the garden about 2 weeks after the last frost date, when the soil is warm. You can also sow seed directly into the garden after the last frost date. Space transplants or thin seedlings to stand 1–1½ feet (30–45 cm) apart. Plants may self-sow in areas with a mild climate.

Pest and disease prevention No specific problems.

Landscape uses Plant clumps in the middle of flower beds and borders for a colorful filler.

Moluccella laevis

Best site
Full sun; moderately fertile, well-drained soil.

Height
3 feet (90 cm)

Spread
1 foot (30 cm)

Flowering time
Summer.

Bells of Ireland

BELLS OF IRELAND ARE GROWN FOR THEIR UNUSUAL, LARGE GREEN CALYCES THAT LOOK QUITE SPECTACULAR FRESH OR DRIED.

Description These tall, moderately frost-hardy annuals have flower spikes that are surrounded by large, shell-like, apple-green calyces, or bells, that appear along the length of the plant's stem. The tiny, white, fragrant flowers are almost insignificant, as they lie at the base of each calyx. The growing habit is upright and branching.

Growing guidelines Propagate from seed sown directly into the garden in spring, when the soil is warm. Keep the soil evenly moist and fertilize established plants.

Pest and disease prevention No specific problems.

Landscape uses This plant is an obvious choice for the cutting garden. Plant bells of Ireland at the back of beds and borders to add height and color contrast.

Monarda citriodora

LAMIACEAE

Best site
Full sun; average, well-drained soil.

Height
2 feet (60 cm)

Spread
1⅓ feet (40 cm)

Flowering time
Midsummer to early autumn.

Lemon mint

A close relative of bee balm, lemon mint is a favorite for flavoring teas and for use in potpourri; the fragrant leaves retain their scent after drying.

Description Lemon mint is a frost-hardy annual herb with an erect, branching habit. The curved, tubular flowers bloom in white and shades of pink or purple. The midgreen, veined leaves are narrow and elongated.

Growing guidelines For best results, sow lemon mint directly into the garden. Sow seed after your last frost date in cooler areas or in early spring in warm-summer climates, when the soil is warm. Thin seedlings to stand 8–10 inches (20–25 cm) apart. Don't overwater young plants, as the stems may rot. Lemon mint doesn't need rich soil to thrive, but giving it a boost of fertilizer after it is established will encourage healthy plant growth.

Pest and disease prevention No specific problems.

Landscape uses Lemon mint is a must for cottage gardens, as it attracts both bees and butterflies. The pretty blooms are also perfect for using in fresh and dried arrangements.

BEST SITE
Full sun or part shade; fertile, well-drained soil.

HEIGHT
Up to 1 foot (30 cm) or more.

SPREAD
1½–2 feet (45–60 cm)

FLOWERING TIME
Spring through summer.

MONOPSIS

MONOPSIS IS A VERY PRETTY CASCADING PLANT THAT LOOKS ATTRACTIVE GROWING OVER AND DOWN A ROCK GARDEN OR WALL.

Description This tender annual has long, thin, wiry stems with alternate linear to lance-shaped leaves with toothed margins. Bright yellow flowers bloom toward the end of the stems. The flowers are tubular and splay out at the tips into spreading lobes. Each tube is divided all the way from the tip to the base on the top side.

Growing guidelines Start seed indoors 4–6 weeks before your last frost date. Plant seed ⅛ inch (3 mm) deep; keep the pots under glass until seedlings appear. Plant out in spring or after all danger of frost has passed. Alternatively, sow seed directly into the garden after your last frost date. Space plants or thin seedlings to stand at least 1 foot (30 cm) apart. Pinch out spent blooms to extend flowering. Water during dry spells.

Pest and disease prevention No specific problems.

Landscape uses Monopsis works well in flower beds and borders or cascading out of window boxes and containers. Try planting some in terraced beds to take advantage of its trailing habit.

BEST SITE
Partial shade; average to moist, well-drained soil with added organic matter.

HEIGHT
1–1½ feet (30–45 cm)

SPREAD
8–10 inches (20–25 cm)

FLOWERING TIME
Midspring through early summer.

FORGET-ME-NOT

FORGET-ME-NOTS ARE INVALUABLE FOR SPRING COLOR IN SHADY GARDENS. THEY MAKE IDEAL COMPANIONS FOR SPRING BULBS AND OTHER EARLY ANNUALS.

Description These short-lived perennials are usually grown as hardy biennials or annuals. Plants form dense clumps of narrow, lance-shaped, hairy leaves. Sprays of many ⅓-inch (8-mm) wide flowers bloom over the leaves. The flowers are sky blue with white or yellow centers, but the flowers can also be pink or white.

Growing guidelines To grow forget-me-nots as biennials, sow seed outdoors in pots or in a nursery bed in spring or summer. Plant seed ⅛ inch (3 mm) deep. Move plants to the garden in early autumn. For bloom the same year, buy plants in early spring, or start seed indoors 4–6 weeks before your last frost date. Set plants out around your last frost date. Space plants or thin seedlings to stand 6 inches (15 cm) apart. Shearing off spent flowers promotes rebloom. Plants often self-sow freely.

Pest and disease prevention No specific problems.

Landscape uses Try them as early-season groundcovers under shrubs, or in beds and borders with short tulips and other spring bulbs for stunning color combinations.

BEST SITE
Full sun to partial shade (especially in warm- and hot-summer areas); evenly moist, well-drained soil with added organic matter.

HEIGHT
1–2 feet (30–60 cm)

SPREAD
6–8 inches (15–20 cm)

FLOWERING TIME
Winter to early summer (depending on climate).

NEMESIA

NEMESIA USUALLY STOPS FLOWERING IN WARM WEATHER, BUT PLANTS MAY REBLOOM IF YOU CUT THEM BACK BY HALF, WATER WELL AND THEN GIVE THEM A DOSE OF FERTILIZER.

Description Nemesia is a tender, cool-weather annual grown for its beautiful flowers. Plants form clumps of branched stems with pairs of narrow, slightly toothed, green leaves. Clusters of trumpet-shaped, lipped flowers bloom atop the stems. The 1-inch (2.5-cm) wide flowers bloom in a range of colors, including white, pink, red, orange, yellow, lilac and even light blue.

Growing guidelines Start seed indoors 6–8 weeks before your last frost date. (In mild-winter areas, you can also sow in autumn for winter bloom.) Sow seed ⅛ inch (3 mm) deep. Set plants out 4–6 inches (10–15 cm) apart after the last frost date. Push short pieces of twiggy brush into the soil around young plants to support the stems as they grow. Pinch off stem tips to promote branching and more flowers.

Pest and disease prevention No specific problems.

Landscape uses Nemesia makes an attractive edging for flower beds and borders. It also makes a great show planted in masses for early-summer color. Try planting a few in containers and window boxes, too.

BEST SITE
Full sun to partial shade (morning sun and afternoon shade is ideal); moist, well-drained soil with added organic matter.

HEIGHT
6–8 inches (15–20 cm)

SPREAD
1 foot (30 cm)

FLOWERING TIME
Summer.

BABY BLUE-EYES

SOW BABY BLUE-EYES AMONG THE EMERGING SHOOTS OF SPRING BULBS TO FORM A COLORFUL, FAST-GROWING CARPET THAT WILL COVER THE RIPENING BULB FOLIAGE AFTER BLOOM.

Description Baby blue-eyes is a hardy annual that forms sprawling mounds of slender, trailing stems and small, finely cut, green leaves. The 1-inch (2.5-cm) wide, bowl-shaped flowers are sky blue with a white center.

Growing guidelines For an extra-early start, sow seed indoors 4–6 weeks before your last frost date. Plant seed 1/8 inch (3 mm) deep. Set plants out 12 weeks before the last frost date. Alternatively, sow seed in the garden in early spring (or even in autumn in mild-winter areas). Sow seed again every 2–3 weeks from spring through early summer to extend the bloom season. Set plants or thin seedlings to stand 6 inches (15 cm) apart. If plants stop blooming in midsummer, shear back halfway and water thoroughly to promote rebloom. Plants often self-sow.

Pest and disease prevention Soggy or poorly drained soil causes the plants to rot and die.

Landscape uses A charming filler or edging for shady flower beds and borders. It also looks great trailing out of pots and planters.

BEST SITE
Full sun to partial shade; average to moist, well-drained soil with added organic matter.

HEIGHT
1½–3 feet (45–90 cm)

SPREAD
1 foot (30 cm)

FLOWERING TIME
Midsummer until frost.

FLOWERING TOBACCO

HYBRIDS AND RED-FLOWERED TYPES OFTEN HAVE LITTLE OR NO SCENT, BUT OLD-FASHIONED, WHITE-FLOWERED TYPES TEND TO BE QUITE FRAGRANT, ESPECIALLY AT NIGHT.

Description This tender perennial is usually grown as a half-hardy annual. Plants form lush rosettes of broad, oval to pointed, green leaves and many-branched stems; both the stems and leaves are sticky and hairy. Trumpet-shaped flowers to 2 inches (5 cm) across bloom atop the stems. Flowers come in a range of colors, including white, pink, purple and red.

Growing guidelines Buy transplants in spring, or grow your own by starting seed indoors 6–8 weeks before your last frost date. Don't cover the fine seed; just press it into the soil and enclose the pot in a plastic bag until seedlings appear. Set seedlings out 10–12 inches (25–30 cm) apart after the last frost date. Water during dry spells. Trim out spent stems to prolong the bloom season. Plants may self-sow.

Pest and disease prevention No specific problems.

Landscape uses Excellent as a filler or accent in beds and borders. Grow flowering tobacco in the cutting garden for fresh flowers. Try compact types in containers.

Nicotiana sylvestris

SOLANACEAE

BEST SITE
Light shade to deep shade; fertile, well-drained soil.

HEIGHT
5 feet (1.5 m)

SPREAD
2 feet (60 cm)

FLOWERING TIME
Summer.

NICOTIANA

NICOTIANA IS ONE OF THE FEW SUMMER-FLOWERING ANNUALS THAT THRIVE IN THE SHADE. ITS FLOWERS REMAIN OPEN EVEN IN DEEP SHADE OR ON OVERCAST DAYS.

Description Although tall and robust, this tender annual cannot survive frosts. The upright, impressive flowering stems arise from a mass of large, fleshy, bright green foliage at the base of the plant. The long, tubular white flowers hang from the stems and give off a beautiful scent, especially on warm summer evenings.

Growing guidelines Sow seed directly into the garden in spring, when all danger of frost is past and the soil is warm. Thin seedlings to stand 6 inches (15 cm) apart. Keep soil moist but don't overwater. Fertilize established plants once or twice during flowering. Pinch off spent blooms to encourage a longer bloom season. Wear gloves and long sleeves when handling if you have sensitive skin.

Pest and disease prevention Check plants regularly for snails and caterpillars; pick them off by hand.

Landscape uses Nicotiana looks fabulous at the back of beds and borders, or in cottage gardens. Take full advantage of its height and scent by planting it against a wall near the house or an outdoor sitting area, for evening enjoyment.

BEST SITE
Full sun to partial shade; average, well-drained soil.

HEIGHT
1½–2 feet (45–60 cm)

SPREAD
6–8 inches (15–20 cm)

FLOWERING TIME
Summer through early autumn.

LOVE-IN-A-MIST

LOVE-IN-A-MIST WILL CONTINUE TO BLOOM THROUGH EARLY AUTUMN IF YOU SOW SEED EVERY 3 TO 4 WEEKS FROM EARLY SPRING TO EARLY SUMMER.

Description Also known as fennel flower and devil-in-the-bush, this fast-growing, hardy annual forms bushy mounds of slender stems and threadlike, bright green leaves. Single or double, 1–2-inch (2.5–5-cm) wide flowers are nestled into the leaves at the tops of the stems. The blue, pink or white flowers are followed by swollen, striped seedpods with short, pointed horns.

Growing guidelines For the earliest flowers, you could start seed indoors 6–8 weeks before your last frost date. Sow seed (just barely cover it with soil) in peat pots. Move plants to the garden after the last frost date. In most cases, though, you'll get better results by sowing directly into the garden, starting in early spring. Space transplants or thin seedlings to stand 6 inches (15 cm) apart. Established plants are care-free. Plants may self-sow.

Pest and disease prevention No specific problems.

Landscape uses Grow as a filler in beds, borders and cottage gardens. Use some of the flowers in fresh arrangements; leave the rest to mature into the puffy seedpods.

Ocimum basilicum

LAMIACEAE

BEST SITE
Full sun; fairly rich, moist, well-drained soil.

HEIGHT
1–2 feet (30–60 cm)

SPREAD
1½ feet (45 cm)

FLOWERING TIME
Summer to early autumn (later in mild-winter areas).

BASIL

BASIL IS ONE OF THE MOST POPULAR HERBS IN HOME GARDENS, MAINLY DUE TO ITS STRONG FLAVOR. THERE ARE MANY DIFFERENT VARIETIES; ANISE BASIL (PICTURED) HAS A DISTINCTLY LICORICE FLAVOR.

Description Basil is a leafy, tender annual with an upright, branching habit. The leaves are long and oval to lance-shaped, and branch off the length of the stem. The tiny white blooms are carried on green spikes at terminal buds.

Growing guidelines Sow seed after all danger of frost has passed. Plant ⅛ inch (3 mm) deep; thin seedlings to stand 6 inches (15 cm) apart. Alternatively, buy plants in spring and pot them up or plant them out. Prune away flowers to maintain best foliage flavor. Side-dress sweet basil with compost in midseason to enhance production. In autumn, cover with plastic to prolong the season and to protect the plant from the earliest frosts.

Pest and disease prevention Mulch with light materials, such as straw, to conserve soil moisture. Pick caterpillars off by hand.

Landscape uses Basil is a must for herb gardens, or as part of a mixed cottage garden. Harvest leaves every week, pinching terminal buds first to encourage branching. Leaves can be used fresh or dried.

BEST SITE
Full sun; average, well-drained to dry soil. Grows poorly in hot weather.

HEIGHT
1–1½ feet (30–45 cm)

SPREAD
4–6 inches (10–15 cm)

FLOWERING TIME
Early spring to early summer, depending on climate.

ICELAND POPPY

THE STRIKING COLORS OF ICELAND POPPIES MAKE A GREAT EARLY-SUMMER SHOW, PLANTED ON THEIR OWN OR IN MASSES.

Description This short-lived perennial is almost always grown as a hardy biennial or annual. Plants form compact rosettes of hairy, deeply cut, gray-green leaves. Long, slender, leafless stems are topped with plump, hairy, nodding buds that open to bowl-shaped, four-petaled flowers. The 2–4-inch (5–10-cm) wide, lightly fragrant flowers have crinkled petals. They bloom in white, pink, red, orange and yellow.

Growing guidelines Easiest to grow from seed sown directly into the garden. Plant in late autumn or very early spring for summer bloom. (In hot-summer areas, sow this cool-loving plant in late summer to early autumn for spring bloom.) Scatter the fine seed over the soil and rake it in lightly. Thin seedlings to stand about 6 inches (15 cm) apart. Leave a few flowers to mature so that plants can self-sow.

Pest and disease prevention Overwatering can induce gray mold. In areas with a dry spring, they are more susceptible to spotted wilt virus; remove infected plants.

Landscape uses Plant Iceland poppies for early color in beds and borders. They are also suitable for rock gardens and for cutting.

BEST SITE
Full sun; average, well-drained soil.

HEIGHT
2–3 feet (60–90 cm)

SPREAD
6–8 inches (15–20 cm)

FLOWERING TIME
Summer.

CORN POPPY

ALSO KNOWN AS FLANDERS POPPY AND SHIRLEY POPPY, CORN POPPY IS A NATURAL FOR ADDING SPARKLE TO MEADOW GARDENS.

Description Plants form clumps of ferny, blue-green leaves. Bowl-shaped flowers with four silky, crinkled petals open from plump, hairy buds atop thin, hairy stems. The 2–4-inch (5–10-cm) wide summer blooms are most often a glowing scarlet. Shirley poppy is a strain that has been selected for single or double flowers in a wider range of colors, including white, pink, red and bicolors.

Growing guidelines Corn poppy is rewardingly easy to grow from seed sown directly into the garden in late autumn or early spring. A second sowing in midspring can help extend the bloom season. Scatter the fine seed over the soil surface, then rake it in lightly. Thin out seedlings to stand 6–8 inches (15–20 cm) apart. Leave a few flowers at the end of the season and plants will most likely self-sow.

Pest and disease prevention No specific problems.

Landscape uses Corn poppies look good as fillers in beds and borders, or as cut flowers. Pick them just as the buds are starting to open, then sear the ends of cut stems over a gas flame or dip them in boiling water to prolong their vase life.

BEST SITE
Full sun to light shade; average, well-drained soil.

HEIGHT
1 foot (30 cm)

SPREAD
2–4 feet (60–120 cm)

FLOWERING TIME
Spring and summer.

IVY GERANIUM

IVY GERANIUM IS AN EXCELLENT CHOICE FOR HANGING BASKETS AND WINDOW BOXES. IT OFFERS BRIGHT GREEN, IVY-LIKE LEAVES, GRACEFULLY CASCADING STEMS AND DELICATELY MARKED BLOOMS.

Description Ivy geranium is always grown as an annual, except in frost-free areas. It is a shrubby plant with long, trailing stems and glossy, green leaves. Clusters of single or double white, pink or lavender flowers bloom atop the stems.

Growing guidelines Start from seed sown indoors 10 weeks before your last frost date. Scatter the seed on the surface of seed-raising mix and press down firmly. Water gently until seedlings appear; keep the seedlings in a very warm position. Set plants out in spring or after your last frost date. Space plants 1½ feet (45 cm) apart. Deadhead faded flowers and pinch back growing tips several times in late spring and early summer to encourage branching. Bring container-grown plants indoors for winter and put them outdoors again the following summer.

Pest and disease prevention Not watering enough can cause wilting and leaf drop, so allow the soil to dry somewhat between waterings, but not to dry out completely.

Landscape uses Ivy geranium makes a good groundcover or spillover planting in cottage gardens.

BEST SITE
Full sun to partial shade; average, well-drained soil.

HEIGHT
1–2 feet (30–60 cm)

SPREAD
1–1½ feet (30–45 cm)

FLOWERING TIME
Late spring until frost.

ZONAL GERANIUM

COLORFUL AND DEPENDABLE, ZONAL GERANIUMS ARE A MAINSTAY OF SUMMER GARDENS. YOU CAN ALSO BRING THEM INDOORS FOR OVERWINTERING.

Description The sturdy, branched stems carry hairy, rounded, bright to dark green leaves with scalloped margins. The leaves are pungent and often marked with dark green or brown, curved bands (zones). Plants produce thin but sturdy stems topped with rounded clusters of many 2-inch (5-cm) wide flowers. The single or double flowers are white or shades of pink, red, salmon and bicolors.

Growing guidelines Set out transplants in early spring or sow seed indoors 8–10 weeks before your last frost date. Plant seed ⅛ inch (3 mm) deep in pots and set in a very warm place until seedlings appear. Move to normal room temperature, then separate the seedlings into individual pots when they're large enough to handle. Set out plants 1–1½ feet (30–45 cm) apart. Pinch off spent blooms to extend the flowering season.

Pest and disease prevention No specific problems.

Landscape uses Grow in masses, or tuck into beds and borders with other annuals and perennials as accents or fillers. Zonal geraniums look great in container gardens and window boxes.

PETUNIA

PETUNIAS ARE TENDER PERENNIALS USUALLY GROWN AS HALF-HARDY ANNUALS. THEY MAY SELF-SOW, BUT THE SEEDLINGS SELDOM RESEMBLE THE PARENT PLANTS.

Description Plants form clumps of upright or trailing stems with oval, green leaves; both the leaves and stems are hairy and somewhat sticky. Funnel-shaped, single or double flowers bloom in nearly every color of the rainbow; some have stripes, streaks or bands of contrasting colors. Petunias are usually divided into groups, based on their flower forms. Grandifloras have the largest flowers (up to 4 or 5 inches [10–12.5 cm] across). They are very showy but tend to be damaged easily by heavy rain. Multifloras have smaller flowers (about 2 inches [5 cm] across), but produce many durable blooms on each plant. Floribundas are an intermediate type, with 3-inch (7.5-cm) wide flowers on fast-growing plants.

Growing guidelines Petunias are among the most popular annuals, and many types are sold as transplants each spring. You can also grow your own from seed, although the fine, dustlike seed can be hard to handle. If you want to try, sow seed indoors 8–10 weeks before your last frost date. Don't cover the seed; just press it lightly into the soil and enclose the pot

Petunias are available in just about every color, except orange.

Best site
Full sun (can take light shade); average to moist, well-drained soil.

Height
6–10 inches (15–25 cm)

Spread
1 foot (30 cm)

Flowering time
Early summer until frost.

in a plastic bag until seedlings appear. Move plants to the garden 2–3 weeks after your last frost date, spacing them 8–12 inches (20–30 cm) apart. Water during dry spells. To keep your petunias bushy and free flowering, shear them back by one third, water thoroughly and fertilize after the first flush of blooms.

Pest and disease prevention Insect damage is not usually a problem, but overwatering or poor soil drainage will quickly cause yellowing and death of the plants.

Landscape uses Petunias come in an amazing range of flower forms and colors. With literally dozens of cultivars available, it's best to check with your local nursery before deciding what to buy. Generally, petunias are favorites for flower beds and borders; they are particularly good for filling in gaps left by spring-flowering annuals and bulbs. Grandiflora types look great spilling out of containers, hanging baskets and window boxes. Look for the cultivars with fancy blooms; some have wavy, crinkly edges or striking, bicolored petals, such as the one pictured above.

BEST SITE
Full sun; average, well-drained soil.

HEIGHT
About 6–8 feet (1.8–2.4 m), depending on the size of the support the vine is growing on.

SPREAD
6–8 feet (1.8–2.4 m)

FLOWERING TIME
Midsummer until frost.

SCARLET RUNNER BEAN

SCARLET RUNNER BEANS ARE EQUALLY AT HOME IN THE FLOWER GARDEN AND THE VEGETABLE GARDEN. THE FAST-GROWING VINES PRODUCE SHOWY ORANGE-RED BLOOMS AND EDIBLE SEEDPODS.

Description This tender perennial climber is grown as a half-hardy annual. The twining stems carry broad, green, compound leaves with three leaflets. The showy clusters of 1-inch (2.5-cm) long, orange-red, pealike flowers are followed by long, silvery green pods that are quite tasty, especially when young (cook them like snap beans).

Growing guidelines Before planting, make sure you have a sturdy support, such as a fence or stout posts, already in place. This fast-growing vine is easy to start from seed sown directly into the garden. Wait 2–3 weeks after the last frost date, when the soil is warm; then plant the seed 1 inch (2.5 cm) deep. Thin seedlings to stand about 8 inches (20 cm) apart. Water during dry spells.

Pest and disease prevention No specific problems.

Landscape uses Scarlet runner bean is a good vine to grow as a screen for quick shade or privacy. It's also excellent as a temporary solution for covering an ugly section of fence or screening an unpleasant view. Train it up a tripod of stakes.

Phlox drummondii

POLEMONIACEAE

BEST SITE
Full sun; average, well-drained soil.

HEIGHT
About 6–18 inches (15–45 cm), depending on the cultivar.

SPREAD
6–8 inches (15–20 cm)

FLOWERING TIME
Midsummer to autumn.

ANNUAL PHLOX

ANNUAL PHLOX IS A HARDY ANNUAL GROWN FOR ITS COLORFUL FLOWERS. IF PLANTS STOP BLOOMING, CUT THEM BACK BY HALF AND WATER THOROUGHLY; THEY SHOULD RESPROUT AND REBLOOM IN AUTUMN.

Description Plants form bushy clumps of narrow, lance-shaped, green leaves. From midsummer to autumn, the leafy stems are topped with clusters of flat, five-petaled flowers, each ½–1 inch (12–25 mm) across. Blooms are a wide range of colors, including white, pink, red, pale yellow, blue and purple; some have a contrasting eye.

Growing guidelines For earliest bloom, buy transplants in spring, or grow your own by starting seed indoors 6–8 weeks before the last frost date. Sow seed ⅛ inch (3 mm) deep in individual pots. Set plants out around the last frost date. You can also sow seed directly into the garden around the last frost date. Set plants or thin seedlings to stand 6 inches (15 cm) apart. Pinch off spent flowers and water during dry spells to prolong the bloom season.

Pest and disease prevention No specific problems.

Landscape uses An excellent filler for flower beds and borders. Try the compact cultivars in container gardens and window boxes. Tall-stemmed cultivars are excellent as cut flowers.

BEST SITE
Full sun or part shade; moist, well-drained soil.

HEIGHT
3 feet (90 cm)

SPREAD
3 feet (90 cm)

FLOWERING TIME
Summer.

CAPE GOOSEBERRY

THE COLORFUL BERRY FRUITS OF CAPE GOOSEBERRY ARE EDIBLE; THEY RIPEN WHEN THE CALYCES START TO DRY OUT. THEY ALSO MAKE WONDERFUL DRIED DECORATIONS.

Description Cape gooseberry is a moderately frost-hardy perennial that is often treated as an annual. It is grown for its edible berries, which ripen from bright yellow to purple. The oval to heart-shaped leaves grow up to 4 inches (10 cm) long. Purple flowers with yellow blotches are ½ inch (12 mm) wide, and are encased by the calyces soon after blooming.

Growing guidelines Prepare the soil before sowing by digging in compost. Cape gooseberry is best grown from seed sown directly into your garden. Sow seed 2–3 weeks after your last frost date. Thin seedlings to stand about 1½ feet (45 cm) apart. Water regularly when plants become established, but don't overwater. Harvest for drying when the calyces have deepened in color. Dry upside-down in a cool, well-aired place.

Pest and disease prevention No specific problems.

Landscape uses Cape gooseberry is an obvious choice for a cutting garden or at the back of beds and borders. Its upright, leafy habit also makes it suitable for growing as part of a cottage garden.

Best site
Full sun; average, well-drained to dry soil.

Height
6 inches (15 cm)

Spread
6–8 inches (15–20 cm)

Flowering time
Early summer through autumn.

Rose moss

ROSE MOSS COMES IN MANY VIBRANT COLORS, INCLUDING WHITE, PINK, RED, ORANGE, YELLOW AND MAGENTA. THE FLOWERS TEND TO CLOSE BY AFTERNOON AND STAY CLOSED ON CLOUDY DAYS.

Description A low-growing, tender annual, rose moss forms creeping mats of fleshy, reddish, many-branched stems with small, thick, almost needle-like leaves. The 1-inch (2.5-cm) wide flowers are single or double.

Growing guidelines For earliest bloom, buy transplants in spring, or start your own by sowing seed indoors 6–8 weeks before your last frost date. Don't cover the seed; just press it lightly into the soil and enclose the containers in a plastic bag until seedlings appear. Set plants out 2–3 weeks after the last frost date, when the soil is warm; space them about 6 inches (15 cm) apart. You can also sow the fine seed directly into the garden after the last frost date; keep the soil moist until seedlings appear. Thin seedlings only if they're crowded. Established plants may self-sow.

Pest and disease prevention No specific problems.

Landscape uses Makes a great groundcover for dry, rocky slopes. It also looks charming as an edging for sunny beds and borders or cascading out of hanging baskets.

BEST SITE
Part shade; fertile, moist, well-drained soil.

HEIGHT
1 foot (30 cm)

SPREAD
1 foot (30 cm)

FLOWERING TIME
Late winter through midspring in warmer areas; summer in cooler areas.

FAIRY PRIMROSE

IT'S BEST TO REMOVE FAIRY PRIMROSES ONCE THEY ARE PAST THEIR BEST. THEY SELF-SEED READILY BUT THE FOLLOWING YEAR'S FLOWERS MAY VARY FROM THE PARENT PLANT.

Description This tender perennial is usually grown as a tender annual. Small, double or single, open flowers bloom in spiral masses in shades ranging from white to cerise to magenta. The oval, light green leaves are slightly hairy, as is the upright stem.

Growing guidelines Sow seed indoors in late summer; in warmer areas, you can continue to sow through to early autumn. Scatter the dustlike seed into trays; don't cover it, just press it in lightly. Keep the trays or pots under plastic until seedlings appear. Plant out 2–3 weeks after your last frost date. Space seedlings to stand about 1⅓–1⅔ feet (40–50 cm) apart. Keep soil moist throughout growing season, but don't overwater.

Pest and disease prevention Watch out for snails and slugs; they love to eat fairy primrose seedlings.

Landscape uses Fairy primrose adapt to just about every garden design. They make unbeatable fillers in beds and borders, or in rock gardens and along the edges of walkways. Plant them in masses for a really stunning effect, harmonizing the various shades of color.

Best site
Part shade; fertile, moist, well-drained soil.

Height
8–10 inches (20–25 cm)

Spread
8 inches (20 cm)

Flowering time
Late winter to spring.

Polyanthus primrose

These cheerful little plants can add a bright spot of color to those neglected, shady parts of your garden. They look especially good when grown as part of a rock garden.

Description Polyanthus primrose is a hardy perennial that is often grown as a hardy annual in warmer climates. Large, flat, scented flowers bloom in just about every color, including a pure blue, with bright yellow centers. The flowers arise from neat clusters of bright green, deeply veined, oval leaves.

Growing guidelines Set out the transplants after your last frost date, or sow seed indoors in late summer, as the plants are slow to grow and flower. Sow the very fine seed onto the surface of trays or pots and barely cover with soil. Enclose in plastic and keep in a warm position until seedlings appear. Water from below the trays or pots. Plant out at 6–8-inch (15–20-cm) intervals. Keep soil moist at all times, but never let it get soggy. Fertilize mature plants every 2 weeks or so. Pinch off spent blooms regularly to prolong the flowering season.

Pest and disease prevention Pick off slugs and snails by hand.

Landscape uses They make neat fillers in beds and borders, whether growing in the ground or in a pot. Try planting them in masses, too.

Rhodanthe anthemoides ASTERACEAE

BEST SITE
Part shade (in hot-summer areas), full sun elsewhere; fertile, well-drained soil.

HEIGHT
1 foot (30 cm)

SPREAD
1–2 feet (30–60 cm)

FLOWERING TIME
Autumn to late spring, depending on climate.

STRAWFLOWER

ALTHOUGH STRAWFLOWER IS NOT PARTICULARLY LONG LASTING AS A FRESH CUT FLOWER, IN THE GARDEN IT HAS A LONG SEASON OF INTEREST.

Description This plant is a squat, bushy perennial that can be grown as an annual in areas where the winter temperatures fall below 23°F (-5°C). The yellow-centered, white flowers have stiff, papery petals that can be cut and dried for lasting arrangements. The leaves are gray-green and give off a strong aroma of chamomile when crushed.

Growing guidelines For best results, sow seed directly into the garden about 2–3 weeks after your last frost date. Keep the soil evenly moist; fertilize established plants regularly during flowering. Shear off spent blooms to prolong flowering and to keep the plants dense and compact. Don't deadhead after late summer, because flower buds will be starting to form around that time.

Pest and disease prevention Usually pest-free, but if you spot any caterpillars, pick them off by hand or spray them with BT, a microbial insecticide.

Landscape uses Plant in masses as a showy groundcover. Also look good in beds and borders, rock gardens or along edges of paving stones. Try some in hanging baskets or as part of a container garden.

BEST SITE
Full sun; poor, well-drained soil.

HEIGHT
2 feet (60 cm)

SPREAD
6 inches (15 cm)

FLOWERING TIME
Late spring through summer.

RHODANTHE

A NATIVE OF AUSTRALIA, RHODANTHE'S DAISY-LIKE, EVERLASTING FLOWERS BLOOM IN SHADES OF LIGHT AND DARK PINK, AND WHITE. THEY ARE EAGERLY SOUGHT AFTER FOR FRESH AND DRIED ARRANGEMENTS.

Description Rhodanthe is a marginally frost-hardy annual. The flower heads are made up of white to pink bracts surrounding a bright yellow center. It has an upright, branching habit. The midgreen, slender and slightly pointed leaves arise from a central stem.

Growing guidelines For best results, sow seed directly into the garden in early spring or after your last frost date. In mild-winter areas, seed can be sown in early autumn. Thin seedlings to stand about 6–8 inches (15–20 cm) apart. Use a light mulch, such as straw, around the base of plants to discourage growth of weeds. There is no need to fertilize mature plants; allow the soil to dry out before watering again. Deadhead regularly to prolong the bloom season.

Pest and disease prevention No specific problems.

Landscape uses Rhodanthe is a must in the cutting garden. It is also suited to bed and border plantings, and containers. After harvesting, hang the cut flowers upside-down in a dry, well-ventilated place until the blooms are completely dried out.

BEST SITE
Full sun; average to moist, well-drained soil.

HEIGHT
6 feet (1.8 m)

SPREAD
3–4 feet (90–120 cm)

FLOWERING TIME
Summer.

CASTOR BEAN

THE SEEDS OF CASTOR BEAN ARE POISONOUS IF EATEN, SO AVOID PLANTING THEM IN OR AROUND CHILDREN'S PLAY AREAS.

Description This tender perennial is usually grown as a half-hardy annual. The huge, fast-growing plants produce thick, sturdy stems with large, deeply lobed, green or purplish brown leaves. Small, ½ inch (12-mm) wide, creamy-looking, petal-less flowers bloom in spiky clusters along the upper part of the stems. Flowers are followed by showy, spiny, reddish burs.

Growing guidelines For an early start, sow seed indoors 6–8 weeks before your last frost date. Soak the large, speckled seeds in warm water overnight, then sow seed ¾ inch (18 mm) deep in individual pots (two or three seeds per pot). If all of the seeds germinate, thin to one plant per pot. Set plants out 2–3 weeks after your last frost date. You can also sow seed directly into the garden after the last frost date. Space plants or thin seedlings to stand about 3 feet (90 cm) apart then water them during dry spells. Plants may self-sow.

Pest and disease prevention No specific problems.

Landscape uses Grow castor beans as accents or in the background of beds and borders, or as a temporary but fast-growing screen or hedge.

BEST SITE
Full sun (can take light shade); average, well-drained to dry soil.

HEIGHT
2–3 feet (60–90 cm)

SPREAD
1 foot (30 cm)

FLOWERING TIME
Summer into autumn.

BLACK-EYED SUSAN

ALSO KNOWN AS GLORIOSA DAISY, BLACK-EYED SUSANS ARE A TRUSTY STAPLE IN ANNUAL GARDENS. THEY MAKE EXCELLENT CUT FLOWERS IN FRESH ARRANGEMENTS.

Description This short-lived perennial or biennial is usually grown as a hardy annual. Plants form clumps of long, hairy leaves that taper to a point. Stiff, hairy stems are topped with 2–3-inch (5–7.5-cm) wide flowers. The daisy-like blooms have golden yellow outer petals and a purple-brown or black, raised center.

Growing guidelines For earliest bloom, sow seed indoors 8–10 weeks before your last frost date; just barely cover the seed. Set plants out 2–3 weeks before the last frost date (protect plants if there's a chance of heavy frost). You can also sow seed directly into the garden after the last frost date, although those plants probably won't bloom until the following year. Space plants or thin seedlings to stand 1 foot (30 cm) apart. Plants often self-sow; if this is a problem, remove the spent flowers before they set seed.

Pest and disease prevention No specific problems.

Landscape uses Black-eyed Susans look bright and cheerful in flower beds and borders. They're also a natural choice for meadow gardens.

Salpiglossis sinuata

SOLANACEAE

Best site
Full sun with wind protection; rich, well-drained soil.

Height
1½–2 feet (45–60 cm)

Spread
1⅓ feet (40 cm)

Flowering time
Summer and early autumn.

Painted tongue

FAST-GROWING PAINTED TONGUE IS QUITE A TRICKY PLANT TO GROW, BUT PATIENT GARDENERS WHO ENJOY A CHALLENGE WILL BE MORE THAN REWARDED BY A STUNNING DISPLAY OF FLOWERS ALL SUMMER.

Description This tender annual has brilliantly colored trumpet-shaped, 2-inch (5-cm) wide flowers that bloom in red, orange, yellow, blue and purple. The petals are distinctively marked with patterned veins. The light green lanceolate leaves arise from a central stem.

Growing guidelines Painted tongue is really only suitable for growing in warmer climates, unless you have a greenhouse. It is best to sow seed directly into the garden, as seedlings often transplant poorly. Sow seed outdoors in spring in warmer areas, or about 6 weeks after your last frost date, when the soil is warm. Thin seedlings to stand 8 inches (20 cm) apart. Fertilize mature plants; deadhead regularly.

Pest and disease prevention Prone to attack by aphids; treat any affected plants with a spray of soap solution. Overwatering causes root rot and death of the plant.

Landscape uses Painted tongue provides all the color you could ask for in beds and borders. Plant it in masses to display the vast range of colors. In colder climates, it can be enjoyed as a greenhouse plant.

BEST SITE
Full sun; average, well-drained soil.

HEIGHT
1½–2 feet (45–60 cm)

SPREAD
1 foot (30 cm)

FLOWERING TIME
Midsummer until frost.

MEALY-CUP SAGE

MEALY-CUP SAGE IS FAIRLY DROUGHT-TOLERANT BUT APPRECIATES WATERING DURING EXTENDED DRY SPELLS. THE PLANTS SOMETIMES LIVE THROUGH MILD WINTERS; THEY MAY ALSO SELF-SOW.

Description Also known as blue salvia, this tender perennial is usually grown as a half-hardy annual. Plants produce bushy clumps of narrow, lance-shaped, green leaves with slightly toothed edges. Stiff, purple-blue stem tips are topped with long spikes of dusty blue buds. These buds open to ½-inch (12-mm) long, blue flowers.

Growing guidelines Buy transplants in spring, or grow your own by starting seed indoors 8–10 weeks before your last frost date. Soaking the seed overnight before planting can promote quicker sprouting. Don't cover the sown seed; just press it lightly into the soil and enclose the pot in a plastic bag until seedlings appear. Set plants out after the last frost date; space them 1 foot (30 cm) apart.

Pest and disease prevention No specific problems.

Landscape uses Looks great alone in masses or mixed with other annuals, perennials and roses in beds, borders and cottage gardens. These neat, shrubby plants are ideal for pots, too. The spiky blooms are useful for fresh or dried arrangements.

Best site
Full sun; average, well-drained soil.

Height
3–4 feet (90–120 cm)

Spread
1 foot (30 cm)

Flowering time
Midsummer until frost.

Scarlet sage

ALTHOUGH SCARLET SAGE ENJOYS A SITE WITH FULL SUN, IN WARMER CLIMATES IT IS BEST TO POSITION IT IN PARTIAL SHADE, AS THE BRIGHT COLORS HOLD BETTER THERE.

Description This tender perennial is grown as a half-hardy annual. Plants form clumps of upright stems with oval, deep green leaves that have pointed tips and slightly toothed edges. The stems are topped with thick, showy spikes of colorful petal-like bracts and 1½-inch (3.5-cm) long, tubular flowers that most often bloom in red, but in also white, pink, salmon and purple.

Growing guidelines Widely sold as transplants in spring. If you want to grow your own, sow seed indoors 8–10 weeks before your last frost date. Don't cover the seed; just press it lightly into the soil and enclose the pot in a plastic bag until seedlings appear. Set plants out after the last frost date; space them 8–12 inches (20–30 cm) apart. Fertilize regularly during summer.

Pest and disease prevention Poor drainage and overwatering causes the plants to rot and die.

Landscape uses If you enjoy mixing bright colors, grow scarlet sage as an edging or filler for flower beds and borders. For a more restrained effect, surround with leafy green herbs and ornamental grasses.

BEST SITE
Full sun; average, well-drained to dry soil.

HEIGHT
6 inches (15 cm)

SPREAD
1½ feet (45 cm)

FLOWERING TIME
Midsummer until frost.

CREEPING ZINNIA

PLANT CREEPING ZINNIA WHERE IT CAN TRAIL OVER WALLS, OR ALLOW IT TO CASCADE OUT OF CONTAINERS, RAISED BEDS, WINDOW BOXES AND HANGING BASKETS.

Description Creeping zinnia is usually grown as a half-hardy annual. Plants form spreading or trailing mounds of branching stems and oval green leaves that taper to a point. The mounds are covered with many ¾-inch (18-mm) wide flowers that resemble miniature black-eyed Susans. The raised, purple-brown centers are surrounded by a ring of golden yellow petals.

Growing guidelines For earliest bloom, sow seed indoors 6–8 weeks before your last frost date. Sow in individual pots so you won't have to disturb the roots at transplanting time. Don't cover the fine seed; just press it lightly into the soil and enclose the pots in a plastic bag until seedlings appear. Set plants out after your last frost date. You can also sow seed directly into the garden after your last frost date. Space plants or thin seedlings to stand 8–12 inches (20–30 cm) apart.

Pest and disease prevention No specific problems.

Landscape uses Creeping zinnia makes a great groundcover in dry, sunny spots. It's also useful as an edging or filler for flower beds and borders.

BEST SITE
Full sun; well-drained, slightly alkaline soil.

HEIGHT
2½ feet (75 cm)

SPREAD
2 feet (60 cm)

FLOWERING TIME
Summer to early autumn.

SCABIOUS

THE TALL STEMS AND DELICATELY HONEY-SCENTED BLOOMS OF SCABIOUS MAKE IT A MUCH SOUGHT-AFTER CUT FLOWER. IT ALSO MAKES A WONDERFUL ADDITION TO A BUTTERFLY OR MEADOW GARDEN.

Description This short-lived, tender perennial is more often grown as a tender annual. The flowers of scabious bear multiple florets with protruding filaments. They are borne on long stems and bloom in mauve, violet and rose. The bright green, deeply veined leaves form a basal rosette.

Growing guidelines For best results, propagate from seed sown directly into the garden in spring after all danger of frost has passed. You can also sow seed indoors 6–8 weeks before your last frost date. Cover the seed with a light layer of soil and enclose the pots or trays in plastic bags until seedlings appear. Transplant seedlings 2–3 weeks after the last frost date. Thin seedlings or space plants to stand about 1½–2 feet (45–60 cm) apart.

Pest and disease prevention No specific problems.

Landscape uses Scabious looks attractive planted in masses or as a filler in beds and borders. Its delicate scent makes it a must for the cutting garden or an informal mixed planting, such as a cottage or meadow garden.

Best site
Full sun to semi-shade, with wind protection; fertile, well-drained soil.

Height
1½ feet (45 cm)

Spread
1 foot (30 cm)

Flowering time
Spring to summer.

Poor man's orchid

Poor man's orchid looks a little like an orchid, hence the name. It is also known as butterfly flower because of its elaborate gold-colored markings.

Description Poor man's orchid is a tender annual with fernlike foliage and slightly flared, tubular, two-lipped flowers that bloom in white, blue, pink or reddish brown. The center of each flower head is usually flushed a bright yellow with dark markings.

Growing guidelines These plants do not like extremes of heat or cold and generally do best outdoors in a mild, frost-free climate. For best results, sow seed directly into the garden 2–3 weeks after your last frost date, when the soil is warm. Thin seedlings to stand 6–8 inches (15–20 cm) apart. Pinch out the tips of young plants (when they are about 4 inches [10 cm] high) to encourage bushy growth. Keep plants well watered at all times, but be careful not to let the soil become soggy. Fertilize a couple of times during the growing season, until flower buds form. Deadhead regularly to prolong flowering.

Pest and disease prevention No specific problems.

Landscape uses It makes a great show planted in masses, or trailing out of window boxes, containers and hanging baskets.

BEST SITE
Full sun; average, well-drained soil.

HEIGHT
8–24 inches (20–60 cm)

SPREAD
1 foot (30 cm)

FLOWERING TIME
Summer.

DUSTY MILLER

DUSTY MILLER CAN LIVE THROUGH MILD WINTERS, BUT SECOND-YEAR PLANTS TEND TO BE MORE OPEN. FOR USE IN EDGINGS, START WITH NEW PLANTS EACH YEAR.

Description This tender perennial is usually grown as a half-hardy annual. Plants form shrubby mounds of deeply lobed leaves that are covered with matted, white hairs. The plants may produce clusters of daisy-like yellow flowers, but they are usually removed so they won't detract from the silvery foliage. Dusty miller is also listed in seed catalogs as *Cineraria maritima.*

Growing guidelines Transplants are easy to find for purchase in spring. They grow slowly from seed, but if you want to raise your own, sow seed indoors 8–10 weeks before your last frost date. Don't cover the seed; just press it lightly into the soil and enclose the pot in a plastic bag until seedlings appear. Set plants out after the last frost date; space them 8 inches (20 cm) apart. Pinch out stem tips in early summer to promote bushy growth.

Pest and disease prevention No specific problems.

Landscape uses Dusty miller's silvery foliage is invaluable as an edging or accent for flower beds, borders and all kinds of container plantings. The silvery leaves and stems also dry well.

Silene armeria CARYOPHYLLACEAE

Best site
Full sun to part shade; fertile, well-drained soil.

Height
1 foot (30 cm)

Spread
6 inches (15 cm)

Flowering time
Summer.

Campion

Campion is an attractive, marginally frost-hardy annual or biennial that is commonly found in gardens across temperate and cool regions.

Description Campion is grown for its bright pink, five-petaled, bell-shaped flowers; each petal has a distinctive notch. It has slender, upright, branching stems and elongated, midgreen, silky leaves.

Growing guidelines Propagate from seed sown in spring or early autumn, or from cuttings taken in spring. Sow seed indoors 6–8 weeks before your last frost date. Enclose the pots in a plastic bag and keep in a warm place until seedlings appear. Transplant or sow seed directly into your garden 2–3 weeks after your last frost date. Space plants or thin seedlings to stand about 6 inches (15 cm) apart. Fertilize every 2 weeks or so during the growing season. Pinch out spent blooms to improve appearance and prolong flowering.

Pest and disease prevention No specific problems.

Landscape uses Campion is best suited to cottage gardens and rockeries. It also grows well in container gardens and can be taken indoors for overwintering.

Coleus

KEEP FAVORITE COLEUS PLANTS FROM YEAR TO YEAR BY TAKING CUTTINGS IN SUMMER; THEY'LL ROOT QUICKLY IN WATER. POT UP THE CUTTINGS FOR WINTER, THEN PUT THEM OUTDOORS IN SPRING.

Description The most distinctive aspect of coleus, also known as flame nettle or painted leaves, is its soft-textured, multicolored foliage that comes in a wide variety of color combinations. These frost-tender perennials are usually grown as bushy, frost-tender annuals. Their sturdy, square stems carry showy, patterned leaves with scalloped or ruffled edges. Each leaf can have several different colors, with zones, edges or splashes in shades of red, pink, orange, yellow and cream. Small blue or purple flowers may appear but add very little to the leafy display; it's usual practice to pinch out or trim the inconsequential flower heads, but it's not necessary if you like the way they look.

Growing guidelines Transplants are readily available for purchase in spring, or start your own by sowing seed indoors 8–10 weeks before your last frost date. Don't cover the seed; just press it lightly into the soil and enclose the seed tray or pot in a plastic bag until seedlings appear. Set plants out 8–12 inches (20–30 cm) apart after your last frost date. During the summer, water

Variations in color and form are the main attraction of coleus.

BEST SITE
Full sun to part shade; humus-rich, moist, well-drained soil.

HEIGHT
Up to 2 feet (60 cm).

SPREAD
1 foot (30 cm)

FLOWERING TIME
Summer to early autumn.

copiously during dry spells, otherwise the leaves will be small and stunted. Fertilize regularly throughout the growing season to encourage healthy leaf growth. Once the plants have flowered, leaf growth stops; pinching off the spikes of the blue flowers promotes more leafy growth. In warm areas, you can leave coleus in the garden for the following year, but the leafy display will not be as lush or dense without significant effort on your part. They would need to be cut right back, watered and fertilized continuously during the following spring and summer to encourage the vigorous growth that results in a showy display.

Pest and disease prevention Watch out for slugs and snails eating young plants. Trap them in shallow pans of beer or sprinkle commercial slug and snail deterrent at the base of the plants.

Landscape uses Coleus are great for adding all-season color to beds, borders and container plantings. Groups of mixed leaf patterns can look too busy when combined with flowering plants, so grow them alone in masses, or consider sticking with a single leaf pattern. This approach works particularly well when coleus is used as an edging plant. Coleus also makes a handy filler between shrubs.

Tagetes hybrids

ASTERACEAE

Best site
Full sun; average, well-drained soil. Light afternoon shade can help prolong bloom in hot-summer areas, especially for creamy-flowered cultivars.

Height
6–36 inches (15–90 cm)

Spread
6–18 inches (15–45 cm)

Flowering time
Summer.

Marigold

Marigolds can add bright color to any sunny spot. Mix them with other annuals and perennials, or grow them alone in masses. They often self-sow.

Description These popular half-hardy annuals are grown for their bright, 2–4-inch (5–10-cm) wide flowers and bushy mounds of lacy, green leaves. African or American marigolds *T. erecta* are larger plants, with 1½–3-foot (45–90-cm) stems and large, usually double, yellow or orange flowers. French marigolds *T. patula* are much daintier, with many smaller, single or double flowers in yellow, orange or red on 1-foot (30-cm) tall plants. There are many hybrid variations.

Growing guidelines For earliest bloom (especially for tall-growing types), start seed indoors 4–6 weeks before your last frost date. Plant seed ⅛–¼ inch (3–6 mm) deep. Set plants out after your last frost date. You can also sow seed of small, early-blooming types directly into the garden after your last frost date. Fertilize mature plants regularly.

Pest and disease prevention Watch out for mites and whiteflies; try hosing them off first, but if that doesn't work, spray them with soap solution or an insecticide.

Landscape uses Grow as a summer filler or edging for flower beds, borders and containers.

BEST SITE
Full sun to partial shade; average, well-drained soil.

HEIGHT
1–2½ feet (30–75 cm)

SPREAD
1–1½ feet (30–45 cm)

FLOWERING TIME
Early to midsummer.

FEVERFEW

FEVERFEW IS PRETTY BUT CAN BECOME A PEST BY DROPPING LOTS OF SEED. CUTTING OFF BLOOM STALKS AFTER THE FLOWERS FADE WILL PREVENT THIS PROBLEM AND PROMOTE NEW LEAFY GROWTH.

Description This short-lived perennial or biennial is often grown as a hardy annual. The plants form ferny mounds of deeply cut, aromatic, green leaves. The leafy stems are topped with 1-inch (2.5-cm) wide, single or double flowers, mainly in early to midsummer. The yellow or white, daisy-like flowers have yellow centers.

Growing guidelines Starts easily from seed sown in the garden in mid- to late spring. You can also start seed indoors 6–8 weeks before your last frost date. Plant the fine seed in a pot, press it lightly into the soil, and enclose the pot in a plastic bag until seedlings appear. Move young plants outdoors after the last frost date. Space plants or thin seedlings to stand 8–12 inches (20–30 cm) apart.

Pest and disease prevention No specific problems.

Landscape uses Grow feverfew in flower beds and borders, herb gardens and container gardens. It looks especially charming with roses in cottage gardens. The sprays of small flowers are great in fresh arrangements, too.

Thunbergia alata

ACANTHACEAE

Best site
Full sun to partial shade; average to moist, well-drained soil.

Height
6 feet (1.8 m)

Spread
About 6 feet (1.8 m), depending on the support the vine is growing on.

Flowering time
Late summer until frost; they look their best from late summer to early autumn.

Black-eyed Susan vine

If you plan to grow black-eyed Susan vine as a climber, install some type of support—such as plastic netting or a trellis—before planting.

Description This tender perennial is grown as a tender annual. Plants produce twining vines with heart- to arrowhead-shaped, green leaves. Pointed buds open to rounded, flattened, 3-inch (7.5-cm) wide flowers. The orange-yellow flowers have a deep purple to black center.

Growing guidelines For earliest flowers, start seed indoors 6–8 weeks before your last frost date. Sow seed ¼ inch (6 mm) deep in peat pots (two or three seeds per pot); thin to leave one seedling per pot. Set plants out 2–3 weeks after the last frost date. You can also start plants from seed sown directly into the garden after the last frost date. Set plants or thin seedlings to stand 1 foot (30 cm) apart. Mulch plants to keep the roots cool. Water during dry spells.

Pest and disease prevention No specific problems.

Landscape uses Black-eyed Susan vine is a good, fast-growing screen for shade or privacy. It also makes a unique feature in a hanging basket, where it will climb up the support wires to create a pyramid of foliage and flowers.

Tithonia rotundifolia ASTERACEAE

BEST SITE
Full sun; average, well-drained soil with added organic matter.

HEIGHT
4–6 feet (1.2–1.8 m)

SPREAD
4–6 feet (1.2–1.8 m)

FLOWERING TIME
Summer.

MEXICAN SUNFLOWER

ALSO KNOWN AS TORCH FLOWERS, MEXICAN SUNFLOWERS ARE POPULAR WITH BEES AND BUTTERFLIES, AND THEY MAKE GOOD CUT FLOWERS FOR FRESH ARRANGEMENTS.

Description Mexican sunflower is a half-hardy annual with colorful blooms. Plants produce tall, sturdy, hairy stems with velvety, lobed or broadly oval, pointed, dark green leaves. During flowering time, the shrubby clumps are accented with many 3-inch (7.5-cm) wide, glowing orange, daisy-like flowers.

Growing guidelines For earliest flowers, start seed indoors 6–8 weeks before your last frost date. Sow seed 1/4 inch (6 mm) deep in individual pots (two or three seeds to each pot); thin to leave one seedling per pot. Set plants out after the last frost date. They also grow quickly and easily from seed sown directly into the garden about 2 weeks after the last frost date. Set plants or thin seedlings to stand 1½ feet (45 cm) apart. Water during dry spells. Plants growing in exposed sites may need staking. Pinch off spent blooms to extend the flowering season.

Pest and disease prevention No specific problems.

Landscape uses Makes an attractive screen or hedge and looks great as a tall accent or background plant in beds and borders.

BEST SITE
Partial shade; moist, well-drained soil. Plants can take more sun in cooler areas.

HEIGHT
1 foot (30 cm)

SPREAD
6–8 inches (15–20 cm)

FLOWERING TIME
Early summer through autumn.

WISHBONE FLOWER

WISHBONE FLOWERS ARE USUALLY PURPLISH BLUE WITH A YELLOW THROAT; THEY MAY ALSO BE WHITE OR PINK. THE MOUTH OF EACH BLOOM HAS TWO SHORT, CURVED STAMENS THAT RESEMBLE A WISHBONE.

Description Also known as bluewings, this tender, shade-loving annual forms clumps of upright, many-branched stems with oval, pointed to narrow, toothed, green leaves that take on reddish purple tints in autumn. The stems are topped with trumpet-shaped, lipped blooms to 1 inch (2.5 cm) long.

Growing guidelines Sow seed indoors 8–10 weeks before your last frost date. Don't cover the seed; just press it lightly into the soil. Enclose the pot in a plastic bag and set it in a warm, dark place. When seedlings appear (in about a week), remove the bag and set the pot in a bright place. Set plants out after the last frost date; space them to stand 6 inches (15 cm) apart. Water during dry spells. If plants start to flop, shear them back by about half to promote branching.

Pest and disease prevention No specific problems.

Landscape uses Wishbone flower is lovely as an edging or filler for shady beds and borders. It also looks good in containers and window boxes.

Tropaeolum majus

TROPAEOLACEAE

Best site
Full sun; average, well-drained to dry soil.

Height
Height of vining types to about 8 feet (2.4 m), bushy types to about 1 foot (30 cm).

Spread
1–3 feet (30–90 cm)

Flowering time
Early summer through autumn.

Nasturtium

Nasturtiums are half-hardy annuals with brightly colored flowers. Bushy types are great as edgings or fillers for beds and borders.

Description Plants grow either as a climbing or trailing vine or as a bushy mound. Each rounded, light green leaf grows from a leaf stalk that emerges from the center of the leaf. The plants bear showy, fragrant, five-petaled flowers to 2 inches (5 cm) wide that bloom in a range of colors, including cream, rose, red, orange and yellow.

Growing guidelines If you're growing vining types, put up some kind of support such as string, wires, netting or a trellis before planting. For an extra-early start, you can sow seed indoors 4–6 weeks before your last frost date. Soak the seed overnight before planting; then sow it ¼–½ inch (6–12 mm) deep in peat pots. Set plants out after the last frost date. Alternatively, sow seed directly into the garden 2–3 weeks before your last frost date. Set plants or thin seedlings to stand 6–12 inches (15–30 cm) apart.

Pest and disease prevention Wash away aphids with a spray of water. For persistent populations, spray with insecticidal soap.

Landscape uses Use climbing types to quickly cover trellises; grow the compact types in containers.

Pansy

To keep pansies happy, mulch the soil around them and water during dry spells to keep the roots moist. Pinching off spent flowers can prolong bloom; leave a few to self-sow.

Description These short-lived perennials are usually grown as hardy annuals or biennials. Plants form tidy clumps of oval to narrow, green leaves with rounded teeth. Flat, five-petaled flowers bloom just above the clumps, mainly in spring but also sometimes in autumn. The 2–5-inch (5–12.5-cm) wide flowers bloom in a range of colors, including white, pink, red, orange, yellow, purple, blue and near black; many have contrasting faces.

Growing guidelines For bloom the same year, purchase plants in early spring or start seed indoors 8–10 weeks before your last frost date. Sow seed ⅛ inch (3 mm) deep; the fine seed only needs to be lightly covered. Before planting out into your garden, prepare the soil by digging in plenty of compost or manure. Set seedlings out 2–3 weeks before your last frost date, by which time they should be about 1–2 inches (2.5–5 cm) high. Set transplants or thin seedlings to stand about 6–8 inches (15–20 cm) apart. To grow pansies as biennials, for earlier spring bloom, sow seed outdoors in a nursery bed in late spring; move plants to the garden

Pansies are invaluable for early color in beds and borders.

BEST SITE
Full sun to partial shade; moist, well-drained soil.

HEIGHT
6–8 inches (15–20 cm)

SPREAD
8–12 inches (20–30 cm)

FLOWERING TIME
Mainly in spring but also sometimes in autumn.

in midautumn. Pansies need regular watering to promote plant strength and optimal flowering; a deep watering once a week should be enough, unless you live in a dry, windy area. Fertilize established plants every 2 weeks. Dig out the plants once they start to look ragged and untidy. Deadhead spent flowers regularly to prolong flowering.

Pest and disease prevention Pansies are relatively free of pest problems, but overwatering can cause rotting and death of the plants. Ensure the garden soil is well drained before planting and check pot bases to make sure that there are enough drainage holes drilled into them.

Landscape uses Pansies are another classic staple in annual gardens. They make wonderful fillers for flowering beds and borders, or in massed plantings to show off the incredible variety of color and form found in different cultivars. They are also well suited to life in container gardens, hanging baskets and window boxes. Pansies make a good cut flower; try arranging them in float bowls for an unusual decoration on a table, or simply in little posies.

BEST SITE
Full sun; average, well-drained to dry soil.

HEIGHT
8–12 inches (20–30 cm)

SPREAD
1–2 feet (30–60 cm)

FLOWERING TIME
Midsummer until frost.

NARROW-LEAVED ZINNIA

NARROW-LEAVED ZINNIA IS A TENDER ANNUAL THAT IS GROWN FOR ITS COLORFUL FLOWERS. ESTABLISHED PLANTS ARE EASY-CARE AND RELATIVELY TROUBLE-FREE.

Description Plants form loose mounds of slender, dark green leaves. The mounds are covered with open, daisy-like, 1½-inch (3.5-cm) wide blooms. The flowers are most often bright orange with a gold stripe in the center of each petal; white- and yellow-flowered types are also available. Narrow-leaved zinnia is also listed in catalogs under the name *Z. linearis*.

Growing guidelines For earliest flowers, sow seed indoors 3–4 weeks before your last frost date. Plant seed ¼–½ inch (6–12 mm) deep in peat pots (two or three seeds per pot). Thin seedlings to leave one per pot. Set plants out after your last frost date. It's also easy to start these fast growers from seed sown directly into the garden 2–3 weeks after your last frost date, when the soil is warm. Space plants or thin seedlings to stand 10–12 inches (25–30 cm) apart.

Pest and disease prevention No specific problems.

Landscape uses Grow in masses as a groundcover, or combine it with other plants as an edging or filler for beds and borders.

BEST SITE
Full sun; average, well-drained soil with added organic matter.

HEIGHT
From 6–36 inches (15–90 cm), depending on the cultivar.

SPREAD
1–2 feet (30–60 cm)

FLOWERING TIME
Midsummer until frost.

COMMON ZINNIA

COMMON ZINNIAS ARE EXCELLENT FOR REPLACING EARLY-BLOOMING ANNUALS AND FILLING IN GAPS LEFT BY DORMANT SPRING-FLOWERING BULBS AND PERENNIALS.

Description Plants produce stiff, sturdy stems with pairs of oval to pointed, green leaves. The stems are topped with blooms in nearly every color (except true blue). Common zinnias come in a range of flower forms, from 1–6 inches (2.5–15 cm) across. The single or double blooms may have petals that are quilled (curled), ruffled or flat.

Growing guidelines Buy transplants in spring, or sow seed indoors 3–4 weeks before your last frost date. Plant seed ¼–½ inch (6–12 mm) deep in peat pots (two or three seeds per pot). Thin seedlings to leave one per pot. Set plants out after last frost date. They also grow quickly from seed sown directly into the garden 1–2 weeks after last frost date, when the soil is warm. Space plants or thin seedlings of compact types about 1 foot (30 cm) apart; leave 1½–2 feet (45–60 cm) between tall cultivars.

Pest and disease prevention Powdery mildew can be a problem; treat with sulfur or other plant fungicides.

Landscape uses Grow common zinnias alone in masses, or mix them with other plants in flower beds, borders and cottage gardens.

Part Five

Plant Directory

~

Bulbs

Allium christophii

LILIACEAE

SITE AND CLIMATE
Full sun; humus-rich, well-drained soil. Zones 5–8.

HEIGHT
1–1½ feet (30–45 cm)

SPREAD
1 foot (30 cm)

FLOWERING TIME
Early to midsummer.

STAR-OF-PERSIA

THE STRIKING FLOWER HEADS OF STAR-OF-PERSIA MAKE AN UNUSUAL ACCENT AT THE BACK OF BEDS AND BORDERS. PLANT IT WITH ORNAMENTAL GRASSES, SUCH AS JAPANESE SILVER GRASS, TO HEIGHTEN THE EFFECT.

Description Star-of-Persia produces 1½-foot (45-cm), strap-shaped, blue-green leaves that arch outward from the bulbs. Starry, lilac-pink flowers carried in 10-inch (25-cm) globose heads radiate from stout 1–1½-foot (30–45-cm) stalks.

Growing guidelines Plant new bulbs shallowly in autumn, with their necks above ground level, and leave to slowly multiply into spectacular flowering clumps. Plants go dormant after flowering. Divide in mid- to late summer as plants go dormant. Sow ripe seed outdoors in summer or autumn. Fertilize in spring. Star-of-Persia naturalizes.

Pest and disease prevention No specific problems.

Landscape uses Use it as a striking accent in almost any garden design. Star-of-Persia is a natural choice for cottage and meadow gardens. It also grows well in containers and makes a great cut flower in fresh or dried arrangements.

Allium giganteum

LILIACEAE

SITE AND CLIMATE
Full sun is ideal, but can take light shade; average, well-drained soil. Zones 5–8.

HEIGHT
Height of leaves usually 6–12 inches (15–30 cm); flower stems grow to 5 feet (1.5 m).

SPREAD
1 foot (30 cm)

FLOWERING TIME
Early to midsummer

GIANT ONION

PLANT PERENNIALS OR SUMMER-BLOOMING ANNUALS AT THE BASE OF GIANT ONION TO FILL IN WHEN THE BULBS GO DORMANT.

Description Wide, flat, sprawling, blue-green leaves emerge in mid- to late spring; they have an oniony odor when bruised. A tall, slender stem rises from the center of the leaves in late spring. By early to midsummer, the stem is topped with a 6-inch (15-cm) globe densely packed with small, reddish purple flowers. The leaves yellow and die back to the ground by midsummer.

Growing guidelines Plant bulbs in early to midautumn or in early spring. Set them in individual holes or larger planting areas dug 8 inches (20 cm) deep. Space bulbs 8–12 inches (20–30 cm) apart. In Zones 5 and 6, protect bulbs over winter with a loose mulch, such as straw or evergreen boughs; remove the mulch in spring. Cut down spent flower stems, unless you want to collect seed or use the dried seed head for arrangements. Leave established bulbs undisturbed.

Pest and disease prevention No specific problems.

Landscape uses Giant onion is a showstopping accent for the back of flower beds and borders. Clumps of six or more giant onions look great with shrubs.

Allium moly

LILIACEAE

SITE AND CLIMATE
Full sun to partial shade; moist, fertile, well-drained soil. Zones 7–9.

HEIGHT
1½ feet (45 cm)

SPREAD
10 inches (25 cm)

FLOWERING TIME
Late spring or early summer.

LILY LEEK

ALSO KNOWN AS GOLDEN GARLIC, LILY LEEK IS A CLOSE RELATIVE OF GIANT ONION AND STAR-OF-PERSIA. LIKE THEM, IT IS A RELATIVELY EASY-CARE PLANT TO GROW.

Description Lily leek is a deciduous summer bulb that bears flat, blue-green leaves and slightly rounded clusters of star-shaped, golden yellow flowers. Flower stems are about 8–12 inches (20–30 cm) tall.

Growing guidelines Plant in autumn, spacing bulbs about 4 inches (10 cm) apart and 4 inches (10 cm) deep. Keep soil moist from winter through spring. Fertilize in spring. Deadhead spent flowers regularly to prolong the bloom season. Mulch around the base of the plant to keep the soil evenly moist in warmer areas and to protect from frost in cooler areas. Propagate by division, offsets, bulbils in autumn or seed in spring.

Pest and disease prevention No specific problems.

Landscape uses Lily leek looks great planted in beds, borders or as part of an informal planting, such as a meadow or woodland garden. Try planting some as an accent in a rock garden, or in a container. Lily leek is inclined to spread, so don't plant it in a position where this is likely to become a problem.

Amaryllis belladonna

AMARYLLIDACEAE

SITE AND CLIMATE
Full sun; rich, well-drained soil. Zones 8–11.

HEIGHT
2 feet (60 cm)

SPREAD
10–12 inches (25–30 cm)

FLOWERING TIME
Late summer through early autumn.

NAKED-LADY

ALSO KNOWN AS BELLADONNA LILY, NAKED-LADY IS AN ELEGANT AND SUBSTANTIAL ADDITION TO INDOOR AND OUTDOOR GARDENS, EITHER IN POTS OR IN THE GROUND.

Description Naked-ladies are deciduous summer bulbs. The strap-shaped, dull green leaves appear in clumps after flowering. The pink or white, 3–4-inch (7.5–10-cm) multiple flowers are trumpet shaped and lightly scented. They perch atop a tall, reddish-colored central stalk.

Growing guidelines Plant in late spring to early summer, spacing bulbs 8–12 inches (20–30 cm) apart, at soil level. Where winter temperatures fall below freezing for extended periods, plant bulbs 6 inches (15 cm) below ground. If you are planting in containers, you'll need to position the bulbs slightly above the soil level. Naked-ladies are not difficult to grow, but you need to keep them moist from midsummer to early spring; fertilize until buds form. Propagate by offsets; divide the bulbs only when crowded.

Pest and disease prevention No specific problems.

Landscape uses These plants look attractive in most garden situations, including tropical gardens. Keep some available for cutting, as the fresh flowers last a long time in water. Naked-ladies also thrive indoors in containers.

Anemone blanda RANUNCULACEAE

SITE AND CLIMATE
Full sun to partial shade (ideally under deciduous trees and shrubs); average to moist, well-drained soil. Zones 5–8.

HEIGHT
6 inches (15 cm)

SPREAD
4–6 inches (10–15 cm)

FLOWERING TIME
Spring.

GRECIAN WINDFLOWER

GRECIAN WINDFLOWERS BLOOM IN MID- TO LATE SPRING IN MOST AREAS; IN WARMER CLIMATES, THEY MAY APPEAR IN LATE WINTER OR EARLY SPRING.

Description Grecian windflowers grow from knobbly tubers to produce carpets of deeply lobed, toothed, green leaves. Daisy-like blue, pink or white spring flowers to 2 inches (5 cm) across bloom just above the ferny leaves.

Growing guidelines Buy and plant the tubers in late spring through early autumn. Soak them overnight before planting, and set them in individual holes or larger planting areas dug about 2 inches (5 cm) deep. It can be hard to tell which side is up: If you can see a shallow depression on one side, plant with that side up. Otherwise, plant the tubers on their sides or just drop them into the hole. Space the tubers 4–6 inches (10–15 cm) apart. Grecian windflowers propagate themselves by spreading and self-sowing.

Pest and disease prevention No specific problems.

Landscape uses Naturalize masses of Grecian windflowers under trees for sheets of spring color, or combine them with daffodils. Also try them in pots and window boxes.

Anemonella thalictroides

RANUNCULACEAE

SITE AND CLIMATE
Bright, dappled shade, ideally under lightly foliaged or high-canopied trees; well-drained, rich soil with added organic matter. Zones 5–9.

HEIGHT
6–10 inches (15–25 cm)

SPREAD
8–10 inches (20–25 cm)

FLOWERING TIME
Spring.

RUE ANEMONE

RUE ANEMONE IS NATIVE TO THE EASTERN UNITED STATES, EXTENDING AS FAR WEST AS OKLAHOMA. IT IS A WOODLAND PLANT THAT SHOULD NOT BE DISTURBED ONCE IT IS ESTABLISHED.

Description Rue anemone grows from short, brown, tuberous roots, with three-lobed leaves that appear in early spring. The 1-inch (2.5-cm) wide flowers appear in mid- to late spring and are usually white, but also occasionally pink.

Growing guidelines Plant tubers in early autumn just below the surface of the soil, spacing them about 8 inches (20 cm) apart. Adding a very thin layer of rotted organic matter to the surface after planting helps to simulate the plant's natural woodland soils. Water it once, then leave it to nature. When leaves appear, resume watering and keep moist until flowering finishes. In summer, give the plants an occasional deep watering. If soil is fertile, no feeding is necessary. Rue anemone does not thrive in hot areas with low rainfall.

Pest and disease prevention Watch out for snails in early spring when fresh leaves are emerging. Pick them off by hand.

Landscape uses Naturalize under deciduous trees, but not where shade is dense. Plant rue anemone as an edging plant beside paths, too.

SITE AND CLIMATE
Partial shade to full shade; rich, well-drained soil. Zones 6–10.

HEIGHT
1–1½ feet (30–45 cm)

SPREAD
1 foot (30 cm)

FLOWERING TIME
Spring.

ITALIAN ARUM

BY LATE SUMMER, THE FLOWERS OF ITALIAN ARUM MATURE INTO COLUMNS OF REDDISH ORANGE BERRIES. THESE COLORFUL SPIKES REMAIN UNTIL NEW LEAVES APPEAR IN AUTUMN.

Description Grows from tubers. It blooms in mid- to late spring and has a greenish white, hoodlike spathe sheltering a narrow column known as the spadix. The flowers are interesting, but the plant is mainly grown for its arrowhead-shaped, semiglossy, dark green leaves that are marked with creamy white. The leaves emerge in autumn, flourish in winter and die back in summer.

Growing guidelines Plant in late summer or early autumn. Set the tubers into individual holes or larger planting areas dug 2–3 inches (5–7.5 cm) deep. Space the tubers 8–12 inches (20–30 cm) apart. Keep the soil moist during leaf growth and flowering. Divide in early autumn; otherwise, allow plants to form handsome clumps.

Pest and disease prevention No specific problems.

Landscape uses Italian arum looks great planted in masses in woodland gardens. It also adds multiseason interest when planted under trees to emerge through beds of English ivy *Hedera helix* or common periwinkle *Vinca minor*. Try combining it with snowdrops *Galanthus nivalis*, too.

SITE AND CLIMATE
Partial shade; evenly moist but well-drained soil with added organic matter. Hardy in Zone 10; elsewhere, grown as annuals or stored indoors in winter.

HEIGHT
1½ feet (45 cm)

SPREAD
1–1½ feet (30–45 cm)

FLOWERING TIME
Summer through autumn.

HYBRID TUBEROUS BEGONIAS

HYBRID TUBEROUS BEGONIAS BLOOM IN A WIDE RANGE OF COLORS, EXCEPT FOR BLUES AND PURPLES; MANY ARE EDGED OR SHADED WITH OTHER COLORS.

Description Hybrid tuberous begonias grow from flattened, circular, light brown tubers. These tubers produce fleshy, upright or trailing stems with pointed oval to heart-shaped, hairy, toothed, green leaves. The bushy plants produce an abundance of gorgeous single or double flowers up to 4 inches (10 cm) across.

Growing guidelines Buy thick tubers that are 1½–2 inches (3.5–5 cm) across. Start them growing indoors about 4 weeks before your last frost date. Plant them in pots of moist potting soil with their pressed-in side up. Cover with ½ inch (12 mm) of potting soil. Raise them under bright light and keep soil evenly moist. Space 1½ feet (45 cm) apart when night temperatures stay above 50°F (10°C). Water and mulch to keep the soil evenly moist. Fertilize several times during the season. To keep over the winter, lift tubers before or just after the first frost, then store in a frost-free place.

Pest and disease prevention No specific problems.

Landscape uses Hybrid tuberous begonias look beautiful in shaded beds, borders and hanging baskets.

SITE AND CLIMATE
Partial shade; moist but well-drained soil with added organic matter. Hardy in Zone 10; elsewhere, grown as annuals or stored indoors for winter.

HEIGHT
1–2 feet (30–60 cm)

SPREAD
2 feet (60 cm)

FLOWERING TIME
The foliage is handsome from late spring until frost.

CALADIUM

CALADIUMS ARE GROWN FOR THEIR SHOWY LEAVES; PINCH OFF ANY OF THE SMALL, HOODED FLOWERS THAT APPEAR IN SUMMER. THESE SHADE-LOVING PLANTS THRIVE IN HEAT AND HUMIDITY.

Description Caladiums grow from tubers. They produce bushy clumps of long-stalked and heart-shaped leaves. The lush leaves are shaded and veined with various combinations of green, white, pink and red.

Growing guidelines Start the tubers indoors in early spring. Set them with the knobby side up in pots of moist potting mix, and cover with 2 inches (5 cm) more of mix. Keep them in a warm, bright spot and keep the soil evenly moist. Move plants out to the garden when night temperatures stay above 60°F (16°C); space them about 1 foot (30 cm) apart. Mulch and water as needed to keep soil moist until late summer. When leaves die back, dig the tubers up and store them in a cool (not cold), dark place.

Pest and disease prevention No specific problems.

Landscape uses Caladiums are invaluable for summer color in shady beds and borders, especially in warm- and hot-summer areas with long growing seasons. Grow them in containers to add a tropical touch to decks, porches and patios.

SITE AND CLIMATE
Full sun to partial shade; sandy, well-drained loam. Zones 5–8.

HEIGHT
2½ feet (75 cm)

SPREAD
10 inches (25 cm)

FLOWERING TIME
Spring through early summer.

GLOBE LILY

TO COMBAT ATTACK ON GLOBE LILY BULBS BY RODENTS AND OTHER ANIMAL PESTS, IT HELPS TO USE ONLY UNSCENTED ORGANIC FERTILIZER. AVOID USING BONEMEAL, FISH MEAL OR FISH EMULSION.

Description This deciduous spring bulb has oval to lance-shaped, short to midlength green leaves. The upright, sometimes nodding flowers are cup-shaped and 1–2 inches (2.5–5 cm) long. They bloom in shades of pink, purple, red, white and yellow.

Growing guidelines Plant in the garden in autumn, spacing bulbs about 1–1½ feet (30–45 cm) apart and 3–5 inches (7.5–12.5 cm) deep. Keep the soil moist from autumn through spring, then let it go dry. Fertilize the first year in spring. Deadhead spent blooms and flower stalks regularly to promote a longer season of interest. Mulch base of plants to keep soil evenly moist. Lift the bulbs out in wet-summer areas and store in a dark, cool place in a net bag or woven cane basket. Propagate by offsets or seed.

Pest and disease prevention To prevent globe lily bulbs being eaten or dislodged by animal pests, plant them in underground, open-topped wire cages.

Landscape uses Globe lily makes a wonderful accent in beds and borders. It's good for cutting, too.

SITE AND CLIMATE
Full sun to partial shade; well-drained, sandy loam. Zones 5–8.

HEIGHT
2½ feet (75 cm)

SPREAD
10 inches (25 cm)

FLOWERING TIME
Spring to early summer.

MARIPOSA TULIP

MARIPOSA TULIP IS ALSO COMMONLY KNOWN AS STAR TULIP BECAUSE OF ITS UNUSUAL STARLIKE FLOWERS. THESE ATTRACTIVE BLOOMS HAVE MADE THIS PLANT AN OLD FAVORITE WITH BULB FANCIERS.

Description Mariposa tulip is a deciduous spring bulb with oval to lance-shaped, midlength green leaves. The stunning, upright flowers are about 1–2 inches (2.5–5 cm) long and bloom in shades of purple, lilac and yellow.

Growing guidelines Plant in autumn; space bulbs about 1–1½ feet (30–45 cm) apart and 3–5 inches (7.5–12.5 cm) deep. In container plantings, space 1 inch (3.5 cm) apart and 2–3 inches (5–7.5 cm) deep. Keep the soil evenly moist from autumn to spring, but let it dry out in summer. Fertilize the first year in spring and deadhead spent blooms and flower stalks regularly. Propagate by offsets or seed.

Pest and disease prevention To avoid having them eaten or dislodged by rodents, plant the bulbs in containers or in underground wire cages, which keep burrowing animal pests out.

Landscape uses Mariposa tulip makes an interesting and attractive accent in rock and container gardens. Plant some as an addition to the cutting garden, too, for use in fresh arrangements.

SITE AND CLIMATE
Full sun to partial shade; humus-rich, moist (but not waterlogged) soil. Zones 5–9.

HEIGHT
1–1½ feet (30–45 cm)

SPREAD
1½ feet (45 cm)

FLOWERING TIME
Late spring.

BLUE CAMASS

ALL CAMASS SPECIES ARE POISONOUS, SO MAKE SURE THAT YOU DON'T PLANT IT IN CHILDREN'S PLAY AREAS, OR NEAR YOUR PET'S FAVORITE SPOT IN THE GARDEN.

Description Blue camass is a deciduous spring bulb with narrow, strap-shaped, long, midgreen leaves. Multiple, star-shaped, lightly fragrant 1–2-inch (2.5–5-cm) wide flowers bloom in rows vertically along the upright stalks.

Growing guidelines Plant bulbs in early autumn, spacing them about 6–10 inches (15–25 cm) apart and 4–6 inches (10–15 cm) deep. These bulbs are relatively easy to care for, just keep the soil moist from spring through early autumn. Fertilize in spring. Propagate by division or seed. It's not necessary to lift and store blue camass bulbs after their season; they are best left undisturbed.

Pest and disease prevention Avoid animal pest damage by planting the bulbs in underground wire cages. When naturalizing, use unscented fertilizers; avoid using bonemeal or fish emulsion.

Landscape uses These plants are a natural choice for making a groundcover in meadow and woodland gardens because they naturalize. They also look good in mixed bed and border plantings. Keep a few in the cutting garden for use in fresh arrangements.

Camassia quamash HYACINTHACEAE

SITE AND CLIMATE
Full sun to partial shade; moist, but not waterlogged, soil. Zones 4–8.

HEIGHT
2–2½ feet (60–75 cm)

SPREAD
1 foot (30 cm)

FLOWERING TIME
Late spring.

COMMON CAMASS

IN FULL SUN, STEADY SOIL MOISTURE IS CRITICAL FOR GROWING COMMON CAMASS SUCCESSFULLY. IN LIGHTLY SHADED SPOTS, THE BULBS CAN TAKE DRIER CONDITIONS.

Description Grassy clumps send up leafless stems topped with dense, spiky flower clusters. These spikes are made up of many 1–2-inch (2.5–5-cm) wide, starry flowers in white, or pale to deep blue.

Growing guidelines These bulbs usually aren't available for sale at garden centers, so you'll probably have to buy them from a mail-order source. Plant the bulbs in autumn, in individual holes or in larger planting areas dug about 4 inches (10 cm) deep. Space the bulbs about 8–10 inches (20–25 cm) apart. Cut down faded flower stems after bloom for appearance.

Pest and disease prevention
Common camass is susceptible to attack from rodents. Try planting the bulbs in open-top, underground wire cages.

Landscape uses Plant common camass in low spots, along streams and ponds, or with moisture-loving shrubs and perennials.

SITE AND CLIMATE
Full sun to partial shade; average to moist, well-drained soil with added organic matter. Usually hardy in Zones 8–10; elsewhere, grown as annuals or stored indoors in winter.

HEIGHT
2–6 feet (60–180 cm)

SPREAD
1–2 feet (30–60 cm)

FLOWERING TIME
Mid- through late summer.

CANNA

CANNAS ARE DROUGHT TOLERANT, BUT THEY GROW EVEN BETTER WITH MULCHING AND WATERING DURING DRY SPELLS. PINCH OFF SPENT FLOWERS TO PROLONG BLOOM.

Description Cannas grow from thick rhizomes. They produce tall, sturdy stems with large, oval, green or reddish purple leaves from spring until frost. The stems are topped with showy clusters of broad-petaled flowers up to 5 inches (12.5 cm) across. The flowers bloom in shades of pink, red, orange and yellow, as well as bicolors.

Growing guidelines For the earliest show, start rhizomes indoors in pots about 1 month before your last frost date. Set out started plants 2–3 weeks after your last frost date. Or plant rhizomes directly into the garden around that time, setting them 3–4 inches (7.5–10 cm) deep and 1–1½ feet (30–45 cm) apart. North of Zone 8 (and in Zone 8, if you want to ensure survival), dig up the rhizomes before or just after the first frost and store them indoors for winter. In warm areas, divide the rhizomes every 3–4 years in spring.

Pest and disease prevention No specific problems.

Landscape uses Grow them alone in masses, or plant them with annuals and perennials in beds and borders. Cannas also grow well in containers.

SITE AND CLIMATE
Part shade; rich, moist, well-drained soil with added organic matter. Zones 6–8.

HEIGHT
Up to 1 foot (30 cm)

SPREAD
2 feet (60 cm)

FLOWERING TIME
Late summer.

HIMALAYAN LILY

AN UNDERSTORY PLANT OF THE MOIST AND HUMID BUT COOL MOUNTAIN WOODLANDS OF THE HIMALAYAS, HIMALAYAN LILY TAKES AT LEAST 5 YEARS TO FLOWER FROM SEED. AFTER BLOOM, THE PLANT DIES, BUT NOT BEFORE PRODUCING MANY OFFSETS.

Description Himalayan lily grows from a basal rosette of leaves from which tall, upright stems emerge each year. The stems grow through summer then die back before winter. Each year the stems become taller. The stunning flowers are trumpet shaped and lightly fragrant.

Growing guidelines Plant the bulbs in late autumn, winter or early spring. The tops of the bulbs should sit at soil level. If possible, buy bulbs of various sizes and ages in order to get flowers over successive years. Keep soil evenly moist. After bloom, lift the clump, discard the parent bulb and replant the offsets, about 3 feet (90 cm) apart.

Pest and disease prevention Aphids, slugs, snails and thrips are often a problem. Bait snails and slugs with shallow pans of beer at soil level. Use insecticidal soap or systemic insecticide to fight aphids and thrips.

Landscape uses Himalayan lily is striking and showy when naturalized through a woodland garden. Always plant it where the light is filtered during the hottest part of the day.

Chionodoxa luciliae HYACINTHACEAE

SITE AND CLIMATE
Full sun to partial shade; moist, well-drained, average garden soil.
Zones 5–8.

HEIGHT
3–6 inches (7.5–15 cm)

SPREAD
8 inches (20 cm)

FLOWERING TIME
Early spring to summer.

GLORY-OF-THE-SNOW

ELEGANT GLORY-OF-THE-SNOW IS AN ENDANGERED SPECIES, WHICH MAKES IT AN ATTRACTIVE OPTION—YOU CAN ENJOY ITS BEAUTY WHILE ALSO PROTECTING AND PROPAGATING IT FOR FUTURE GARDEN LOVERS.

Description Glory-of-the-snow is a deciduous spring bulb with narrow, short, dark green leaves. The multiple, six-pointed, star-shaped, 1-inch (2.5-cm) wide flowers bloom in blue, pink or white, with white centers. The flower heads appear in rows vertically along the stalk, with about six to 10 flowers per stalk.

Growing guidelines Plant in autumn, spacing bulbs about 2 inches (5 cm) apart and 4 inches (10 cm) deep. Fertilize until buds form on flower stalks. Keep the soil quite moist throughout autumn and spring and damp in summer. Mulch at the base of the plant to retain soil moisture (especially in Zones 7–8), and to protect against frost in cooler areas.

Pest and disease prevention This bulb is susceptible to animal pest damage, so plant it in open-top, underground wire cages and use only unscented fertilizers; avoid bonemeal, fish meal or fish emulsion.

Landscape uses Enjoy the cheerful flowers of glory-of-the-snow in mixed borders and cottage and container gardens, or naturalized in woodland and meadow gardens.

SITE AND CLIMATE
Full sun to partial shade; average, well-drained soil. Zones 4–9.

HEIGHT
Leaves to about 8 inches (20 cm); flowers to 4–6 inches (10–15 cm).

SPREAD
6 inches (15 cm)

FLOWERING TIME
Late summer through early autumn.

SHOWY AUTUMN CROCUS

SHOWY AUTUMN CROCUS GROWS FROM LARGE, PLUMP CORMS. ONCE ESTABLISHED, EACH CORM WILL PRODUCE A PROFUSION OF ROSY PINK FLOWERS.

Description Wide, flat, glossy green leaves emerge in late autumn or early spring, elongate through spring, then turn yellow and die to the ground in early summer. Rosy pink, 4-inch (10-cm) wide, goblet-shaped, stemless flowers rise directly from the ground.

Growing guidelines Plant corms in mid- to late summer, as soon as they are available; they may begin to bloom even before you plant them if you delay. Set the corms in individual holes or in larger planting areas dug about 4 inches (10 cm) deep. Space corms 6 inches (15 cm) apart. Propagate by division after the leaves have died down.

Pest and disease prevention Plant corms in open-top, underground cages to protect against animal pest damage. Avoid using scented fertilizers, such as bonemeal.

Landscape uses Showy autumn crocus is beautiful but a little tricky to site effectively. It's usually best coming up through low groundcovers or under shrubs, where the coarse spring leaves won't detract from or smother other flowers.

SITE AND CLIMATE
Full sun; moist, humus-rich soil. Zones 7–10.

HEIGHT
2–3 feet (60–90 cm)

SPREAD
1–2 feet (30–60 cm)

FLOWERING TIME
Summer and early autumn; varies with individual cultivars.

CROCOSMIA

CROCOSMIA IS A BRIGHTLY COLORED PERENNIAL WITH VIVID RED OR ORANGE SUMMER FLOWERS AND FANS OF SWORDLIKE LEAVES THAT RESEMBLE GLADIOLUS. THEY GROW FROM BUTTON-LIKE CORMS.

Description Tubular orange or red flowers are carried on erect, sparsely branched, zigzagging stems. The flowers form tiers vertically along one side of angled, branching spikes.

Growing guidelines Easy-care crocosmias spread to form broad clumps of tightly packed foliage fans. Plant in spring, spacing 4–6 inches (10–15 cm) apart and 2–4 inches (5–10 cm) deep. Fertilize in spring. Remove spent stalks after flowering. Divide overgrown clumps in spring. If you store corms over winter, replant them when temperatures become moderate again. Store them in a dark, cool (but not cold) place in a net bag or open basket of dry peat moss. Propagate by offsets or seed.

Pest and disease prevention Spider mites and thrips cause white or brown stippling or streaks on the leaves. Spray with insecticidal soap or a botanical insecticide, such as pyrethrin. Cut damaged plants to the ground and destroy infested portions.

Landscape uses Use crocosmia as an accent along walls with shrubs, or in mixed perennial plantings.

Crocus chrysanthus

IRIDACEAE

SITE AND CLIMATE
Full sun to partial shade; moist, average, well-drained soil. Zones 4–8.

HEIGHT
3–6 inches (7.5–15 cm)

SPREAD
6 inches (15 cm)

FLOWERING TIME
Late winter to early spring.

SNOW CROCUS

THE DELICATE BLOOMS OF SNOW CROCUS ARE SINGLE, WHITE AND CUP-SHAPED, GIVING THEM A VERY SIMILAR APPEARANCE TO THE WHITE STRAINS OF DUTCH CROCUS.

Description Snow crocus is a deciduous spring corm with short, grasslike, dark green leaves. The 1½–3-inch (3.5–7.5-cm) long flowers appear to be stemless, arising directly from soil level. The flowers are sometimes lightly scented.

Growing guidelines Plant in autumn, spacing corms about 1–3 inches (2.5–7.5 cm) apart and 3–5 inches (7.5–12.5 cm) deep. Keep the soil moist; mulch in warmer areas or windy sites. Fertilize when shoots appear. Propagate by division in autumn. It's best to transplant container plants into the garden for bloom the following year. Divide corms if they become overcrowded.

Pest and disease prevention Watch out for rodents and animal pests; plant in pots or in underground wire cages to discourage damage or dislocation of the corms. Avoid using scented fertilizers.

Landscape uses Snow crocus looks great in most garden situations. Plant it in beds or as an edging. It works especially well mass planted in cottage, meadow and woodland gardens. You can also enjoy snow crocus in containers during the first season of bloom.

SITE AND CLIMATE
Full sun; average, well-drained soil. Zones 5–9.

HEIGHT
Leaves to 6 inches (15 cm); flowers to 4–6 inches (10–15 cm).

SPREAD
2 inches (5 cm)

FLOWERING TIME
Early to mid-autumn; the plants go dormant by midsummer.

SHOWY CROCUS

IF YOU GROW SHOWY CROCUS IN LAWN AREAS, WAIT UNTIL THE LEAVES TURN YELLOW TO START MOWING IN SUMMER, AND STOP MOWING IN EARLY AUTUMN—AS SOON AS THE FIRST FLOWER BUDS APPEAR.

Description Showy crocus grows from a small corm. Thin, green, grasslike leaves with a white center stripe rise in spring, grow and go dormant by midsummer. The goblet-shaped, 1–2-inch (2.5–5-cm) wide blooms are usually lavender-purple with violet-purple veins.

Growing guidelines Plant in late summer, as soon as they are available. Set corms in individual holes or larger planting areas dug about 3 inches (7.5 cm) deep. Space the corms 4–6 inches (10–15 cm) apart. Established clumps of showy crocus will spread and reseed to cover large areas. Propagate by division in autumn. Divide only when they are too crowded.

Pest and disease prevention Discourage animal pests by planting in open-top, underground cages; avoid using scented fertilizers.

Landscape uses Looks charming popping out of low groundcovers, such as English ivy *Hedera helix* or common periwinkle *Vinca minor*. It's also excellent for naturalizing in low-maintenance areas.

Site and climate
Full sun to partial shade (under deciduous trees and shrubs); average, well-drained soil. Zones 3–8.

Height
Leaves to 8 inches (20 cm); flowers to 4 inches (10 cm).

Spread
1–3 inches (2.5–7.5 cm)

Flowering time
Late winter to early spring.

Dutch crocus

Dutch crocus are a welcome sight after a long, cold winter. After bloom, the leaves continue to elongate until they ripen and die back to the ground in early summer.

Description Dutch crocus grow from small corms. The leaves and flowers appear at the same time. Grasslike leaves are thin and green with a white center stripe. Goblet-shaped, stemless flowers up to 3 inches (7.5 cm) across bloom just above the leaves. The flowers are white, lilac, purple or yellow; they may also be striped with contrasting colors.

Growing guidelines Plant the corms in autumn, pointed side up, in individual holes or larger planting areas dug 2–4 inches (5–10 cm) deep. Space the corms 2 inches (5 cm) apart. Dutch crocus usually return year after year and spread to form showy clumps.

Pest and disease prevention Interplanting crocus corms with daffodil bulbs (which are toxic if eaten) may help discourage damage from mice.

Landscape uses Plant in beds and borders for early color. Grow them in containers for outdoor spring bloom or winter forcing indoors. They are excellent for naturalizing in lawn if you can wait until late spring (when the leaves have yellowed) before you start mowing.

SITE AND CLIMATE
Partial shade; average, well-drained soil. Zones 5–9.

HEIGHT
4–6 inches (10–15 cm)

SPREAD
4–6 inches (10–15 cm)

FLOWERING TIME
Early autumn.

HARDY CYCLAMEN

HARDY CYCLAMEN GROW WELL UNDER SHRUBS AND TREES—EVEN IN DRY SUMMER SHADE—AND ARE ATTRACTIVE THROUGH MOST OF THE YEAR. TOP-DRESS WITH A THIN LAYER OF COMPOST IN LATE SUMMER.

Description Hardy cyclamen grow from smooth tubers. The leafless flower stalks are topped with pink or white flowers. The 1-inch (2.5-cm) long, nodding flowers have upward-pointing petals. Heart-shaped, silver-marked, green leaves emerge shortly after the blooms finish. The leaves die back by midsummer but return again by midautumn.

Growing guidelines Buy only nursery-propagated tubers or start your own from seed. (Some commercial cyclamen sellers will try to sell wild-collected tubers; avoid supporting this irresponsible practice.) Set plants into the garden in spring or summer. Or plant dormant tubers shallowly in summer, with the smooth, unmarked side toward the bottom. The top of the tuber should be about 1 inch (2.5 cm) below the soil surface. Space tubers 6 inches (15 cm) apart.

Pest and disease prevention No specific problems.

Landscape uses Hardy cyclamen look good in shady spots with ferns and hellebores *Helleborus* spp.

DAHLIA

PINCH OFF STEM TIPS IN EARLY SUMMER TO PROMOTE BUSHY GROWTH AND MORE (BUT SMALLER) FLOWERS. OR, TO GET THE LARGEST FLOWERS, PINCH OFF SIDESHOOTS TO LEAVE ONE OR TWO MAIN STEMS.

Description Dahlias grow from long, slender, tuberous roots. Some types, known as bedding dahlias, form compact, bushy plants; others produce the tall, large-flowered border favorites. Both types have upright stems with divided, green (or sometimes purple-tinted) leaves. Dahlia flowers are 1–8 inches (2.5–20 cm) wide and come in almost every color but true blue—even in near black and bicolors. The flowers are available in many different forms, including spiky-petaled cactus types, daisy-like singles, puffy-centered anemone types and globe-shaped ball and pompon types.

Growing guidelines Start bedding types from seed sown indoors 6–8 weeks before your last frost date. Plant seed ⅛ inch (3 mm) deep. Set plants out in the garden 1–2 weeks after your last frost date; space them 10–12 inches (25–30 cm) apart. In cooler areas, start tuberous roots indoors in large pots 2–3 weeks before your last frost date; set started plants out 1–2 weeks after the last frost date. Elsewhere, plant the roots directly into the garden

There are endless dahlia cultivars to choose from.

SITE AND CLIMATE
Full sun; average, well-drained soil. Hardy in Zones 9 and 10; elsewhere, grown as annuals or stored indoors for winter.

HEIGHT
From 1 foot (30 cm) for bedding types to 5 feet (1.5 m) for border types.

SPREAD
1–4 feet (30–120 cm)

FLOWERING TIME
Midsummer through autumn.

around the last frost date. Dig a hole about 6 inches (15 cm) deep and set in the roots, so the purplish eyes are 2–4 inches (5–10 cm) below the soil surface. When planting tall border dahlias, also insert a stake at planting time to avoid damaging the roots later on. Mulch in summer and water during dry spells. Cut or pinch off spent flowers regularly to prolong the bloom season. Border dahlias can stay in the ground all winter in areas that are generally frost-free. With a thick layer of mulch, they often overwinter in Zone 8 gardens, too (although you may want to dig up your favorites in autumn for indoor storage). In Zones 7 and cooler, treat dahlias as annuals (buy new roots or start new plants from seed each spring). Or dig up the roots in autumn, before or just after the first frost, and store them indoors in a cool but frost-free area. Before replanting in spring, divide the root clumps in half or thirds, making sure each section has some of the stem attached.

Pest and disease prevention Dahlias are susceptible to both animal and insect pests. Watch closely for signs of damage and treat accordingly.

Landscape uses Plant dahlias in beds and borders and in the cutting garden. They make a great accent in cottage gardens, too.

SITE AND CLIMATE
Full sun to partial shade; moist, humus-rich, well-drained soil. Zones 5–8.

HEIGHT
2–6 inches (5–15 cm)

SPREAD
6–10 inches (15–25 cm)

FLOWERING TIME
Late winter to spring.

WINTER ACONITE

WINTER ACONITE IS A NATURAL CHOICE FOR WOODLAND AND MEADOW GARDENS BECAUSE IT NATURALIZES. THE SUNNY YELLOW BLOOMS ALSO THRIVE IN SHADE GARDENS.

Description Winter aconite grows from a spring tuber. It has radiating, slightly upturned, short, bright green leaves and cheerful bright yellow, cup-shaped flowers with a waxy surface. The flowers are 1–1½ inches (2.5–3.5 cm) wide and bloom directly above a collar of foliage.

Growing guidelines Plant the tubers in autumn, spacing them about 2½–3 inches (6–7.5 cm) apart and 2 inches (5 cm) deep. Keep the soil moist year-round, but water a little less after bloom. Fertilize the plants in winter when the shoots first start coming up. Mulch around the base of the plant to keep the soil evenly moist. Propagate by division or seed.

Pest and disease prevention No specific problems.

Landscape uses Plant winter aconite in beds and borders or container gardens. It also looks at home in rock gardens or informal designs, such as cottage gardens.

SITE AND CLIMATE
Bright to filtered shade; moist, rich, well-drained soil. Zones 5–9.

HEIGHT
4–12 inches (10–30 cm)

SPREAD
6–10 inches (15–25 cm)

FLOWERING TIME
Spring.

DOG-TOOTH VIOLET

DOG-TOOTH VIOLET IS A FAIRLY RELIABLE SELF-SEEDER, SO IT'S AN OBVIOUS CHOICE FOR NATURALIZING. PLANT IT IN MASSES AND YOU'LL ENJOY A CARPET OF BLOOMS EACH SPRING FROM YEAR TO YEAR.

Description Dog-tooth violet is a spring corm. Each plant has two tongue-shaped, short to midlength green leaves. The 2-inch (5-cm), star-shaped, nodding flowers appear singly on each stem and bloom in pink, purple, rose and white, and sometimes in contrasting colors.

Growing guidelines Plant in early autumn, spacing corms about 6–8 inches (15–20 cm) apart and 3–4 inches (7.5–10 cm) deep. Keep the soil evenly moist throughout the growing season. Fertilize once in spring and mulch to maintain soil moisture. Propagate by division. The bulbs are best left undisturbed.

Pest and disease prevention No specific problems.

Landscape uses Dog-tooth violet works well in bed and border plantings and in rock, shade and woodland gardens in drifts or mixed plantings. Try some in containers, too.

Site and climate
Full sun or part shade; average, well-drained soil. Zones 6–9.

Height
1 foot (30 cm)

Spread
10 inches (25 cm)

Flowering time
Late winter to early spring.

Sierra fawn lily

Easy-to-grow Sierra fawn lily hails from California's Sierra Nevada ranges. It is one of the lesser known but nonetheless beautiful species of lily.

Description Sierra fawn lily has the unusual habit of producing creeping stems, or stolons. The attractive mottled leaves are highlighted by cream flowers with yellow blotches.

Growing guidelines Plant early in autumn, about 3 inches (7.5 cm) deep. A position that affords a little shade during the hottest part of the day is best, but where summers are mild, full sun is fine. When growth appears in spring, water plants freely but ease off as summer approaches and the plants begin to die back. Apply a thin layer of soil-improving mulch during the growing season. Allow the soil to dry out completely when the leaves turn yellow. Lift and divide the bulbs before the leaves have withered completely. Don't store bulb divisions; replant immediately.

Pest and disease prevention No specific problems.

Landscape uses Grow Sierra fawn lily in pots or massed in the garden. Excellent choice for naturalizing in an open, partly shaded garden. Try planting them in rows in formal flower beds and borders, too.

Fritillaria imperialis LILIACEAE

SITE AND CLIMATE
Full sun; average to sandy, well-drained soil. Zones 5–9.

HEIGHT
2–4 feet (60–120 cm)

SPREAD
1 foot (30 cm)

FLOWERING TIME
Mid- to late spring.

CROWN IMPERIAL

CROWN IMPERIAL MAY TAKE A FEW SEASONS TO ESTABLISH AND BLOOM WELL; MATURE CLUMPS CAN LIVE FOR MANY YEARS. ALL PARTS OF THE PLANT HAVE A MUSKY ODOR.

Description Sturdy shoots of green stems and glossy green leaves emerge from the large, fleshy bulb in early spring and elongate for several weeks. The tall stems are topped with a tuft of green leaves and hanging, bell-shaped, yellow, orange or red flowers about 2 inches (5 cm) long.

Growing guidelines Plant the bulbs in late summer or early autumn. Dig a large hole for each bulb or prepare a generous planting area; make either about 8 inches (20 cm) deep. Loosen the soil at the base of the hole to promote good drainage. When you set the bulb in the hole, tilt it slightly to one side to discourage water from collecting in the depression at the top of the bulb. Space bulbs 1 foot (30 cm) apart. Propagate by division. Soon after bloom, the leaves and stems turn yellow; they die back to the ground by midsummer.

Pest and disease prevention No specific problems.

Landscape uses Plant it at the back of beds and borders for a striking spring accent.

SITE AND CLIMATE
Partial shade; average, well-drained soil. Zones 6–8.

HEIGHT
1 foot (30 cm)

SPREAD
2–4 inches (5–10 cm)

FLOWERING TIME
Midspring.

CHECKERED LILY

THE NODDING FLOWERS OF CHECKERED LILIES ADD A LOVELY TOUCH TO SPRING GARDENS. NATURALIZE THEM IN WILD AREAS, OR PLANT THEM IN CLUMPS IN BEDS AND BORDERS.

Description Slender, arching stems with narrow, gray-green leaves rise in early spring. By midspring, broad, nodding, bell-like blooms dangle from the ends of the nodding stems. The 1–2-inch (2.5–5-cm) long flowers range in color from white to deep purple; many are marked with a checkered pattern. These plants die back to the ground by midsummer.

Growing guidelines Plant in early autumn, as soon as the bulbs are available. Dig the holes or planting areas 2–3 inches (5–7.5 cm) deep. Space bulbs 4–6 inches (10–15 cm) apart. Fertilize during flowering season. Leave established clumps undisturbed to form large sweeps of spring color. Propagate by offsets.

Pest and disease prevention No specific problems.

Landscape uses Checkered lilies look lovely when naturalized in masses in woodland or meadow gardens. Or grow them in beds and borders under deciduous trees; these small bulbs combine well with ferns and hellebores *Helleborus* spp.

Galanthus nivalis

AMARYLLIDACEAE

SITE AND CLIMATE
Full sun to partial shade; average to moist, well-drained soil with added organic matter. Zones 3–9.

HEIGHT
6 inches (15 cm)

SPREAD
2–3 inches (5–7.5 cm)

FLOWERING TIME
Late winter or early spring.

COMMON SNOWDROP

COMMON SNOWDROPS ARE AMONG THE EARLIEST FLOWERS TO BLOOM IN THE SPRING GARDEN. ESTABLISHED BULBS ARE TROUBLE-FREE; THEY WILL SPREAD AND RESEED FREELY.

Description Common snowdrops grow from small bulbs. Each bulb produces two or three flat, narrow, green leaves. Dainty, drop-shaped, nodding flowers to 1 inch (2.5 cm) long bloom at the tips of arching, green flower stems. The single or double flowers are white; each of the shorter, inner petals has a green tip. Plants die back to the ground by early summer.

Growing guidelines Plant bulbs in autumn. Set them in individual holes or larger planting areas dug 3–4 inches (7.5–10 cm) deep. Space bulbs 3–4 inches (7.5–10 cm) apart. Keep the soil evenly moist. Fertilize in spring. Propagate by division during dormant period.

Pest and disease prevention No specific problems.

Landscape uses Grow clumps of common snowdrop in the garden with other early flowers, such as snow crocus and Christmas rose *Helleborus niger*. Or naturalize them in lawns, groundcovers and low-maintenance areas, or under deciduous trees and shrubs. (If you grow them in lawns, you'll have to wait until the leaves have turned yellow or brown to mow.)

Gladiolus x *hortulanus* IRIDACEAE

SITE AND CLIMATE
Full sun; average, well-drained soil. Usually hardy in Zones 7–10; elsewhere, grown as annuals or stored indoors for winter.

HEIGHT
2–5 feet (60–150 cm)

SPREAD
6–12 inches (15–30 cm)

FLOWERING TIME
Summer to early autumn (depending on planting time).

GLADIOLUS

GLADIOLI BLOOM IN NEARLY EVERY COLOR BUT TRUE BLUE; MANY ALSO HAVE SPOTS OR SPLASHES OF CONTRASTING COLORS.

Description Gladioli grow from flattened corms. They produce tall fans of flat, sword-shaped, green leaves. A slender flower stem rises from the center of each fan. The flower stem is topped with a many-budded spike that blooms from the bottom up. The buds produce open, funnel-shaped flowers up to 4 inches (10 cm) across. The leaves yellow several weeks after bloom.

Growing guidelines Start planting the corms outdoors after the last frost date in spring. Set them in individual holes or larger planting areas dug 4–6 inches (10–15 cm) deep. Space the corms 4–6 inches (10–15 cm) apart. To extend the bloom season, plant more corms every 2 weeks until midsummer. Tall-flowering types benefit from staking. In Zone 7 and colder areas, dig the corms before or just after the first frost, and store them in a net bag or an open basket in a cool, dark place.

Pest and disease prevention Spray spider mites and thrips with insecticidal soap, as necessary.

Landscape uses The spiky blooms add excitement to the middle and back of beds and borders. They are also a must for the cutting garden.

Habranthus robustus

AMARYLLIDACEAE

SITE AND CLIMATE
Full sun to partial shade; moist, average, well-drained soil. Zones 9–11.

HEIGHT
10 inches (25 cm)

SPREAD
8 inches (20 cm)

FLOWERING TIME
Summer; may bloom again in autumn.

PAMPAS LILY

BY PLANTING WARMTH-LOVING PAMPAS LILY IN A CONTAINER, YOU CAN MOVE IT AROUND TO TAKE FULL ADVANTAGE OF THE WARMEST PARTS OF YOUR GARDEN OR PATIO.

Description Pampas lily is a tropical plant that grows from a bulb. The midlength green leaves are narrow and strap-shaped. Copper, pink, purple, red or white multiple, trumpet-shaped flowers bloom atop the flower stems. The flowers are 3 inches (7.5 cm) wide.

Growing guidelines Plant in spring, spacing bulbs about 3–6 inches (7.5–15 cm) apart and 1–2 inches (2.5–5 cm) deep. Keep the soil evenly moist (especially in late spring), but allow it to dry out somewhat after bloom. In Zones 9–11, start watering 4 weeks after the previous blooms finish to encourage repeat bloom. Fertilize plants during the growing season. Propagate by offsets or seed.

Pest and disease prevention No specific problems.

Landscape uses Plant pampas lily in beds, borders, containers and cottage gardens. It also works well in rock gardens and mixed plantings, or as an unusual edging.

Daylily

DAYLILIES ARE AMONG THE MOST POPULAR PERENNIALS. ALTHOUGH EACH FLOWER LASTS FOR ONLY ONE DAY, A PROFUSION OF NEW BUDS KEEPS THE PLANTS IN BLOOM FOR A MONTH OR MORE.

Description The colorful flowers of daylily consist of three petals and three narrower, petal-like sepals. The strap-shaped leaves have a central vein that forms a keel when viewed in cross section. The crowns increase from short sideshoots. Daylily flowers vary in color and form. The majority of the wild species are orange or yellow with wide petals and narrow, petal-like sepals. Modern hybrids come in a rainbow of colors with the exception of blues and true white. Many have blazes, eyes and blotches on the petals. Flower shape varies from traditional form to narrow-petaled, spider-like forms and fat, tubular or saucer-shaped flowers.

Growing guidelines Plant container-grown or bareroot plants in spring or autumn, placing the crowns just below the soil surface. Plants take a year to become established, then spread quickly to form dense clumps. Remove spent flowers regularly to keep the plants looking their best. If the leaves turn yellow, grasp them firmly and give a quick tug to remove them from the base. Lift overcrowded, sparse-flowering

To choose the color you want, buy daylilies that are in bloom.

SITE AND CLIMATE
Full sun to light shade; moist, average to rich, well-drained soil. Zones 3–10.

HEIGHT
1–5 feet (30–150 cm)

SPREAD
2–3 feet (60–90 cm)

FLOWERING TIME
Late spring through summer.

clumps and pull or cut the tangled crowns apart. Division is also the way to propagate named cultivars.

Pest and disease prevention
Although daylilies are usually pest-free, aphids and thrips may attack the foliage and flower buds. Wash off aphids with a stream of water or spray them with insecticidal soap or a botanical insecticide, such as pyrethrin. Thrips make small, white lines in the foliage and may deform flower buds if damage is severe. Spray with insecticidal soap or a botanical insecticide.

Landscape uses Daylilies are perfect for massed plantings. Use them in beds and borders, in meadow gardens and at the edge of a woodland with shrubs and trees. Try combining them with ornamental grasses and summer-blooming perennials. Or use them with fine-textured flowers, such as coral bells *Heuchera* spp., baby's breath *Gypsophila paniculata* and yarrows. Plant them with generous quantities of garden phlox *Phlox paniculata*, cranesbills *Geranium* spp., and daisies *Chrysanthemum* spp.

Hippeastrum

SPECTACULAR AND ASTONISHINGLY EASY TO BRING INTO BLOOM, HIPPEASTRUM MAKES A PERFECT WINTER GIFT PLANT. KEEP THE PLANT COOL WHEN IT IS IN BLOOM SO THAT THE FLOWERS WILL LAST LONGER.

Description Hippeastrum grows from a tropical bulb that can be deciduous or evergreen. The large bulb sends up a 2-foot (60-cm) tall, hollow bloom stalk, along with or slightly before the long, broad, arching, strap-shaped green leaves. One to 10 trumpet-shaped, single or double flowers bloom atop the stalk for up to a month. The flowers bloom in orange, pink, red and white and are sometimes lightly fragrant. Each bloom is about 5–10 inches (12.5–25 cm) wide. The bloom stalks can be single or double.

Growing guidelines Plant in autumn to winter. If you are planting directly into the garden, space bulbs about 1–2 feet (30–60 cm) apart and slightly above soil level. Keep the soil evenly moist from spring through autumn. If you are planting indoors or outdoors into a container, set the bulb in a well-drained, all-purpose potting mix. Choose a container that is about 1 inch (2.5 cm) wider than the bulb itself. Position the bulb in the pot so that the top quarter is sticking out of the soil. Fertilize twice a month until buds form. Deadhead flowers

Bring outdoor pots inside in spring for a longer bloom time.

SITE AND CLIMATE
Full sun; rich, well-drained soil. Zones 7–11.

HEIGHT
8–24 inches (20–60 cm)

SPREAD
1–1½ feet (30–45 cm)

FLOWERING TIME
Winter to spring in outdoor gardens; spring to summer indoors.

and withered stalks regularly, for appearance. Lightly mulch around the base of the plant with compost. Propagate by offsets or seed. Allow the bulbs to dry out and cure for a month before storing. Store deciduous bulbs in a cool, dark place in a net bag or open basket. Store evergreen bulbs in a cool, dark place in a porous container, such as a terracotta pot, lined with dampened peat moss.

Pest and disease prevention Hippeastrum is susceptible to damage from rodents and other animal pests. In container gardens this won't be a problem, but if you're planting the bulbs into a garden bed, consider doing so in an open-top, underground cage. Also, avoid using scented fertilizers such as bonemeal, fish meal or fish emulsion.

Landscape uses Hippeastrum is an obvious choice for indoor or outdoor container gardens. Try growing a collection of different cultivars together, or positioning single plants with other flowering bulbs. They make a great accent in beds and borders, as well as in tropical gardens. Grow extras in beds and borders for cutting—they make beautiful fresh arrangements.

SITE AND CLIMATE
Full sun to partial shade; well-drained soil with added organic matter. Zones 4–8.

HEIGHT
Flowers 1–1½ feet (30–45 cm); leaves to 8 inches (20 cm).

SPREAD
6–10 inches (15–25 cm)

FLOWERING TIME
Late spring.

SPANISH BLUEBELL

ESTABLISHED PATCHES OF SPANISH BLUEBELLS INCREASE QUICKLY, OFTEN TO THE POINT OF BECOMING INVASIVE. REMOVING SPENT FLOWER STALKS WILL MINIMIZE RESEEDING; MOW UNWANTED PLANTS.

Description Spanish bluebells grow from small bulbs. In spring, the plants form clumps of sprawling, strap-shaped, green leaves. Upright, leafless flower stems topped with spikes of many bell-shaped blooms appear in late spring. The ¾-inch (18-mm) wide flowers bloom in white, pink or shades of purple-blue. The flowers are fragrant. Plants go dormant by midsummer. Spanish bluebells are still sold under a variety of former names, including *Scilla campanulata*, *S. hispanica* and *Endymion hispanicus*.

Growing guidelines Plant the bulbs in autumn, setting them in individual holes or larger planting areas dug 3–4 inches (7.5–10 cm) deep. Space each bulb 6–8 inches (15–20 cm) apart. Propagate by offsets or division. Divide only when overcrowded.

Pest and disease prevention No specific problems.

Landscape uses Include clumps in beds and borders, combine them with groundcovers or naturalize Spanish bluebells in woodlands and low-maintenance areas.

SITE AND CLIMATE
Full sun to partial shade; well-drained to moist soil. Zones 4–8.

HEIGHT
1⅔ feet (50 cm)

SPREAD
6–10 inches (15–25 cm)

FLOWERING TIME
Spring.

ENGLISH BLUEBELL

THE DELICATE AND FRAGRANT FLOWERS OF ENGLISH BLUEBELLS LOOK MOST AT HOME IN A COTTAGE GARDEN, OR NATURALIZED IN WOODLAND OR MEADOW GARDENS.

Description English bluebells are deciduous spring bulbs with slender, arching, long green leaves. The blue, rose, pink or white bell-shaped flowers are about ¾ inch (18 mm) long, and are borne in vertical layers along a single stalk.

Growing guidelines Plant bulbs in autumn, spacing them about 6–8 inches (15–20 cm) apart and 3–5 inches (7.5–12.5 cm) deep. Keep the soil evenly moist from winter through spring, and damp in summer. Fertilize only when flower buds form. Mulch in Zones 4–6 to protect against frost. Propagate by offsets or division. Divide only when overcrowding is a problem.

Pest and disease prevention No specific problems.

Landscape uses English bluebells look wonderful planted in drifts, or as part of mixed, informal plantings. Keep some in the cutting garden or plant extras in beds and borders for use in fresh arrangements.

Hyacinth

After the first year, hyacinth bloom spikes tend to become smaller; in some cases, they may not flower at all. Plant new hyacinth bulbs every year or two to ensure a good display.

Description Hyacinths grow from plump bulbs. Sturdy shoots with wide, curved-edged, strap-shaped, green leaves and upright flower stalks emerge in early spring. By midspring, each stalk is topped with a dense spike of starry, 1-inch (2.5-cm) wide, powerfully fragrant flowers. Each flower stalk bears the flower heads in close-fitting tiers, vertically along the stalk. The single or double flowers bloom in a wide range of colors, including white, pink, red, orange, yellow, blue and purple. Hyacinths go dormant in early summer.

Growing guidelines Plant the bulbs in autumn. Set them in individual holes or larger planting areas dug about 5–8 inches (12.5–20 cm) deep; space the bulbs about 6–8 inches (15–20 cm) apart. Keep the soil moist throughout spring. Fertilize until flower buds form. Mulch around the base of plants to protect against frost in cooler climates and to retain soil moisture in warmer climates. Double-flowered types may need staking. Remove spent flower stalks. Lift and divide the bulbs after the leaves

A single hyacinth bloom can scent a whole room.

SITE AND CLIMATE
Full sun; average, well-drained soil with added organic matter. Zones 4–8.

HEIGHT
8–12 inches (20–30 cm)

SPREAD
6–8 inches (15–20 cm)

FLOWERING TIME
Midspring.

have yellowed and died down. If you cut off, pull off or bundle the leaves together before they have withered naturally, the bulb won't be able to store the energy it needs, and it may bloom poorly or even die by the next year. Store dormant bulbs in a cool, dark place in a net bag or open basket of dry peat moss. Propagate by offsets.

Pest and disease prevention Watch out for slug and snail damage; set traps by placing shallow pans of beer set flush with the surface of the soil.

Landscape uses Cheerful and colorful hyacinths make a welcome contribution to spring flower beds and borders. Grow them in masses or as part of a mixed planting. Their compact shape and strong colors make them great companions for lots of other spring-flowering bulbs, as well as many early annuals. Try combining them with primroses *Primula* Polyanthus Group and pansies *Viola* x *wittrockiana* for extra excitement. The rich, velvety purples and the hot pinks also look striking with daffodils. Hyacinths grow well in containers and make a wonderful gift plant. Try potting up a few for friends, or enjoy an explosion of color in your own container garden, whether it's indoors or outdoors, by growing masses of colors together.

Ipheion uniflorum

ALLIACEAE

SITE AND CLIMATE
Full sun to partial shade; fertile, well-drained soil. Zones 6–10.

HEIGHT
6–8 inches (15–20 cm)

SPREAD
4 inches (10 cm)

FLOWERING TIME
Early spring.

STARFLOWER

STARFLOWER LOOKS BEAUTIFUL IN FORMAL AND INFORMAL GARDEN DESIGNS. TRY NATURALIZING IT IN WOODLAND GARDENS, OR PLANTING IT IN A COLOR-THEME BORDER WITH EARLY-FLOWERING ANNUALS.

Description Starflower grows from a deciduous bulb. The flat, strap-shaped, midlength green leaves have a slightly oniony scent. The pretty star-shaped flowers are about 1 inch (2.5 cm) wide and bloom in shades of blue or white. There are many cultivars available, with variations in bloom size and color.

Growing guidelines Plant bulbs in autumn, spacing 2–4 inches (5–10 cm) apart and about 2 inches (5 cm) deep. Keep the soil moist from autumn through spring. Fertilize during the growing season until the plants are established. Propagate by division or offsets; divide when crowded. Store dormant bulbs in a cool, dark place in a net bag or a basket lined with dry peat moss.

Pest and disease prevention No specific problems.

Landscape uses Starflower looks attractive in most garden situations. Plant it in beds, borders, drifts, edgings, rock gardens or massed in a meadow garden. It also thrives in containers.

Iris bearded hybrids

SITE AND CLIMATE
Full sun or partial shade; evenly moist, average to humus-rich soil. Zones 3–9.

HEIGHT
1–3 feet (30–90 cm)

SPREAD
1–2 feet (30–60 cm)

FLOWERING TIME
Late spring and early summer; some cultivars rebloom.

BEARDED IRIS

BEARDED IRISES LOOK WONDERFUL IN MOST GARDEN DESIGNS, WHETHER FORMAL OR INFORMAL. PLANT THEM WITH PERENNIALS, ORNAMENTAL GRASSES AND SHRUBS FOR A REALLY STUNNING EFFECT.

Description Bearded irises produce broad fans of wide, flattened leaves and thick, flowering stems from fat, creeping rhizomes. The flowers have three segments, called falls, ringing the outside of each bloom. The falls usually hang downward and bear a fringed "beard." The center of the flower boasts three slender segments called standards. The elegant blooms range in color from white and yellow to blue, violet and purple.

Growing guidelines Set out bareroot irises in late summer or container-grown plants in spring, summer and autumn. Divide every 3–4 years in midsummer to late summer; replant with the top half of the rhizome above the soil line. Cut the foliage back by half. Remove dead foliage in spring and autumn.

Pest and disease prevention No specific problems.

Landscape uses Bearded irises are old-fashioned cottage garden favorites. Combine them with rounded perennials such as peonies, yarrows, pinks *Dianthus* spp., and cranesbills *Geranium* spp.

SITE AND CLIMATE
Partial to full shade (sites with a little sun will produce more blooms); moist, humus-rich soil. Zones 3–9.

HEIGHT
Flowers to 4 inches (10 cm); leaves 6–8 inches (15–20 cm).

SPREAD
3–4 inches (7.5–10 cm)

FLOWERING TIME
Early spring.

DWARF CRESTED IRIS

DWARF CRESTED IRISES ARE DELICATE WOODLAND WILDFLOWERS BELOVED FOR THEIR DIMINUTIVE STATURE, TIDY FOLIAGE AND EXUBERANT BLOOM. THEY FORM EXTENSIVE COLONIES WITH TIME.

Description The flattened, 2-inch (5-cm) wide flowers are blue with a white-and-yellow blaze. Plants grow from a wiry rhizome that creeps on the surface of the soil.

Growing guidelines Plant rhizomes in late summer or autumn. Space them about 1–2 feet (30–60 cm) apart and 2–4 inches (5–10 cm) deep. Or cluster plants about 6 inches (15 cm) apart for a massed planting. Clumps may become so congested that plants bloom less. If this happens, lift them after blooming and tease the rhizomes apart. Replant into prepared soil with added organic matter. Store lifted rhizomes in a cool, dark place in a net bag or a basket lined with dry peat moss.

Pest and disease prevention Watch out for leaf damage as a result of slugs and other foliage feeders. Pick them off by hand or treat with a botanical insecticide, such as pyrethrin.

Landscape uses Plant dwarf crested iris in shade, woodland or rock gardens. Try them planted in masses under flowering shrubs or among the roots of mature trees.

Iris reticulata IRIDACEAE

SITE AND CLIMATE
Full sun to partial shade; average to rich, moist, well-drained soil. Zones 4–8.

HEIGHT
Reaches 3–5 inches (7.5–12.5 cm) in bloom; foliage may reach 1 foot (30 cm).

SPREAD
2–3 inches (5–7.5 cm)

FLOWERING TIME
Late winter and early spring.

Reticulated iris

RETICULATED IRISES RETURN YEAR AFTER YEAR TO GRACE YOUR GARDEN WITH THEIR DELICATE SPRING FLOWERS. TUCK THEM INTO BEDS, BORDERS AND ROCK GARDENS.

Description Reticulated irises grow from small bulbs. The dainty blue, purple or white flowers have three upright petals (known as standards) and three outward-arching petals (known as falls). The falls have gold and/or white markings. The grass-like, dark green leaves are short at bloom time but elongate after the flowers fade; they ripen and die back to the ground by early summer.

Growing guidelines Plant the bulbs in autumn. Set them in individual holes or larger planting areas dug 3–4 inches (7.5–10 cm) deep. Propagate by division; lift and divide the bulbs after the leaves have turned yellow.

Pest and disease prevention No specific problems.

Landscape uses The delicate, lightly fragrant blooms look beautiful in spring beds and borders. For extra color, combine them with Grecian windflowers *Anemone blanda* and early crocus. Reticulated irises also grow well in pots for spring bloom outdoors or winter forcing indoors.

SITE AND CLIMATE
Full sun or partial shade; evenly moist (but not waterlogged), humus-rich soil. Zones 3–9.

HEIGHT
1–3 feet (30–90 cm)

SPREAD
1–2 feet (30–60 cm)

FLOWERING TIME
Early summer flowers; some cultivars rebloom.

SIBERIAN IRIS

PLANT SIBERIAN IRISES WITH PERENNIALS, ORNAMENTAL GRASSES AND FERNS. THEY ARE PERFECT FOR COTTAGE GARDENS AND WATERSIDE PLANTINGS.

Description Siberian irises form tight fans of narrow, swordlike leaves from slow-creeping rhizomes. Flowers range in color from pure white, cream and yellow to all shades of blue, violet and purple. The foliage looks good all season.

Growing guidelines Plant bareroot irises in autumn, spacing them 1–2 feet (30–60 cm) apart. Plant container-grown plants in spring, summer and autumn. If bloom begins to wane or plants outgrow their position, divide them in late summer. Divide named cultivars to propagate. Sow fresh seed outdoors in summer or autumn.

Pest and disease prevention Siberian irises are susceptible to iris borer. Squash the grubs between your fingers while they are in the leaves. Dig up affected plants and cut off infested portions of the rhizome.

Landscape uses Stately Siberian irises are a traditional favorite for most garden designs. They look great along ponds and streams with ferns, hostas and astilbes. Combine the foliage and lovely flowers with rounded perennials such as peonies, baptisias *Baptisia* spp. and cranesbills *Geranium* spp.

Leucocoryne ixioides ALLIACEAE

SITE AND CLIMATE
Full sun; fertile, moist, well-drained soil. Zones 8–10.

HEIGHT
1 foot (30 cm)

SPREAD
8–10 inches (20–25 cm)

FLOWERING TIME
Late spring or early summer.

GLORY-OF-THE-SUN

GLORY-OF-THE-SUN IS QUITE A TRICKY BULB TO GROW, BUT ITS ATTRACTIVE, SWEETLY FRAGRANT BLOOMS ARE AMPLE REWARD FOR ALL YOUR HARD EFFORT.

Description Glory-of-the-sun produces grasslike leaves in autumn. The plant grows through winter and the leaves die down toward the end of spring, just as the heads of mauve-blue and white flowers begin to appear. There is also a form with pure white blooms.

Growing guidelines Plant the bulbs in late summer or earliest autumn about 2 inches (5 cm) deep and 3–4 inches (7.5–10 cm) apart. When the leaves appear, water often enough to keep the soil evenly moist. Feed lightly once or twice during autumn and winter and once more as flower stems appear. After bloom, let the plant dry out. These bulbs like cool and rainy, but not freezing cold, winters. In the garden, they will tolerate a few degrees of frost but in cold-winter areas they must be grown in a greenhouse. Keep soil lightly moist until frosts have finished, then take the pots outside into full sun.

Pest and disease prevention Take care not to overwater during winter, as plants may rot and die.

Landscape uses Plant them in masses or as an edging. They look attractive in wide, shallow pots.

SITE AND CLIMATE
Full sun to partial shade; moist but well-drained soil with added organic matter. Zones 4–10.

HEIGHT
1½ feet (45 cm)

SPREAD
6 inches (15 cm)

FLOWERING TIME
Mid- to late spring.

SUMMER SNOWFLAKE

DESPITE THEIR NAME, SUMMER SNOWFLAKES ACTUALLY BLOOM IN SPRING. PLANT THE SMALL BULBS IN GROUPS AND OVER TIME THEY'LL FORM LARGE CLUMPS.

Description Clumps of strap-shaped, green leaves emerge in early spring. Plants produce slender, green flowering stems tipped with loose clusters of nodding, bell-shaped, ¾-inch (18-mm) wide flowers. The white flowers have a green spot near the tip of each petal. After bloom, the leaves yellow and die back to the ground by midsummer.

Growing guidelines Plant in early autumn; set bulbs in individual holes or larger planting areas dug 4 inches (10 cm) deep. Space them about 6 inches (15 cm) apart. Fertilize once in early spring. Mulch to keep soil evenly moist. Propagate by bulblets or division in early autumn. The bulbs are best left undisturbed. Store dormant bulbs in a cool, dark place in a net bag or basket lined with dry peat moss.

Pest and disease prevention No specific problems.

Landscape uses Grow them with tulips and daffodils in flower beds and borders. Interplant with summer- and autumn-blooming annuals that will fill in when the bulbs go dormant. They look great naturalized in moist meadows and woodland gardens.

Leucojum vernum

SITE AND CLIMATE
Full to filtered sun; moist, well-drained soil. Zones 5–9.

HEIGHT
8–15 inches (20–40 cm)

SPREAD
6 inches (15 cm)

FLOWERING TIME
Late winter to early spring.

SPRING SNOWFLAKE

THE DAINTY, NODDING BLOOMS OF SPRING SNOWFLAKE MAKE WONDERFUL CUT FLOWERS. GROWING EXTRAS IN BED AND BORDER PLANTINGS GUARANTEES A SHOWY DISPLAY OUTSIDE AS WELL AS BEAUTIFUL CUT FLOWERS FOR INDOOR ARRANGEMENTS.

Description Spring snowflake grows from a deciduous bulb. It has strap-shaped, midlength, thin, dark green leaves. The small, white, nodding, bell-shaped flowers arise from a single flower stalk and bloom in layers at the terminal end of the stalk.

Growing guidelines Plant the bulbs in autumn, in individual holes or larger planting areas dug about 4 inches (10 cm) deep. Keep the soil evenly moist from autumn through late spring, then let it dry out in summer to allow the leaves to yellow and die back to the ground. Apply fertilizer once during the growing season. Propagate by bulblets or division. The bulbs are best left undisturbed.

Pest and disease prevention No specific problems.

Landscape uses Spring snowflake is a good choice for beds and borders, or meadow and woodland gardens.

Lily

LILIES MAKE EXCELLENT CUT FLOWERS; PICK THEM WHEN THE FIRST ONE OR TWO BUDS OPEN. YOU MAY WANT TO REMOVE THE ORANGE ANTHERS TO KEEP THE POLLEN FROM STAINING CLOTHES OR SOFT FURNISHINGS.

Description Lilies grow from scaly bulbs. They produce upright, unbranched stems with narrow to lance-shaped, green leaves. By early to late summer (depending on the hybrid), the long, plump flower buds open to showy, flat or funnel-shaped flowers. After bloom, the leaves and stems usually stay green until late summer or early autumn. Asiatic hybrids bloom in early summer in a range of bright and pastel colors. The 4–6-inch (10–15-cm) wide flowers are usually upward facing but can also be outward facing or nodding. They bloom atop sturdy stems usually 2–3 feet (60–90 cm) tall. Aurelian hybrids bloom in midsummer and have large, trumpet-shaped, bowl-shaped, nodding or starry flowers on 4–6-foot (1.2–1.8-m) tall stems. The 6–8-inch (15–20-cm) wide flowers come in a wide range of colors and are usually fragrant. Oriental hybrids bloom in late summer and have large flowers in crimson-red, pink, white or white with yellow stripes; many blooms are spotted with pink or red. The richly fragrant flowers grow to 10 inches (25 cm) long and may

Lily blooms can be plain or shaded with other colors.

SITE AND CLIMATE
Full sun to partial shade; moist, well-drained soil. Zones 4–10.

HEIGHT
From 2–5 feet (60–150 cm), depending on the hybrid.

SPREAD
6–12 inches (15–30 cm)

FLOWERING TIME
Summer.

be bowl-shaped or flat-faced; some have petals with recurved tips.

Growing guidelines Handle the scaly bulbs gently, planting them in autumn or early spring, as soon as they are available. If you plan to plant in spring, it's smart to prepare the planting area in autumn and cover it with a thick mulch so it will be ready when your bulbs arrive. Dig individual holes or larger planting areas 6–8 inches (15–20 cm) deep, and loosen the soil in the bottom. After carefully filling in around the bulbs, water to settle the soil. Mulch to keep the bulbs cool and moist. Water during dry spells, especially before flowering. Pinch off spent flowers where they join the stem. Cut stems to the ground when the leaves turn yellow; divide clumps at the same time only if needed for propagation.

Pest and disease prevention Relatively trouble-free. Trap slugs and snails in shallow pans of beer set flush with the surface of the soil.

Landscape uses Lilies add height and color to any flower bed or border. They're also elegant mixed into foundation plantings, grouped with shrubs or naturalized in woodlands. Combine them with mounding annuals, perennials or groundcovers that can shade the soil and keep the bulbs cool.

SITE AND CLIMATE
Full sun to partial shade; average, well-drained soil that's dry in summer.
Zones 5–10.

HEIGHT
Flowers to 2 feet (60 cm); leaves to 1 foot (30 cm).

SPREAD
6 inches (15 cm)

FLOWERING TIME
Late summer to early autumn.

MAGIC LILY

MAGIC LILY BULBS PRODUCE LEAVES IN SPRING AND LEAFLESS FLOWER STALKS BY LATE SUMMER. SOME GARDENERS LIKE TO COMBINE THEM WITH BUSHY PLANTS TO HIDE THEIR BARE STEMS.

Description Slender, greenish brown, leafless stems are topped with loose clusters of funnel-shaped, rosy pink flowers up to 4 inches (10 cm) long. The broad, strap-shaped, green leaves emerge several weeks after the blooms fade. The foliage elongates in spring and dies back in summer, 1–2 months before new blooms appear.

Growing guidelines Plant bulbs as soon as they are available in midsummer. Set them in individual holes or larger planting areas dug 4–5 inches (10–12.5 cm) deep. Space bulbs about 8 inches (20 cm) apart. Water during dry spells in autumn and spring. Protect the leaves over winter with a loose mulch, such as evergreen branches, pine needles or straw. Propagate by division in early to midsummer, as soon as the leaves die back; or, leave the bulbs undisturbed to form large clumps.

Pest and disease prevention No specific problems.

Landscape uses Magic lilies grow best when naturalized on slopes, in groundcovers or as part of a low-maintenance garden.

SITE AND CLIMATE
Full sun to partial shade (under deciduous trees and shrubs); average, well-drained soil. Zones 4–8.

HEIGHT
6–8 inches (15–20 cm)

SPREAD
3–4 inches (7.5–10 cm)

FLOWERING TIME
Early spring.

GRAPE HYACINTH

ONCE PLANTED, GRAPE HYACINTHS ARE TROUBLE-FREE. THEY NATURALIZE WELL UNDER TREES AND SHRUBS, AND LOOK QUITE ATTRACTIVE COMBINED WITH GROUNDCOVERS.

Description Grape hyacinths grow from small bulbs. The narrow, grasslike, green leaves appear in autumn and elongate through the spring. The clumps are accented by short, leafless stems topped with dense spikes of grapelike blooms. The individual purple-blue, white-rimmed flowers are only 1/4 inch (6 mm) wide. The leaves yellow and die back by early summer.

Growing guidelines Plant bulbs in early to midautumn, as soon as they are available. Set them in individual holes or larger planting areas dug 2–3 inches (5–7.5 cm) deep. Space the bulbs about 4 inches (10 cm) apart. For propagation, divide just after the leaves die back in early summer. Otherwise, leave the bulbs undisturbed to form sweeps of spring color.

Pest and disease prevention No specific problems.

Landscape uses Scatter the bulbs liberally throughout flower beds and borders. Mix them with primroses, pansies, daffodils and tulips for an unforgettable spring show. You can also grow them in containers for outdoor bloom in spring or indoor forcing in winter.

Daffodil

It's hard to imagine a garden without at least a few daffodils for spring color. Grow them in borders, plant them under trees or naturalize them in low-maintenance areas.

Description Daffodils grow from large, pointed bulbs. Clumps of flat, strap-shaped, green leaves emerge in early spring, along with leafless flower stalks. The flowers are sometimes fragrant. Each flower has a cup or trumpet (technically known as a corona) and an outer ring of petals (known as the perianth). The single or double blooms are most commonly white or yellow but may also have pink, green or orange parts or markings. The leaves usually remain green until midsummer, at which time they turn yellow and die back to the ground.

Growing guidelines Plant the bulbs in early to midautumn. Set them in individual holes or larger planting areas dug 4–8 inches (10–20 cm) deep. (Use the shallower depth for smaller bulbs; plant large bulbs deeply to discourage them from splitting and to promote larger flowers.) Space small types 3–4 inches (7.5–10 cm) apart and large types 8–10 inches (20–25 cm) apart. Top-dress the planted bulbs with compost in early spring. Pinch off developing seed capsules. Allow

Daffodils are seldom bothered by insects.

Site and climate
Full sun to partial shade; average, well-drained soil with added organic matter. Zones 4–9.

Height
From 6–20 inches (15–50 cm), depending on the cultivar.

Spread
4–8 inches (10–20 cm)

Flowering time
Early, mid- or late spring.

the leaves to turn yellow before cutting them back or pulling them out; braiding or bundling the leaves with rubber bands can interfere with ripening and weaken the bulbs. For propagation, divide clumps after the leaves die back.

Pest and disease prevention Plant in a well-drained position to deter root rot. Trap slugs and snails in shallow pans of beer set flush with the surface of the soil.

Landscape uses Create unforgettable combinations by grouping daffodils with other early bloomers, including pansies, crocuses, Siberian squill *Scilla sibirica*, grape hyacinths *Muscari* spp., and Grecian windflower *Anemone blanda*. Daffodils grow especially well with groundcovers, such as Japanese pachysandra *Pachysandra terminalis* and common periwinkle *Vinca minor*, which can mask the ripening leaves. Grow some daffodils in containers for spring bloom outdoors or winter forcing indoors. And don't forget to include some in the cutting garden for spring arrangements. The cut stems release a thick sap that can harm other flowers, so collect daffodils separately and let the stems sit in cool water overnight before mixing them with other blooms in a vase.

SITE AND CLIMATE
Full sun; moist, well-drained soil. Zones 8–10.

HEIGHT
2 feet (60 cm)

SPREAD
10 inches (25 cm)

FLOWERING TIME
Autumn.

GUERNSEY LILY

MAKE A POINT OF PLANTING GUERNSEY LILIES IN THE CUTTING GARDEN; THE BEAUTIFUL, LONG-LASTING BLOOMS MAKE EYE-CATCHING FRESH ARRANGEMENTS.

Description Guernsey lily grows from a deciduous or evergreen bulb. It has strap-shaped, mid-length, deep green leaves. The multiple, flared, pink, white or red flowers bloom atop a long, single flower stalk. The blooms are 2–3 inches (5–7.5 cm) wide and form ruffled clusters.

Growing guidelines Plant in late summer to autumn. Space bulbs about 10–12 inches (25–30 cm) apart, just above soil level. Guernsey lilies are easy to care for, just make sure that the soil is kept moist from autumn through spring. Allow deciduous bulbs to dry out in summer. Fertilize during the growing season, until plants become established. Mulch around the base of the plants. Propagate by offsets; the bulbs are best left undisturbed.

Pest and disease prevention No specific problems.

Landscape uses Guernsey lilies make a great accent in beds and borders. They also adapt well to life in containers, small-space gardens or in greenhouses.

Ornithogalum thyrsoides HYACINTHACEAE

SITE AND CLIMATE
Full sun to partial shade; moist, fertile, well-drained soil. Zones 5–10.

HEIGHT
1–3 feet (30–90 cm)

SPREAD
10–12 inches (25–30 cm)

FLOWERING TIME
Spring or summer.

STAR-OF-BETHLEHEM

THE BULB AND FOLIAGE OF STAR-OF-BETHLEHEM ARE POISONOUS IF INGESTED: TAKE CARE NOT TO PLANT IT NEAR CHILDREN'S PLAY AREAS OR YOUR PET'S FAVORITE GARDEN SPOT.

Description Star-of-Bethlehem grows from a deciduous bulb. The strap-shaped, arching, glossy green leaves form at the base of the plant. The 2–5-inch (5–12.5-cm) wide flowers bloom in tiers, vertically, along single flower stalks. The multiple, six-petaled, fragrant flowers bloom in orange, yellow, white and sometimes green-white.

Growing guidelines Plant in autumn. Space bulbs 6–8 inches (15–20 cm) apart and 3–5 inches (7.5–12.5 cm) deep. Keep the soil moist from autumn through spring. Fertilize during growing season until established. Propagate by offsets or by seed. Store dormant bulbs in a cool to warm place, in a net bag or a basket lined with dry peat moss.

Pest and disease prevention No specific problems.

Landscape uses Plant star-of-Bethlehem in beds, borders and cutting gardens. It also works well naturalized in meadow and woodland gardens.

SITE AND CLIMATE
Full sun to partial shade; moist, fertile, well-drained soil. Zones 7–9.

HEIGHT
3–4 inches (7.5–10 cm)

SPREAD
6–8 inches (15–20 cm)

FLOWERING TIME
Winter to summer.

MOUNTAIN SOURSOP

FROM HIGH IN THE CHILEAN ANDES, MOUNTAIN SOURSOP IS A CHARMING PLANT WITH THE SAME LOW, TIGHT HABIT OF MANY OTHER ALPINE PLANTS.

Description Mountain soursop grows from a tuberous root. It is a low, mound-forming plant with rosettes of compact, gray-green leaves topped with pretty pink flowers that bloom atop short flower stems.

Growing guidelines Plant the tubers in early autumn about 1 inch (2.5 cm) deep and 6 inches (15 cm) apart. Keep the soil barely moist during winter, but increase watering and liquid fertilizer as spring approaches. Reduce watering after bloom but don't let the tubers go completely dry in summer. Propagate by division in late summer (this won't be necessary for several years in garden-grown plants).

Pest and disease prevention No specific problems.

Landscape uses Mountain soursop makes an ideal rock garden plant. Or, grow it in stone troughs, wide pots or raised beds. It also works well planted between paving stones.

SITE AND CLIMATE
Full sun to partial shade; average, well-drained soil. Zones 5–10.

HEIGHT
1½ feet (45 cm)

SPREAD
10 inches (25 cm)

FLOWERING TIME
Early spring or summer, depending on climate.

RANUNCULUS

ALSO KNOWN AS PERSIAN BUTTERCUP, RANUNCULI ARE AVAILABLE IN MIXTURES OF COLORS AS WELL AS STRAIGHT COLORS. THE BEST VARIETIES HAVE TIGHTLY PACKED PETALS, RATHER LIKE A CAMELLIA.

Description Ranunculi grow from a tuberous root. The leaves are fernlike, deeply toothed and dark green. The many-petaled flowers bloom on straight stems about 1–1½ feet (30–45 cm) high. The 3-inch (7.5-cm) wide flowers bloom in pink, white, crimson, cerise, yellow and orange.

Growing guidelines Plant tubers in autumn; soak the tubers for 24 hours before you plant. Space 4–6 inches (10–15 cm) apart and 1–2 inches (2.5–5 cm) deep. Keep the soil evenly moist from autumn through spring, and damp from late spring through summer. Fertilize in spring. Mulch to prevent the soil from caking. Propagate by division.

Pest and disease prevention Pick slugs and snails off by hand, or trap them by placing shallow pans of beer set flush with the surface of the soil. Take care not to let the soil become soggy or the tubers will rot.

Landscape uses Plant ranunculi in beds, borders, containers and drifts in cottage, cutting or rock gardens. They look superb planted in masses, but second-year flowerings may not be as impressive as the first year.

SITE AND CLIMATE
Full sun to partial shade; rich, moist, well-drained soil. Zones 8–11.

HEIGHT
2 feet (60 cm)

SPREAD
1 foot (30 cm)

FLOWERING TIME
Summer to late autumn.

RIVER LILY

WATER-LOVING RIVER LILIES THRIVE IN CONTAINER GARDENS AS WELL AS IN THE GROUND. THEY MAKE WONDERFUL CUT FLOWERS FOR FRESH ARRANGEMENTS.

Description River lily grows from a rhizome. It always occurs near water where its roots can be kept constantly moist. Plants have narrow, grasslike leaves and tall stems of satiny, 1-inch (2.5-cm) wide flowers in pink or red.

Growing guidelines Plant the rhizomes in early spring, 1–2 inches (2.5–5 cm) deep and about 3 inches (7.5 cm) apart. Fertilize once in spring, summer and early autumn. River lilies will tolerate cooler temperatures, but where winters are very cold, they'll need the protection of a greenhouse. They can be grown on the edges of areas with boggy soil, but they do not do well in waterlogged soil.

Pest and disease prevention No specific problems.

Landscape uses Grow river lily next to ponds or in clumps or drifts in rich, moist soil.

SITE AND CLIMATE
Full sun to partial shade; moist, humus-rich, well-drained soil. Zones 4–8.

HEIGHT
4–18 inches (10–45 cm)

SPREAD
2–10 inches (5–25 cm)

FLOWERING TIME
Early spring.

PERUVIAN SQUILL

ALTHOUGH PERUVIAN SQUILL NATURALIZES, IT LOOKS BEST IN SMALL-SCALE PLANTINGS, SUCH AS COTTAGE GARDENS, OR AS PART OF A ROCK GARDEN.

Description Peruvian squill grows from a deciduous bulb. The dark green leaves are midlength and strap-shaped. Multiple, star-shaped, 1-inch (2.5-cm) wide flowers bloom in tight groups, tiered along a single flower stalk. The flowers are blue, purple, pink or white.

Growing guidelines Plant in autumn, spacing the bulbs 4–6 inches (10–15 cm) apart and 4 inches (10 cm) deep. Peruvian squill is relatively easy-care, just make sure that the soil is kept evenly moist from autumn through summer. Fertilize once a month during the growing season, until the plants are established. Propagate by offsets or by seed.

Pest and disease prevention No specific problems.

Landscape uses Peruvian squill is a good choice for beds, borders, container gardens or as an edging in a formal garden. Try some in the cutting garden, too.

SITE AND CLIMATE
Full sun to partial shade; average, well-drained soil. Zones 3–8.

HEIGHT
6 inches (15 cm)

SPREAD
2–3 inches (5–7.5 cm)

FLOWERING TIME
Early to midspring.

SIBERIAN SQUILL

THE DEEP BLUE BLOOMS OF SIBERIAN SQUILL LOOK WONDERFUL IN MASSES. THEY ALSO COMBINE BEAUTIFULLY WITH OTHER SPRING-FLOWERING BULBS, ANNUALS AND PERENNIALS.

Description Siberian squills grow from small bulbs. They produce narrow, strap-shaped, green leaves and leafless flower stems starting in late winter. The flower stems are topped with clusters of nodding, starry or bell-shaped blue flowers to ½ inch (12 mm) across. By early summer, the leaves gradually turn yellow and die back to the ground.

Growing guidelines Plant bulbs in early to midautumn, as soon as they are available. Set them in individual holes or larger planting areas dug 3–4 inches (7.5–10 cm) deep. Established bulbs are trouble-free. For propagation, divide bulbs after the leaves turn yellow; otherwise, leave them undisturbed to spread into large clumps.

Pest and disease prevention No specific problems.

Landscape uses Tuck them into beds and borders with pansies, primroses and daffodils. They are also excellent for naturalizing in lawns and low-maintenance areas and under trees and shrubs; just wait until the bulb leaves have turned yellow to mow. Grow them in containers for spring bloom outdoors or winter forcing indoors.

Sternbergia lutea AMARYLLIDACEAE

SITE AND CLIMATE
Full sun; moist, rich, well-drained soil. Zones 7–9.

HEIGHT
1 foot (30 cm)

SPREAD
6 inches (15 cm)

FLOWERING TIME
Autumn.

AUTUMN DAFFODIL

AUTUMN DAFFODIL IS ALSO COMMONLY KNOWN AS AUTUMN CROCUS AND LILY-OF-THE-FIELD. IT IS ONE OF THE MOST ATTRACTIVE AUTUMN-FLOWERING BULBS.

Description Autumn daffodil grows from a deciduous bulb. The green leaves are midlength and strap-shaped. Glossy, bright yellow, 1½-inch (3.5-cm) wide flowers bloom on short stems. The single flowers look a little like crocuses and form berry-like seeds.

Growing guidelines Plant in late summer, spacing bulbs 4–6 inches (10–15 cm) apart and 4–6 inches (10–15 cm) deep. Keep the soil evenly moist autumn through spring and let it dry out in summer. Fertilize during growing season, until the plants are established. Propagate by division, offsets or seed. Once established, leave undisturbed for as long as possible. Store dormant bulbs in a cool, dry place in a net bag or basket lined with dry peat moss.

Pest and disease prevention Spider mites can be a problem; if you see yellow stippling on leaves, spray with soap solution.

Landscape uses Autumn daffodils look great just about anywhere. Plant them as accents in beds and borders, or as an edging plant in a meadow garden. They thrive in containers, too.

SITE AND CLIMATE
Full sun; moist, average, well-drained soil. Zones 7–10.

HEIGHT
3 feet (90 cm)

SPREAD
4–6 inches (10–15 cm)

FLOWERING TIME
Summer through autumn.

TIGER FLOWER

ALSO KNOWN AS MEXICAN SHELL FLOWER, TIGER FLOWER MAKES A STUNNING ACCENT IN MIXED TROPICAL GARDENS. THE UNUSUAL BLOOMS LAST FOR JUST ONE DAY.

Description Tiger flower grows from a corm. The long, thin green leaves are swordlike with characteristic vertical ribs. The stunning orange, pink, purple, red, white or yellow flowers are open, three-petaled, cuplike blooms that have a triangular appearance. The inner petals are curved and sometimes speckled with contrasting colors. The blooms each last for one day.

Growing guidelines Plant in late spring, spacing the corms 4–6 inches (10–15 cm) apart and about 2–3 inches (5–7.5 cm) deep. Fertilize during growing season. Mulch in Zones 4–8, to protect against frost. Lift and store in Zones 4–6. Store in a cool to warm, dry place in a net bag or open basket lined with dry peat moss. Propagate by cormlets, offsets or seed.

Pest and disease prevention To discourage rodents and other animal pests from eating or dislodging the corms, plant them in open-top, underground cages. Also, avoid using scented fertilizer, such as bonemeal or fish emulsion.

Landscape uses Plant tiger flower in beds, borders and containers. It looks best in small-scale plantings.

SITE AND CLIMATE
Partial to full shade; moist, rich, well-drained soil. Zones 4–8.

HEIGHT
6–20 inches (15–50 cm)

SPREAD
1–1⅓ feet (30–40 cm)

FLOWERING TIME
Spring.

WAKE ROBIN

WAKE ROBIN IS SUSCEPTIBLE TO BEING EATEN OR DISLODGED BY ANIMAL PESTS. TO GUARD AGAINST DAMAGE, PLANT THE RHIZOMES IN AN OPEN-TOP, UNDERGROUND CAGE.

Description Wake robin grows from a rhizome. The oval, midlength, green leaves are whorled in groups of three. The solitary, three-petaled flowers are 2–3 inches (5–7.5 cm) wide and bloom in purple, pink, white and yellow.

Growing guidelines Plant in autumn, spacing the rhizomes 6–12 inches (15–30 cm) apart and about 4 inches (10 cm) deep. Keep the soil moist year-round. Fertilize once a year, in spring. Lightly mulch around the base of the plants. Propagate by division or seed. Store dormant rhizomes in a cool, dry place in a porous container, such as a terracotta pot, lined with dampened peat moss.

Pest and disease prevention Watch out for animal pests. In open areas, such as woodland or meadow gardens, don't use scented fertilizer.

Landscape uses Wake robin looks best planted in informal gardens. Plant it in mounds in natural, rock, shade and woodland gardens. Or, use it as an accent in bed and border plantings.

TULIP

HYBRID TULIPS OFTEN BLOOM POORLY AFTER THE FIRST YEAR. FOR A GREAT SHOW EACH YEAR, PULL THEM OUT AFTER BLOOM AND REPLACE THEM WITH SUMMER ANNUALS; PLANT NEW TULIPS EVERY AUTUMN.

Description The multitude of tulip hybrids available are the most popular of all spring bulbs. They grow from plump, pointed bulbs that produce broad, dusty-green leaves that are sometimes striped with maroon in early to midspring. The slender, upright, usually unbranched flower stems are topped with showy single or double flowers up to 4 inches (10 cm) across. By midsummer, leaves gradually turn yellow and die back to the ground. Tulips grow in almost every color, except true blue. They may have complex flower heads with fringes or scalloped petals, or the simple egg-shaped blooms that are so familiar.

Growing guidelines Plant bulbs in mid- to late autumn. Set them in individual holes or larger planting areas dug 4–6 inches (10–15 cm) deep. (If possible, planting 8 inches [20 cm] deep is even better, since it can discourage bulbs from splitting and, in turn, promote better flowering in following years.) Space bulbs about 6 inches (15 cm) apart. Fertilize twice a month in spring. Protect plants in windy sites. Pinch

The choice of tulip colors and forms is endless.

SITE AND CLIMATE
Full sun to partial shade; average, well-drained soil that's dry in summer. Usually best in Zones 3–10.

HEIGHT
From 6–30 inches (15–90 cm), depending on the cultivar.

SPREAD
6–10 inches (15–25 cm)

FLOWERING TIME
Early to midspring.

off the developing seedpods after flowering, and allow the leaves to yellow before removing them. In Zones 9 and 10, treat hybrid tulips as annuals and plant precooled bulbs each year in late autumn or early winter. Propagate by offsets in late summer or autumn. Store dormant bulbs in a cool, dry place in a net bag or a basket lined with dry peat moss.

Pest and disease prevention
Although tulips are relatively easy-care, they are susceptible to damage caused by insect pests. Trap snails and slugs by placing shallow pans of beer at the base of plants, flush with the soil. Pick off any you see by hand. Spray aphids and thrips with insecticidal soap.

Landscape uses Tulips' stately, colorful flowers are an indispensable part of the spring garden. In flower beds and borders, grow them with daffodils, pansies, primroses, bleeding hearts *Dicentra* spp., grape hyacinths *Muscari* spp., and forget-me-nots *Myosotis* spp. Some hybrids naturalize; they look wonderful planted in drifts beneath trees. Tulips also make charming cut flowers; pick them when the flowers are fully colored but still in bud. You can also grow tulips in containers and force them for winter bloom indoors.

SITE AND CLIMATE
Full sun to partial shade; moist, rich, well-drained soil. Zones 8–10.

HEIGHT
1–4 feet (30–120 cm)

SPREAD
1–2½ feet (30–75 cm)

FLOWERING TIME
Summer to autumn.

ARUM LILY

ARUM LILIES DON'T MIND HAVING THEIR FEET WET, SO TRY PLANTING SOME AS ACCENTS IN SHALLOW WATER WITH ORNAMENTAL GRASSES, OR AT THE EDGE OF A GARDEN POND TO ACCENT THE WATER FEATURE.

Description Arum lily grows from a tuber. The elongated, heart-shaped, shiny, dark green leaves are sometimes patterned with white speckles. The distinctive white flower heads are made up of a petal-like spiral spathe with a long, thin, yellow, waxy-looking spadix protruding from the center.

Growing guidelines Plant in early autumn, spacing tubers 1–1⅓ feet (30–40 cm) apart and 4 inches (10 cm) deep. Keep the soil damp year-round. Fertilize twice a month during growing season. Use a light mulch to keep the soil moist. Propagate by division, offsets or seed. Store dormant tubers in a cool to warm place in a net bag or a basket lined with dry peat moss.

Pest and disease prevention Animal pests aren't usually a problem but spider mites tend to attack arum lilies. Treat with soap spray solution.

Landscape uses Arum lily makes an elegant addition to formal beds and borders. Keep some in the cutting garden, as they make beautiful bouquets. They also adapt well to life in containers, indoors or out.

Zephyranthes candida AMARYLLIDACEAE

SITE AND CLIMATE
Full sun; moist, average, well-drained soil. Zones 7–10.

HEIGHT
1 foot (30 cm)

SPREAD
8 inches (20 cm)

FLOWERING TIME
Summer to autumn.

RAIN LILY

DAINTY RAIN LILY LOOKS BEST IN INFORMAL GARDEN DESIGNS, SUCH AS MIXED PLANTING ROCK GARDENS, OR AS AN EDGING IN A COTTAGE GARDEN.

Description Rain lily grows from a deciduous bulb. It has grasslike, arching, long, bright green leaves. The solitary, 2–4-inch (5–10-cm) wide, lily-like flowers bloom in pink, red, white and yellow. The petals are shaped like elongated ovals with a slightly pointed tip.

Growing guidelines Plant in spring. Space bulbs 3–4 inches (7.5–10 cm) apart and 2–4 inches (5–10 cm) deep. Keep the soil moist throughout the growing season; allow it to dry for one month after bloom, then water again for rebloom. Fertilize during the growing season. Mulch in Zones 7–8. Propagate by offsets or seed.

Pest and disease prevention No specific problems.

Landscape uses Plant rain lilies as accents in beds and borders. Or, naturalize them in Zones 9–10 in meadow, rock and woodland gardens. They also work well in container gardens.

Plant Hardiness Zone Maps

These maps of the United States, Canada and Europe are divided into ten zones. Each zone is based on a 10°F (5.6°C) difference in average annual minimum temperature. Some areas are considered too high in elevation for plant cultivation and so are not assigned to any zone. There are also island zones that are warmer or cooler than surrounding areas because of differences in elevation; they have been given a zone different from the surrounding areas. Many large urban areas, for example, are in a warmer zone than the surrounding land. Plants grow best within an optimum range of temperatures. The range may be wide for some species and narrow for others. Plants also differ in their ability to survive frost and in their sun or shade requirements.

PACIFIC OCEAN

Average Annual Minimum Temperature °F (°C)

ZONE 1	Below -50°F (Below -45°C)	**ZONE 6**	-10° to 0°F (-23° to -18°C)
ZONE 2	-50° to -40°F (-45° to -40°C)	**ZONE 7**	0° to 10°F (-18° to -12°C)
ZONE 3	-40° to -30°F (-40° to -34°C)	**ZONE 8**	10° to 20°F (-12° to -7°C)
ZONE 4	-30° to -20°F (-34° to -29°C)	**ZONE 9**	20° to 30°F (-7° to -1°C)
ZONE 5	-20° to -10°F (-29° to -23°C)	**ZONE 10**	30° to 40°F (-1° to 4°C)

Canada
ATLANTIC
OCEAN
United States
of America

The zone ratings indicate conditions in which designated plants will grow well, and not merely survive. Many plants may survive in zones that are warmer or colder than their recommended zone range. Remember that other factors, including wind, soil type, soil moisture, humidity, snow and winter sunshine, may have a great effect on growth.

Keep in mind that some nursery plants have been grown in greenhouses, so they might not survive in your garden. It's a waste of time and money, and a cause of heartache, to buy plants that aren't suitable for your climate zone.

Australia and New Zealand

These maps divide Australia and New Zealand into seven climate zones which, as near as possible, correspond to the USDA climate zones used in the United States, Britain and Europe and in this book. The zones are based on the minimum temperatures usually, or possibly, experienced within each zone. This book is designed mainly for cool-climate gardens, but the information in it can be adapted for those in hotter climates. In this book, the ideal zones in which to grow particular plants are indicated and when you read that a plant is suitable for any of the zones 7 through to 10, you will know that it should grow successfully in those zones in Australia and New Zealand. There are other factors that affect plant growth, but temperature is one of the most important. Plants listed as being suitable for zone 10 may also grow in hotter zones, but to be sure, consult a gardening guide specific to your area.

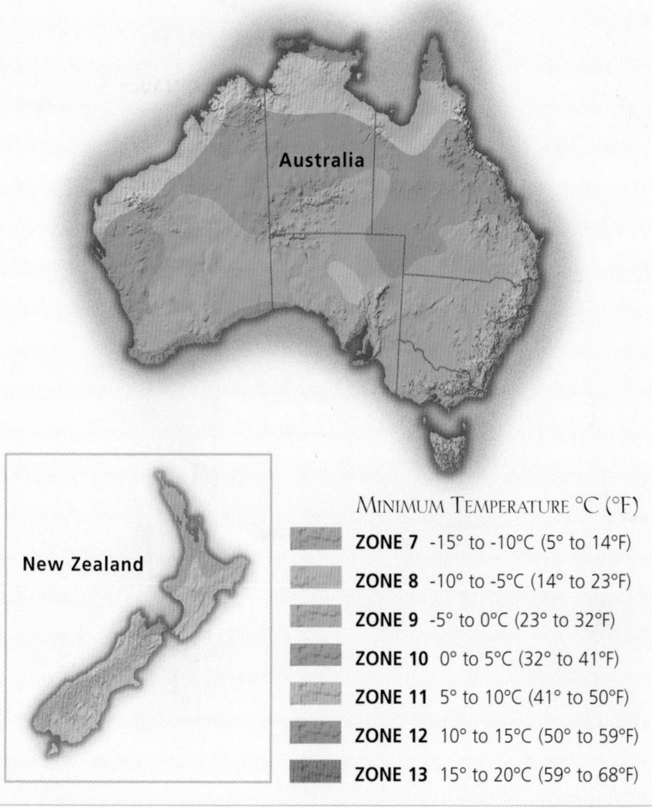

INDEX

Page references in *italics* indicate photos and illustrations.

C

D

E

F

G

Acknowledgments

KEY l=left, r=right, c=center, t=top, b=bottom

APL=Australian Picture Library; BCL=Bruce Coleman Ltd; COR=Corel; CN=Clive Nichols; DW=David Wallace; GP.com=gardenphotos.com; GPL=Garden Picture Library; HSC=Harry Smith Collection; HSI=Holt Studios International; IH=Ivy Hansen; JP=Jerry Pavia; JY=James Young; LC=Leigh Clapp; LR=Lorna Rose; OSF=Oxford Scientific Films; PD=PhotoDisc; PH=Photos Horticultural; SOM=S. & O. Mathews; TE=Thomas Eltzroth; WO=Weldon Owen; WR=Weldon Russell

1t GPL/Lynne Brotchie; c Corbis; b WO/JY **2**c GPL/John Glover **5**c LC **6**t Corbis; c JY **7**t COR; c WO; b COR **10**c GPL/J. Sira **12**bl COR **13**t COR **14**tl PD **15**b COR **16**t Corbis **17**br COR **18**br COR **19**t CN **20**bl WO **21**br CN **22**b JP **23**t GPL/David Cavagnaro **24**tl GPL/Neil Holmes **25**bl WO/JY **26**tl GPL/Brian Carter **27**t WO/JY **28**tl COR **30**bl COR **31**tl COR **32**c LC **34**br WO/JY **36**tl GPL/Howard Rice **37**bl GPL/Michael Howes **39**c GPL/Mayer/Le Scanff **40**tl JY; br GPL/Lamontagne **41**tr WR **42**br Corbis **43**t GPL/Zara McCalmont **44**tl GPL/Brigitte Thomas **45**tl PD **46**bl WO/JY **48** tr PD; bl GPL/Howard Rice **50**bl GPL/Marie O'Hara **51**b Corbis **52**tl WO/JY; bl BCL/Jane Burton **53**cr GPL/Jane Legate **56**bl GPL/Lynne Brotchie **57**tr GPL/John Baker; bl GPL/Brian Carter **58**tl PD; b GPL/John Glover **59**tl GPL/Philippe Bonduel **60**tr COR **60–61**br GPL/John Glover **61**tr COR **62**tl GPL/JP; br GPL/Friedrich Strauss **64**tr GPL/Friedrich Strauss; bl CN **65**tr SOM; bl GPL/Ron Evans **67**c PD **69**tr SOM; bl Andrew Lawson **70**t GPL/Lynne Brotchie **71**t APL/Farkaschowsky **72**c LC **74**tl COR **75**tr GPL/Linda Burgess; bl GPL/Mayer/Le Scanff **77**tr GPL/Lamontagne; bl COR **80**tl WO/JY; br WR/Cheryl Maddocks **82**tl CN **83**br GPL/Michael Howes **84**br APL/Corbis/George D. Lepp **85**tr GPL/Jane Legate **86**t WO/JY **88**tl WO; br PH **90**t COR

91b WO/JY **93**t BCL/Hans Reinhard **94**bl WO/JY **95**tr Corbis **96–7**t CN **97**br SOM **98**br GPL/Lynne Brotchie **99**tr PH **100**b CN **102**tl SOM **103**c PD **104–5**b WO/JY **106**br APL/Geoff Woods **107**tl PD **109**tr CN **110**br GPL/ Brian Carter **111**tl WO/JY; br GPL/Maver/Le Scanff **112**c LC **114**t TE **115**t TE **116**t SOM **117**t TE **118**t GPL/David Cavagnaro **119**t GPL/David Cavagnaro **120**t WO **121**t GPL/Chris Burrows **122**t PH **123**t JP/Joanne Pavia **124**t WO/JY **125**t TE **126**t WO/JY **127**t HSC **128**t Gillian Beckett **129**t SOM **130**t TE **131**t WO/JY **132**t SOM **133**t TE **134**t PH **135**t Tony Rodd **136**t TE **137**t TE **138**t GP.com/Judy White **139**t WO **140**t APL/Corbis/Hal Horwitz **141**t GPL/J. Sira **142**t JP **143**t TE **144**t TE **145**t HSC **146**t TE **147**t WO **148**t TE **149**t GP.com/Graham Rice **150**t TE **151**t JP **152**t WO **153**t GPL/ Mark Bolton **154**t GPL/J. Sira **155**t COR **156**t GPL/Lamontagne **157**t Corbis **158**t JY **159**t WO/JY **160**t GPL/Howard Rice **161**t Random House **162**t TE **163**t Gillian Beckett **164**t PH **165**t TE **166**t TE **167**t WR **168**t GPL/Eric Chrichton **169**t JY **170**t GPL/Geoff Dann **171**t JP **172**t TE **173**t TE **174**t PD **175**t Derek Fell **176**t TE **177**t JP **178**t WO/JY **179**t GPL/Lynne Brotchie **180**t PH **181**t TE **182**t WO/JY **183**t HSC **184**t GPL/Chris Burrows **185**t OSF Frank Huber **186**t WO/JY **187**t GP.com/Judy White **188**t GPL/Brian Carter **189**t GPL/Howard Rice **190**t WO/JY **191**t HSC **192**t GPL/Howard Rice **193**t IH **194**t OSF/Deni Bown **195**t WO/JY **196**t Corbis **197**t WO/JY **198**t WO/JY **199**t GPL/JP **200**t WO/JY **201**t WO/JY **202**t Corbis **203**t WO **204**t WO/JY **205**t COR **206**t WO/JY **207**t TE **208**t TE **209**t JY **210**t OSF/ Harold Taylor **211**t TE **212**t GPL **213**t COR **214**t TE **215**t PH **216**t Gillian Beckett **217**r TE **218**t GP.com/Graham Rice **219**t JP **220**t TE **221**t TE **222**t PH **223**t APL/Corbis/W. Wayne Lockwood **224**t SOM **225**t GPL/JP **226**t WO/JY **227**t SOM **228**t PD **229**t CN **230**t WO/JY **231**t HSC **232**t TE **233**t WO/JY **234**t COR **235**t WO/JY **236**t TE **237**t PD **238**c Corbis **240**t WO/JY **241**t HSC **242**t WO/JY **243**t GPL/John Glover **244**t SOM **245**t WO/JY **246**t GPL/Lamontagne **247**t TE **248**t HSC **249**t APL/Corbis/ Patrick Johns **250**t Random House **251**t GPL/Philippe Bonduel **252**t HSC **253**t TE **254**t GPL/John Glover **255**t GPL/J. Sira **256**t CN **257**t LR **258**t GPL **259**t SOM **260**t COR **261**t Gillian Beckett **262**t JP **263**t WO/JY **264**t GPL/ Howard Rice **265**t GPL/John Glover **266**t John Game **267**t CN **268**t TE **269**t CN **270**t GPL/Brian Carter **271**t Denise Greig **272**t WO **273**t GPL/JP **274**t WO/JY **275**t GPL/ Brian Carter **276**t SOM **277**t GPL/David Askham **278**t COR **279**t WO/JY **280**t GPL/Rex Butcher **281**t Corbis **282**t HSC **283**t CN **284**t WO/JY **285**t PH **286**t TE **286**t GPL/J. Sira **288**t PowerPhotos **289**t WO/JY **290**t Derek Fell **291**t CN **292**t WO/JY **293**t SOM **294**t GPL/ Mark Bolton **295**t PH **296**t GPL/Philippe Bonduel **297**t Corbis **298**t JY **299**t GPL/Howard Rice **300**t WO/JY **301**t HSC **302**t GPL/Brigitte Thomas **303**t GPL/Eric Crichton **304**t Corbis **305**t WO/JY **306**t GPL **307**t GPL.

Illustrations by Tony Britt-Lewis, Edwina Riddell, Barbara Rodanska, Jan Smith, Kathie Smith.

The publishers would like to thank Puddingburn Publishing Services, for compiling the index, and Bronwyn Sweeney, for proofreading.